ARQUEONAUTAS
WORLDWIDE
Arqueologia Subaquatica, S.A.

**PATRIMONIO
INTERNACIONAL SARL**

"The Excavation of the *Nossa Senhora da Consolação* (1608)" by Alejandro Mirabal.

HISTORICAL BACKGROUND BY Torsten Arnold.

SITE PLANS AND VECTORIAL DRAWINGS BY Faure Cambiella and Alejandro Raúl Mirabal.

PRE-CONSERVATION PHOTOS BY Yuri Romero, Carlos Bosch and Manuel Navarro.

POST-CONSERVATION PHOTOS BY Jorge Ponce and Manuel Almeida.

UNDERWATER PHOTOS BY Yuri Romero and Alejandro Mirabal.

ARCHAEOLOGICAL DRAWINGS BY Alejandro Raúl Mirabal.

ARCHAEOLOGICAL DATABASE BY Alina Reyes.

PHOTO MOSAIC PHOTOS BY Alejandro Mirabal, Yuri Romero and Manuel Navarro.

PHOTO MOSAIC IMAGE EDITING BY Alejandro Raúl Mirabal.

3D MODELING AND TEXTURING BY José Brás.

3D RENDERING BY António Bustorff.

TEXT REVISION BY Janette Ramsay.

EDITED BY Miguel Gomes da Costa.

EDITORIAL COORDINATION BY Nikolaus Graf Sandizell.

PUBLISHED BY Arqueonautas Worldwide - Arqueologia Subaquática SA, Rua das Murças, 98, 9000-058 Funchal. Portugal. All rights reserved.

www.aww.pt
ISBN: 978-989-97948-2-5

About the Author

M.Sc. Alejandro Mirabal (1964) is a Marine Archaeologist with a further graduate degree in Marine Biology and a master's degree in Marine Ecology, all by the University of Havana. Born in Cuba and naturalized Portuguese, Alejandro Mirabal has 28 years of work experience worldwide and is the author of several publications. He has worked on more than 300 historical wreck sites as archaeologist, operations manager, surveyor and diver in Cuba, Cape Verde, Mozambique, Vietnam, Brazil and Indonesia, and has clocked up more than 10,000 diving hours. From 1985-98 he worked at the state company CARISUB in Cuba. Since 1999, Alejandro Mirabal has worked for Arqueonautas as an archaeologist where, in close cooperation with Dr. Margaret Rule (CBE, FSA), he worked on the scientific publications of documented shipwrecks in Cape Verde and Mozambique. Besides his duties as Arqueonautas' main archaeologist, since 2005 he has also been Chief Operations Officer (COO) responsible for the Company's marine archaeology expeditions. Additionally, he has played a key role disseminating scientific knowledge, having presented lectures on marine archaeology at local universities in Cuba, Indonesia and Austria, and having participated in scientific events in the United States, United Kingdom, Netherlands, Germany, Mozambique, Cape Verde, Vietnam and Philippines.

Books:

- *"Inés de Soto: Un Hallazgo de Cuatro Siglos"*, CIMEX, Cuba, 1998.
- *"Spanish Coins in Mozambican Waters: The Numismatic Collection of the São José (1622)"*, Arqueonautas, Portugal, 2012.
- *"The Excavation of the Nossa Senhora da Consolação (1608)"*, Arqueonautas, Portugal, 2013.
- *"Swedish Coins in Cape Verdean Waters: The Plate Money of the Schimmelmann (1781)"*, (in preparation).
- *"The Wreck of the Espadarte (1558)"*, (in preparation).
- *"The Marine Archaeology Survey of the Bangka-Belitung Province, Indonesia"*, (in preparation).

For a complete list of his more than 20 publications and archaeological reports visit:
http://publications.aww.pt

Contents

Foreword

When the Consortium Património Internacional SARL/Arqueonautas Worldwide SA signed the concession agreement for the Nampula Province with the Mozambican Government back in 1999, two main objectives were defined and have been pursued since then: Firstly, to protect Mozambican Underwater Cultural Heritage and secondly, to scientifically study that same Underwater Cultural Heritage.

In order to protect Underwater Cultural Heritage we must know exactly what we are aiming to protect and therefore the creation and continuous update of the Archaeological Chart of the Nampula Province territorial waters has been fundamental. This chart now includes more than 40 identified and documented wreck sites. A selected few of these wreck sites were excavated, either because there was clear evidence that they were in danger of being looted or pillaged or because they represented an important or even unique opportunity to study, in detail, shipwrecks that could provide valuable archaeological information.

The excavation of *Nossa Senhora da Consolação* (1608) clearly falls into the latter category. This book and the donation of all artefacts recovered during the excavation, to the Marine Museum of the Island of Mozambique, are perfect examples of how the work of the Consortium Património Internacional/Arqueonautas Worldwide is achieving the goals that were set from the start of this endeavour.

While the knowledge generated is being shared with the academic world and the general public, Mozambique as a country is benefiting from its past as it builds a sustainable future for the nation, with archaeological collections enriching its museums, helping to attract tourists and to create jobs, all without one single cent from the tax payer.

We believe that this is the way to move forward and that this innovative, balanced and pragmatic approach to the protection of Underwater Cultural Heritage, will be recognized internationally for its merits and visionary qualities and will eventually be followed in many more African countries and around the world.

Maputo, January 2013

General Jacinto Veloso
(President of Património Internacional SARL)

Preface

This book, the second from the Scientific Publications Collection to be published by Arqueonautas, illustrates well the commitment and dedication of our consortium with Património Internacional SARL towards the protection and study of Mozambique's Underwater Cultural Heritage. It also further reinforces our continued efforts to share our archaeological work with the academic world.

Our core team has now been based at the Island of Mozambique for 10 years. During the past decade, strong ties have been established with the local community and a relationship of mutual respect has developed into a solid partnership. Our team's dedication and ethical work have strongly contributed to the tangible results we are achieving in our quest for the protection of Underwater Cultural Heritage in the region.

The archaeological excavation of the *Nossa Senhora da Consolação* (1608), led by our archaeologist Alejandro Mirabal and his expert team, revealed a wreck site of extraordinary significance to better understand naval construction during this important period of the discoveries. Natural conditions at the site, with ballast stones covering a large part of the ship's structure, made it possible for much of the wood to survive over centuries despite frequent 'pickings' by local fishermen and the harsh underwater environment. After painstakingly documenting every detail of the structure the site was again covered with its ballast and is therefore protected for future studies.

The story told by this wreck site confirms archival documentation that recounted the fate of the *Nossa Senhora da Consolação*. It also sheds light on many unanswered questions regarding the construction of these fabled ships that annually faced numerous dangers on their journeys to distant ports in the Far East, in order to bring back the spices, silk, precious stones and Chinese porcelain so much in demand in the European markets at the time.

For Mozambique, this publication is another fine example of how a sustainable policy for the protection and study of Underwater Cultural Heritage led by Património Internacional can bear fruit and help the country to establish itself on the world stage as one of the most active African countries in the demanding task of protecting their National Maritime Heritage.

With several other scientific publications in the their final stages of completion, 2013 will be a year when Arqueonautas Worldwide will dedicate a considerable amount of resources to sharing, with the academic world and the general public, the results of our maritime archaeology work and expeditions, not just on-line (www.aww.pt) but now through printed publications as well.

Estoril, January 2013

Nikolaus Graf Sandizell
(Chairman of the Board & CEO of Arqueonautas Worldwide SA)

Acknowledgements

The archaeological excavation of the *Nossa Senhora da Consolação* wreck demanded a more physically demanding effort than usual, from the field team of archaeologists and divers. Around 200 tons of ballast stones had to be removed by hand, one by one, to uncover the surviving wood structure of the ship. This task was done with great care as delicate artefacts were mixed with the stones and without the untiring spirit of the diving team it wouldn't have been at all possible without lowering the quality of the collected data. I want to deeply thank all of them in the first place.

I would also like to express my profound gratitude to, Dr. Margaret Rule, friend and mentor, for her wise and continuous guidance and advice over all these years, as well as:

To the Ministry of Education and Culture of the Republic of Mozambique, for their support on the project.

To Dr. Jacinto Veloso from *Património Internacional* SARL and Urgel Barreira for providing us with liaison and logistics support from Maputo, Mozambique.

To the *Gabinete de Arqueología de la Oficina del Historiador de la Cuidad de La Habana*, Cuba, and especially to its Director Roger Arrazcaeta for the valuable input, providing expertise on naval construction.

To Nikolaus Sandizell, CEO of Arqueonautas Worldwide, for sponsoring this publication and supporting operations from Europe.

To Yuri Romero, Faure Cambiella, Alejandro Raul Mirabal and Alessandro Lopes for their painstaking and meticulous recording of the wood structure of the ship.

Any achievement that this publication may contain is thanks to all of them. The errors that may plague it, are entirely mine.

M.Sc. Alejandro Mirabal Jorge
(Archaeologist / AWW OPS Director)

SECTION 1

Abstract

The shipwreck code-named IDM-003 was found on *Cabeceira* reef, Ilha de Moçambique, in the Province of Nampula, Republic of Mozambique, in 2001 during a systematic archaeological survey of the area. It has been tentatively identified as the *Nossa Senhora da Consolação*, a Portuguese Indiaman, lost at this location on July, 1608 during the Dutch siege of the island. The archaeological excavation of this wreck provided a collection of artefacts from the late 16th and the early 17th centuries giving us a glimpse of life on board those ships. A part of the wood structure survived allowing for the study of 16th century Portuguese naval architecture. The evidence suggests that IDM-003 was a typical Portuguese Indiaman, similar to those described in Portuguese 16th century ship treaties, with a keel of around 27.7m and an overall length of nearly 40m.

Key words: IDM-003, *Nossa Senhora da Consolação*, Ilha de Mozambique, Portugal, wood structure, Portuguese *Nau*.

SECTION 2

Introduction

The first European to arrive at what today is known as *Ilha de Moçambique* was Vasco Da Gama, after an arduous journey from Lisbon. According to the *"roteiro"* of the official journal of the voyage, the fleet set sail from the Tagus River on 8 July, 1497. After a long and difficult trip they arrived at the mouth of the bay, which shelters the Island of Mozambique. It was the afternoon of 1 March, 1498. It was almost eight months since they had left Lisbon, and, as one historian put it, *"a new era in the history of the Indian Ocean had begun"*. (*Bell,* 1974, 201).

During the course of the 16th century, the Island of Mozambique became Portugal's most important station in the whole of Africa and one of the four most important bases in the empire (the others being Goa, Malacca and Macau). Trade with the interior of Africa was never as profitable as the Crown would have liked, but it was still lucrative, and, more importantly, the sheltered bay around the Island, situated as it was, midway down the east coast (and half way between the gold mines to the south and the Swahili city-states to the north) provided a much needed haven for ships, where they could rest, repair and replenish after an arduous voyage around the Cape, or, if in the other direction, make preparations for the battering of the Cape that was to come. Rapidly, the island prospered and became the principal centre of the African trade and the most important nodal point within the western empire. Due to the increasing importance of this harbour, in 1545 the decision was taken to fortify the northern end of the island with the monumental *Fortaleza de São Sebastião*.

This outstanding position of the Island of Mozambique in the European trade with the East left an important cultural mark, above and below the sea surface.

The Arqueonautas' survey team found the wreck site codenamed IDM-003 (as it was the third wreck found in the area) on 3 July 2001, whilst performing a drift dive as part of the systematic archaeological survey in the surrounding waters of *Ilha de Moçambique*. This particular drift dive for visual survey was undertaken during the exceptionally good visibility conditions of that day, taking advantage of the strong incoming current.

SITE DESCRIPTION AND FIRST FINDS

This wreck site was located at a depth of 5m on the north side of the channel, 1,110m in front of the *São Sebastião* fortress and consisted of a ballast stone mound under a coral reef that grew over the wreck. Some unidentified iron objects, heavily concreted, were also present. Six interesting lead ingots were found during small test sondages performed at the site during the 2001 survey. These ingots were boat shaped, had illegible stamped marks and weighed approximately 50kg each. One of these lead ingots was recovered for identification purposes. At that time no wood structure, anchors or cannons were observed at the site. During a later survey in 2003, one heavily concreted iron cannon (G1) was located, partially covered by the ballast.

The entire area around the ballast pile was checked with metal detectors and test sondages were made in order to define the stratigraphy and the depth of the wreck remains. Two of the sondages were stopped as soon as the hull timbers were reached and the third was stopped at the layer where the lead ingots were found with loose wood. Some sample artefacts were recovered to help assess the site and possibly identify the wreck. All the test areas were backfilled at the end of the dives in order to protect the hull remains from further degradation and to help in future detailed study.

SEDIMENT NATURE AND HYDROGRAPHIC CONDITIONS

The area where the wreck site is located is a deposition bank at the edge of the deep channel that is the entry into the Bay of Mozambique. It is an area of counter currents, either incoming or outgoing tides, creating a kind of swirl which concentrates the sediments transported by the water. Therefore the nature of the seabed in this area is made up of very fine grain sand (mostly mud) on the first layer, followed by a thick layer of packed dead shells and coelenterates' skeletons. The surface of the seabed presents some patches of seagrass, mainly *Thalassia hemprichii, Halophila* Sp. and *Syringodium* Sp., over a clean layer of sand. The only coral formation in the area is precisely the one that grew over the wreck, which provides a solid base allowing the coral colonies to conquer the site. This would be impossible on the soft ground of this particular area of the seabed. The coral colonies are of very fast growth with light skeletons and weak attachment to the ground (leaf coral predominantly) and the only big colonies *(Acropora* Sp. and *Isopora* Sp.) were attached to some big iron objects and concretions.

The area is of relatively gentle hydrographic conditions as it is not exposed to important ground swell, surge or heavy swell. Currents are felt during spring tides but they are not strong enough to be taken into consideration with regards to wreck material dispersal, although sedimentation is very fast and objects are buried very deep under the sand quite quickly.

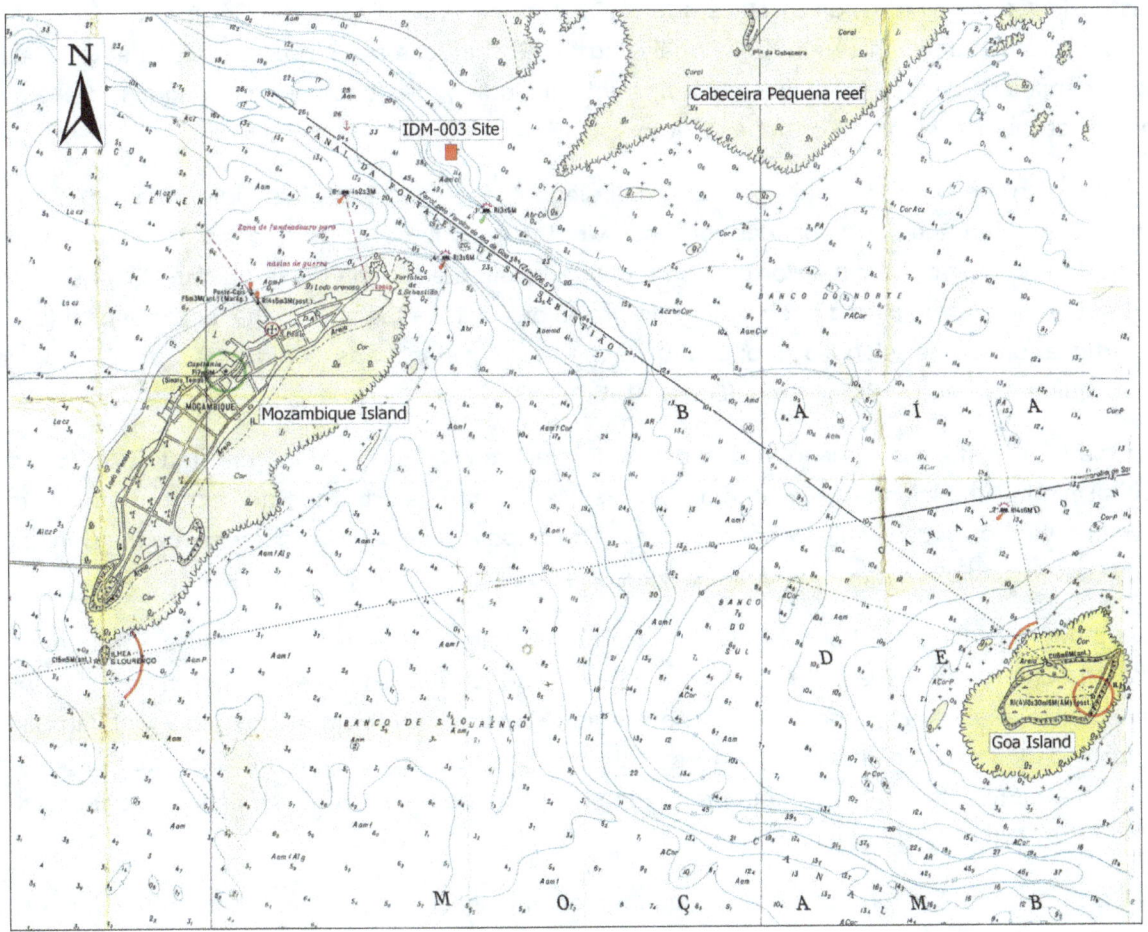

FIG.1
Geographical location of IDM-003 wreck site at Ilha de Moçambique.

SECTION 3

Historical Background

Based on the study of the historic records from the archives in our research, IDM-003 seems most likely to be the *Nossa Senhora da Consolação*, sunk in late July 1608, during an attempt by the Dutch to steal her. The historical records explain that during the Dutch siege of the Island of Mozambique in 1608, the attackers repeatedly attempted to steal the *Nossa Senhora da Consolação*, which was anchored in the bay. Most of her crew had sheltered in the *São Sebastião* fortress, defending the island.

The Portuguese sails dominated the oceans and maritime trade routes for almost a hundred years but this would change at the beginning of the 17th century during the Dual Monarchy of the Spanish kings in Portugal (1580-1640). Although King Philip II of Spain, Philip I of Portugal (1527-198) had suppressed the revolts against the Spanish dominance in the Low Countries, the political situation and the relations between the Low Countries and the Iberian Peninsula were relatively calm (*Murteira*, 2012). The reign of his successor, Philip III was characterized by a policy of embargo of Dutch ships calling at Iberian ports and the rivalries were soon intensified (*idem*). The Portuguese had been dominating the trade of spices and other precious oriental goods, the so-called *Rota do Cabo* (Route of the Cape of Good Hope), which resulted in the founding of the two famous private companies: the British East India Company (EIC) on 31 December 1600 and the Dutch East India Company (VOC), on 20 March 1602, in order to break down this monopoly. Analyzing the Portuguese trade routes, these fleets soon started to chase their enemies and attack them whenever possible, including the attack on the famous fortress of Malacca, established after the outstanding Portuguese victory in 1511.

As part of this plan the Dutch fleets began an initial siege of the Island of Mozambique in 1607, attacking the stronghold of the island, the *São Sebastião* fortress, with the intention of capturing it. The Island of Mozambique was an important port of call for the Portuguese India fleets situated in the Mozambique Channel. Outward and homeward bound fleets would load fresh water and provisions or take the sick to the local hospital (*Boxer*, 1961). The first fortification of the Island of Mozambique, the "*Torre Velha*" was constructed in 1508 but a modern fortress was built between 1548 and 1558 (*Lopes*, 1960).

The first armada of 7 ships commanded by Admiral Paulus van Caerden, which had left Texel (Holland) on 20 April 1606, arrived at the Island of Mozambique on 29 March 1607, started the attempt to conquer the fortress and port where two Portuguese ships were anchored. The ships in Van Caerden's fleet were the *Banda* (Flagship), *Walcheren* (Vice-Flagship), *Bantam, Ceylon, Ter Vere, Zierikzee* and *China* (*Sousa*, 1948).

Almost two months earlier, on 5 February 1607, a Portuguese fleet of three ships - *Nossa Senhora da Penha de França*, *Nossa Senhora de Jesus* and the *São Francisco* – had left Lisbon under the command of Dom Jerónimo Coutinho and were on the way to the Island of Mozambique (*Sousa*, 1948). Unaware of this fact Van Caerden took his ships for re-fitting and replenishing supplies at the Comoro Islands, leaving Mozambique unguarded. When he returned on 4 August, it was only to find that during his absence the Portuguese fleet had entered the harbour and resumed their trip to Goa (*ibidem*).

Having failed to conquer the fortress or to ambush the enemy fleet, Van Caerden decided to leave Mozambique on 20 August attempting to chase the Portuguese ships on their journey to India. The *São Francisco* was lost at the entrance of the Mozambique port (*Murteira*, 2012).

The *Nossa Senhora da Consolação* nau with Diogo de Sousa as Captain was part of the second fleet of four Portuguese ships commanded by João Correia de Sousa, which had left Lisbon on 23 February, 1607, arriving in Mozambique on 24 September. The other ships accompanying her were the *São Felipe e Santiago*, the *Santo André* and *Nossa Senhora do Loreto*. Having arrived too late to continue towards India during that monsoon period, the ship had to remain in Mozambique for almost a year (*Sousa* 1948). Therefore the cargo and in particular the amount of 10,000 *cruzados* meant for the royal pepper trade were stored in the *São Sebastião* fortress (*Rego, Baxter*, 1989).

The second Dutch fleet of nine ships commanded by Admiral Pieter Willemsz Verhoeff, which left Holland on 22 December, 1607, officially had commercial orders but their secret mission was to search and fight against the Portuguese fleet which had left Lisbon in 1607 and arrived in India, as well as the fleet which had left Lisbon before the arrival of the Dutch fleet commanded by Admiral Jacob van Heemskercke (*Sousa*, 1948). Therefore their planned blockade of the Tagus River in 1608 was unsuccessful. Upon arrival at Mozambique on 28 July, 1608, Verhoeff verified that the fortress had not been conquered by Van Caerden in 1607 and that the *Nossa Senhora da Consolação* and at least one other ship of the India trade were anchored in the said port. The *Santo André* had left Mozambique but was lost at the bar of Goa on 27 May (*ibidem*).

Verhoeff sent four boats to capture the ships. Entering the bay very close to the fortress at the southern edge of the entry channel and taking advantage of the low spring tide, the Dutch managed to escape the cannon fire as the artillery masters of the fortress were unable to aim so low (*Nijhoff*, 1930). They soon started to cut the cables of the ships and tow them out of the bay. At this point the Portuguese had corrected their cannons and started a vicious attack leaving the Dutch no choice other than to cut the cables and abandon the two ships; the *Consolação*, pushed by the southern winds helplessly drifted against the northern shores of the channel where she remained stranded (*ibidem*). Unable to organize a coherent salvage at that moment, the captain of the fortress, D. Estevão de Atayde sent a small boat commanded by the master of the *Consolação* to remove as much cargo as possible before setting the ships on fire preventing the Dutch from pillaging them (*Durão, Prestage, Boxer*, 1937).

The capture of the *Nossa Senhora da Consolação* is described in several historical accounts of which the following were used for the research: a Portuguese document called *"Cercos de Moçambique"* and the eye witness account of Johann Verken, a German soldier who was on board a ship which was part of the Verhoeff fleet.

The IDM-003 site showed clear signs of having been extensively salvaged in the past. Evidence of this was the lack of artillery pieces and large elements, such as the anchors. There were some areas where rescue at the time of the accident might have been extremely difficult due to the displacement of the ballast over the starboard side of the ship. The composition of the artefact sample recovered from this wreck during the archaeological excavation was one typical of a Portuguese Indiaman in the India trade. Chinese porcelain, although with little occurrence, *Martaban* jars for the transport of spices, a ceramic flask of Indian manufacture, ornamental beads and pendants and a lead seal with the *"Esfera armilar"* clearly strengthen that hypothesis.

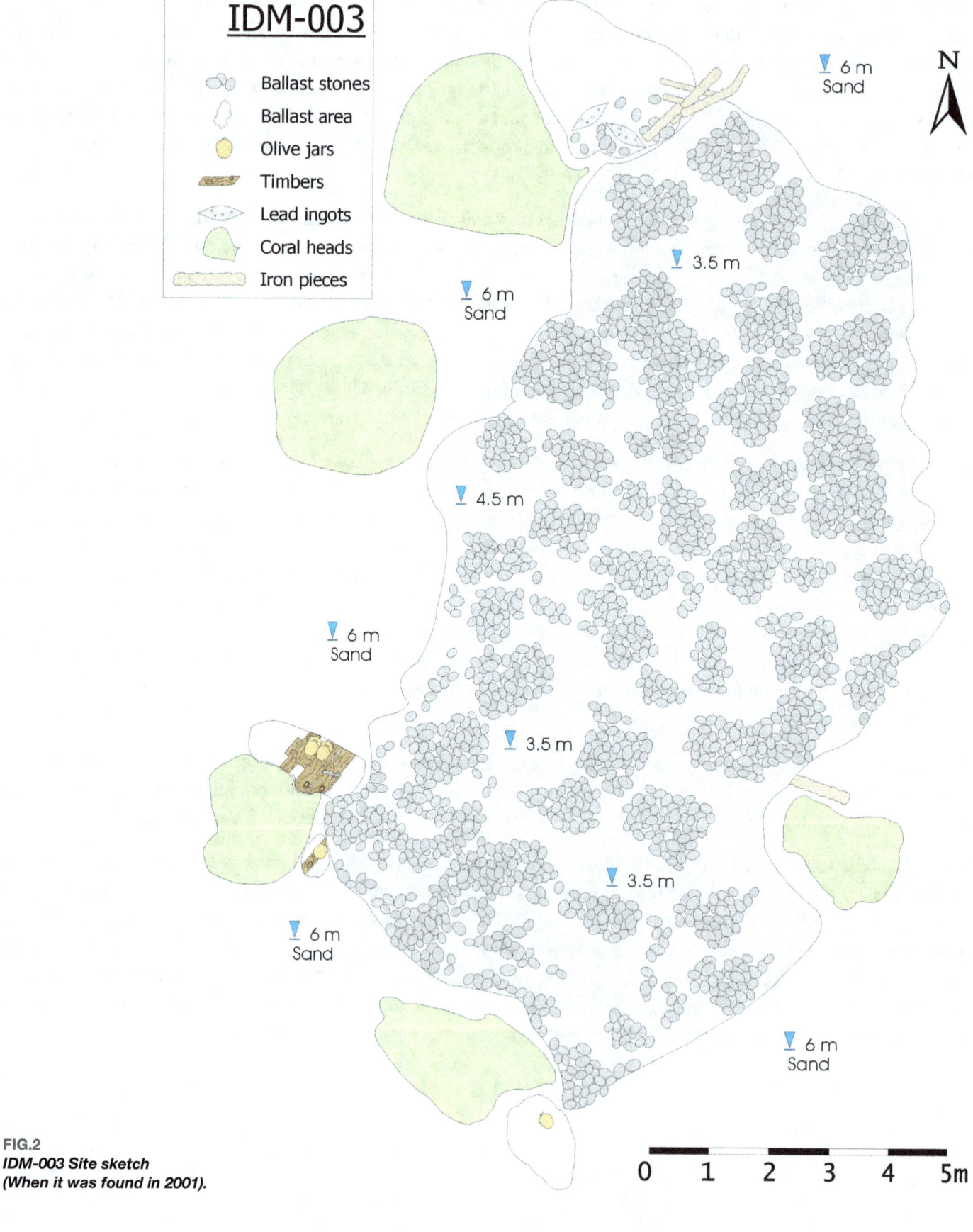

FIG.2
IDM-003 Site sketch
(When it was found in 2001).

Excavation was planned to start in 2005, when a bigger team and adequate equipment could be mobilized, and took place during two seasons (2005 and 2006) with the following statistics:

Days worked on the site	279 days
Dives	2,283 dives
Dive hours	4,357.16 hours
Artefacts recovered	309 artefacts
Excavation status	Completed
Conservation status	Completed
Documentation status	Completed
Backfilling of the archaeological station	Completed

PRE-EXCAVATION WORKS

Before starting excavation in 2005, some work was necessary at the site to prepare the area. As we had previously defined the areas to be excavated, a grid network was deployed over the ballast stones mound. Each quadrant of the grid was 5m x 5m and numbered from S1 to S18 for a total area of 450m^2 to be excavated. The grids were demarcated using plastic ropes of 6mm in diameter and the team marked every meter with a plastic tag and every 5m in black. Vertical datum points were also prepared should stratigraphy play an important role in the understanding of the site.

The main objective of the first phase of excavation was therefore to remove all the ballast from the pile in order to uncover any remains of the hull that may have survived underneath and to begin its study. To achieve that aim, it was necessary to manually remove the ballast stones and transport them away from the site in plastic crates and nets with the help of a 500kg lifting bag. Simultaneously the water dredge was deployed in the removal of the soft sediment from the edges of the ballast pile and from within the timbers.

Due to the soft nature of the sediment within the stones and the fragility of some of the artefacts observed during the test sondages, we decided to use only the water dredge to remove the overburden from the site and the lifting bags to remove the coral heads that were attached to the iron concretions.

All divers were carrying writing slates to record the exact measurements and locations of the artefacts, net bags and plastic rigid boxes to bring the artefacts to the surface and measuring tapes to refer to the depth under the original seabed where the artefacts or structure features were found.

SECTION 4

Excavation

Excavation started on grid S1 from the northern side of the coral head, heading towards the north. We reached the wood structure of the hull found during the previous test pit and excavation continued at that level following the spaces between the timbers until the wood planking underneath.

S1 GRID.

Nature of the overburden	⟶	Fine sand/mud and some shells
Depth of the overburden	⟶	0.30m
Depth of the cultural layer	⟶	0.25m
Average depth excavated	⟶	0.50m
Artefacts observed	⟶	Wood structure, coarse ceramics
Artefacts recovered	⟶	42 artefacts
Excavation status	⟶	Finished

The excavation of this grid started from the southern edge, besides the big coral head, heading east and north first and then to the west, at a depth of 0.35m. The excavation was done in two phases (in this and all other grids); first removing the overburden of the entire grid until a depth of approximately 0.30m, where the first artefacts began to appear. During the second phase, this thin layer was carefully excavated, going deep between the hull timbers until reaching the planking underneath. The southern sector provided most of the artefacts, apparently concentrated there due to the action of the coral head acting as a mechanical barrier for the horizontal dispersion. There was a mixture of cargo, domestic and personal belongings, with a majority of domestic items. There were also burnt timbers, clearly indicating there had been a fire on board. (Fig. 3)

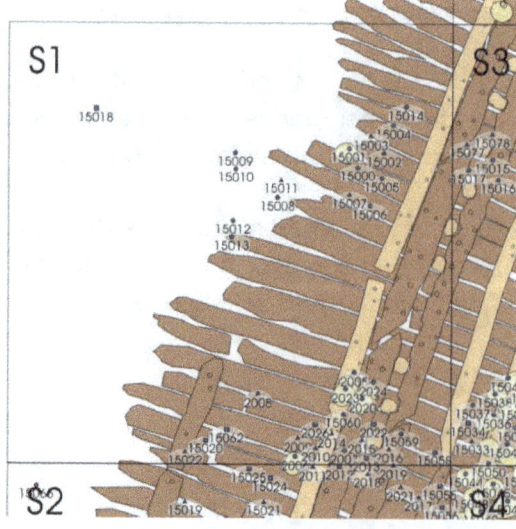

FIG.3

S2 GRID.

Nature of the overburden	——————▶	Fine sand/mud and some shells
Depth of the overburden	——————▶	0.30m
Depth of the cultural layer	——————▶	0.25m
Average depth excavated	——————▶	0.70m
Artefacts observed	——————▶	Wood structure, coarse ceramics, lead seals
Artefacts recovered	——————▶	28 artefacts
Excavation status	——————▶	Finished

We opened S2 to the south, adjacent to S1 surrounding the coral head. The wood structure from S1 continued all along S2 in a south-westerly direction although in the southern section of the grid many loose and smaller timbers started appearing. The hull continued uninterrupted under the coral head, which grew over an unidentified iron object resting on top of the timbers. We studied the possibility of removing this coral to excavate beneath it but this proved to be too risky, endangering the wood structure. We therefore decided to excavate, as best as we could, underneath the coral and left it undisturbed. Most of the artefacts were found in the NE corner of the grid, adjacent to S1, S3 and S4 and were of the same categories as the previous grid. A small group of silver coins found beneath the timbers were of special interest. Two very interesting lead seals were excavated under the timbers, one of them with the Portuguese *"esfera armilar"* and the other one with an unidentified coat of arms, both in relief. On the west sector of the grid the wood structure disappeared, having been broken and burnt at the ends of the timbers; the sediment was deeper at this part of the grid, reaching 1.8m to the sterile layer. Three big concretions produced by iron objects were located in the centre of the grid but were left undisturbed. (Fig. 4)

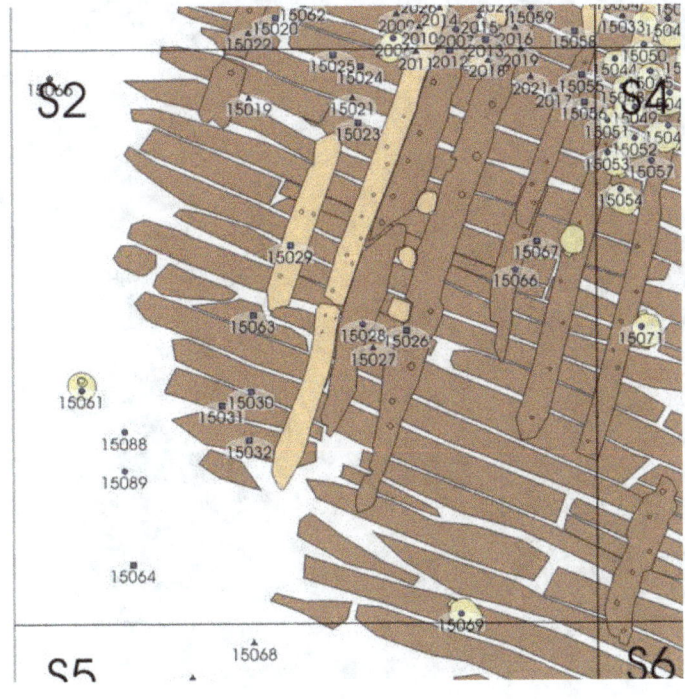

FIG.4

S3 GRID.

Nature of the overburden	————————▶	Fine sand/mud and some shells
Depth of the overburden	————————▶	0.30m
Depth of the cultural layer	————————▶	0.25m
Average depth excavated	————————▶	0.70m
Artefacts observed	————————▶	Wood, olive jars
Artefacts recovered	————————▶	21 artefacts
Excavation status	————————▶	Finished

This grid was excavated following the trail of coarse ceramic artefacts found in the NE corner of S2 at the depth of the wood structure. An interesting concentration of olive jars was found on the SW corner of S3, entering S4 to the south. The olive jars were arranged between the ship timbers in a row of six, with the mouths pointing towards the SE, most of them in the same direction. Several fragments of olive jars were also found in the centre of the grid, apparently broken by ballast stones sliding onto them. The part of the hull exposed from the ballast pile appeared very loose and disorganized. Mainly cargo artefacts were found in this grid, although a few domestic items were excavated in the NW sector of the grid. The excavation to the east stopped when the main body of ballast stones was reached. The body was resting on the timbers and no artefacts were visible on the whole cultural layer. The removal of the ballast was done in the next phase, during the study of the hull underneath. (Fig. 5)

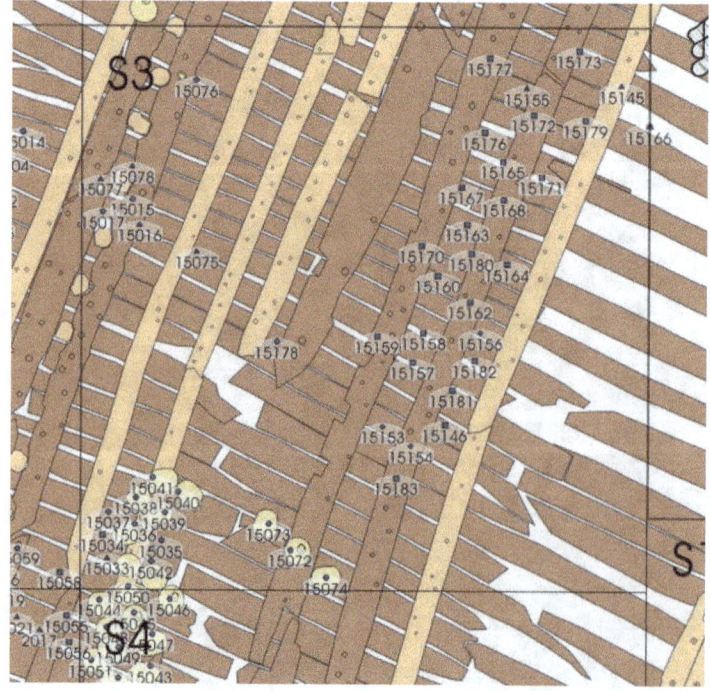

FIG.5

S4 GRID.

Nature of the overburden	⟶	Fine sand/mud and some shells
Depth of the overburden	⟶	0.30m
Depth of the cultural layer	⟶	0.25m
Average depth excavated	⟶	0.70m
Artefacts observed	⟶	Wood, olive jars
Artefacts recovered	⟶	12 artefacts
Excavation status	⟶	Finished

The wood structure in this grid almost disappeared to the southeast of this area and the only artefacts found belonged to the cargo category. Some pieces of round timbers were found in the centre of the grid, apparently transported in the ship for minor repairs of the woodwork. The only concentration of artefacts was the olive jars located in the NW corner of the grid belonging to the group, which had been excavated in S3. The depth of the sediment increases when advancing to the south, but the sterile layer is reached at approximately 0.70m, the same as in the previous grids. (Fig. 6)

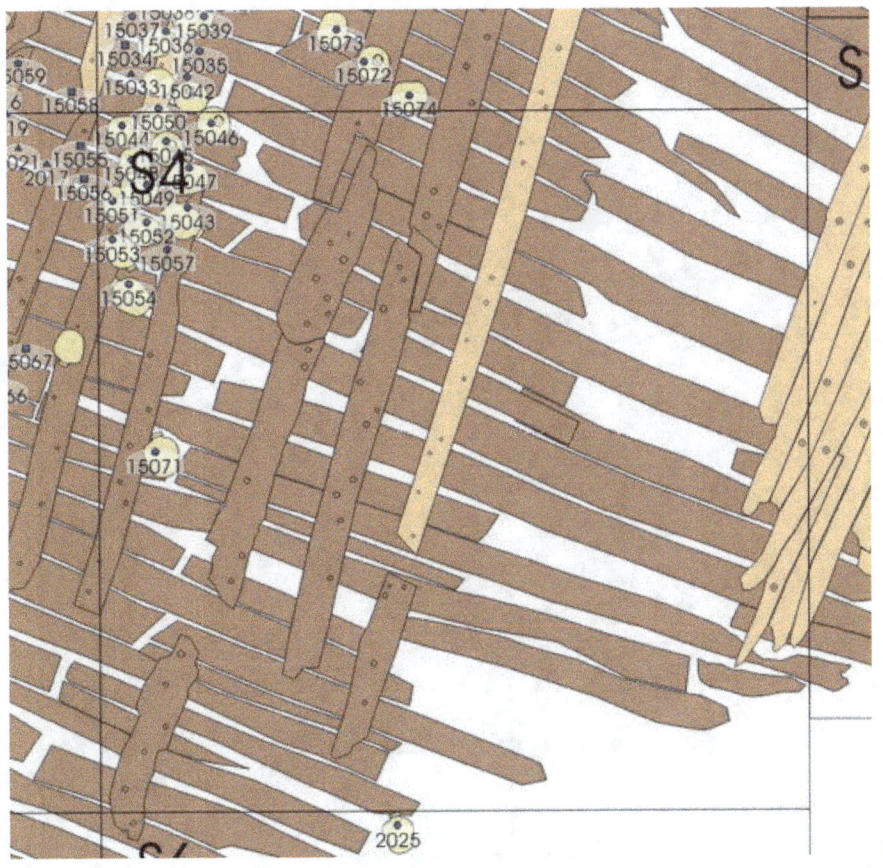

FIG.6

S5 AND S6 GRIDS.

Nature of the overburden	————————▶	Fine sand/mud, sea-grass and some shells
Depth of the overburden	————————▶	0.50m
Depth of the cultural layer	————————▶	0.15m
Average depth excavated	————————▶	1m
Artefacts observed	————————▶	Wood, olive jar
Artefacts recovered	————————▶	2 artefacts (S5) 1 artefact (S6)
Excavation status	————————▶	Finished

These grids completed the southern end of the debris field of this wreck site. The wood structure disappears at the very north of both quadrants and only a few loose pieces of wood were observed. Almost no ballast stones were present in this area, which we believe could be the bow of the ship. Two domestic category artefacts and one olive jar were found on both grids, reinforcing the theory that no more debris is present further to the south. Excavation continued to a depth of 1.90m beneath the sand in order to try to locate any other wreck remains buried deeper but no further wreck evidence was registered. (Fig. 7)

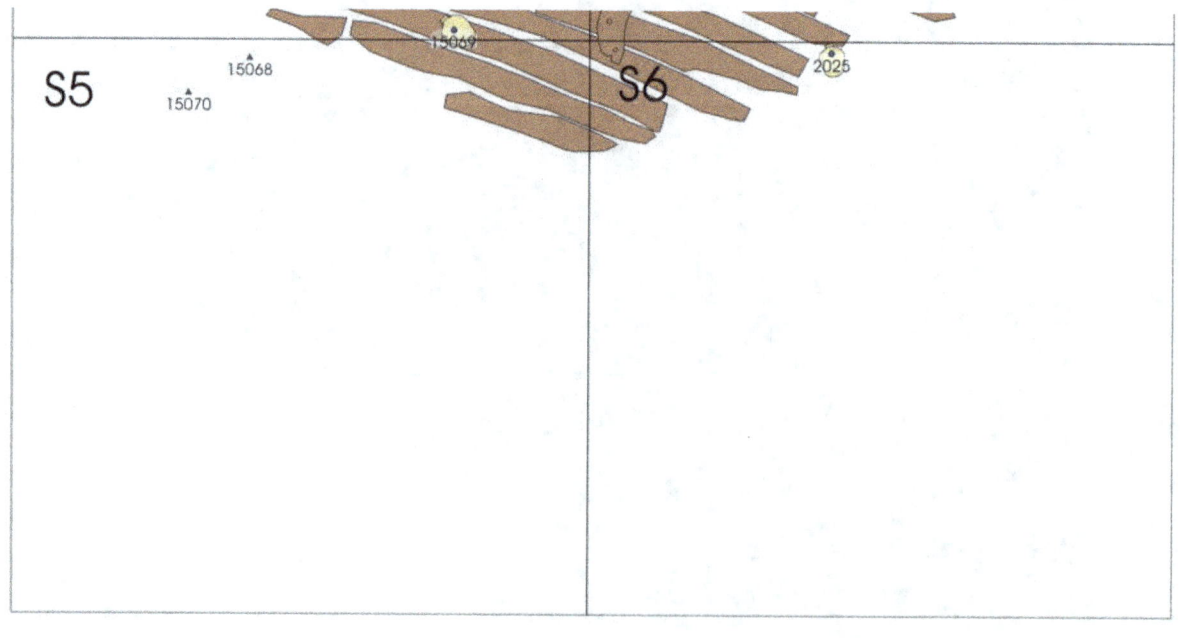

FIG.7

S7 GRID.

Nature of the overburden	——————➔	Fine sand/mud, sea-grass, shells
Depth of the overburden	——————➔	0.40m
Depth of the cultural layer	——————➔	0.40m
Average depth excavated	——————➔	0.90m
Artefacts observed	——————➔	Wood structure, olive jars, tusks
Artefacts recovered	——————➔	37 artefacts
Excavation status	——————➔	Finished

This grid was established at the north and adjacent to S3, following the bigger timbers in the structure of the hull, which were facing SW-NE within this area. The overburden was thicker than in the previous grids and the cultural layer was also wider, mostly to the west of the grid. Several olive jars from the cargo were found, but a higher occurrence of personal belongings and the first professional instruments were also noticed. The most notable artefacts excavated in this grid were an intact statue of Jesus Christ (13cm high, made of pewter), one intact Chinese porcelain ewer (from the Ming Dynasty) and two sets of navigational dividers in fairly good condition. Several fragments of a Chinese porcelain plate were found in different areas of this grid. They were later restored to form the entire piece. The diverse nature of the finds in this grid lead us to believe that we were approaching the stern section of the ship, where most of the cabins were located and therefore more diverse categories of artefacts are to be expected. Some elephant tusks and hippopotamus fangs were located as well but left *in-situ* for further study before excavation. Some small fragments of glass were observed in this grid and one intact drinking glass was recovered. (Fig. 8)

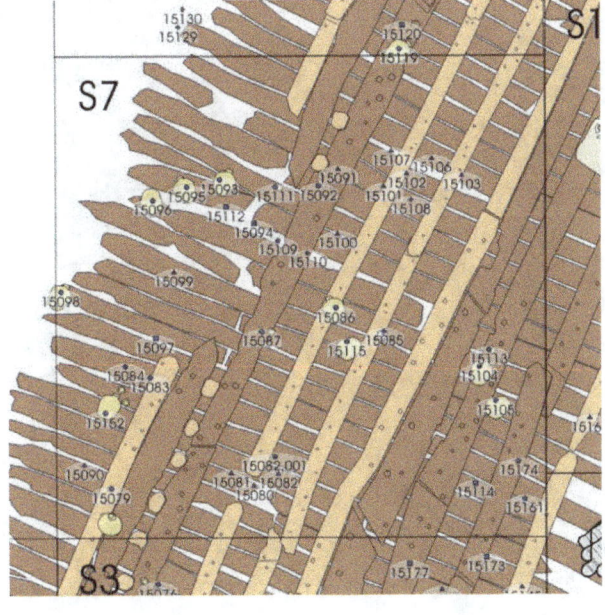

FIG.8

S8 GRID.

Nature of the overburden	⟶	Fine sand/mud, sea-grass, shells
Depth of the overburden	⟶	0.40m
Depth of the cultural layer	⟶	0.60m
Average depth excavated	⟶	1.20m
Artefacts observed	⟶	Wood structure, olive jars, tusks
Artefacts recovered	⟶	17 artefacts
Excavation status	⟶	Finished

This grid was deployed at the north and adjacent to S7, following the timbers in the structure of the hull, which continued with the same orientation as the previous grid. Excavation started from the SE locating the wood structure at 0.45m that continued further north, along with common fragments of coarse ceramics and more abundant Chinese porcelain shards. The fragmented bottom of an unusually large *Martaban* jar was observed in the NE corner of the grid (under the coral) and was partially excavated, but left *in-situ*. The wood structure disappeared towards the west, where some loose portions of unrelated timbers were observed. The depth of the grid increased in that direction, up to 1.20m to reach the cultural layer. More navigational instruments (one intact set of dividers and one intact copper measuring instrument) were found in this area as well as stone shot and iron cannon balls. Two interesting concentrations of lead shot were observed between the timbers, contained between two thinner planks, as if this had been the original location of these items. (Fig. 9)

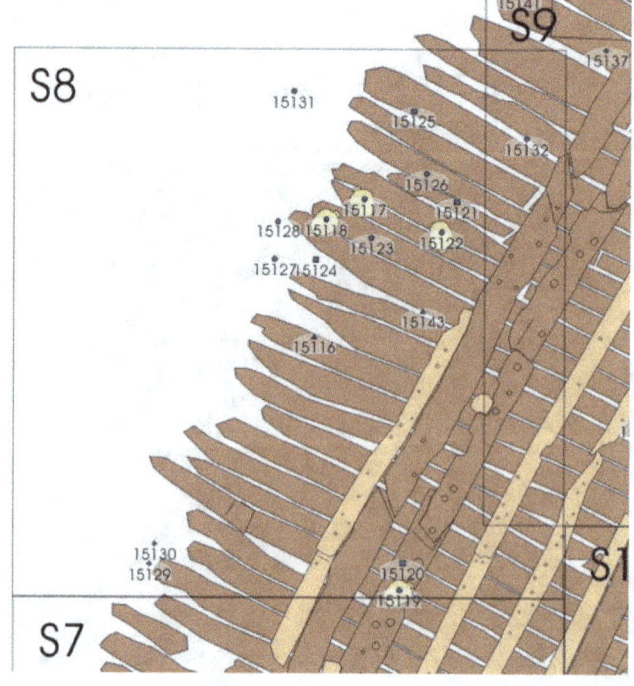

FIG.9

S9 GRID.

Nature of the overburden	⟶	Fine sand/mud, sea-grass, shells
Depth of the overburden	⟶	0.50m
Depth of the cultural layer	⟶	0.30m
Average depth excavated	⟶	1.00m
Artefacts observed	⟶	Wood structure, personal belongings, and lead ingots
Artefacts recovered	⟶	9 artefacts
Excavation status	⟶	Finished

This grid was opened to the east and adjacent to S8, 1m displaced to the north and avoiding the main concentration of ballast stones. The wood structure is less organized in this grid than in the previous ones, but the first evidence of the breaking and collapsing of a side (starboard side of the ship, we believe) was observed under the northern edge of the ballast pile. Further concentration of fragments of ceramics and a large iron concretion lying on the timbers were observed in the western sector of S9 at a depth of 0.35m. Two boat-shaped lead ingots weighing approximately 50kg were located in the northern sector of the grid, but were left *in-situ* for further photography and excavation during the next phase. Small fragments of Chinese porcelain still occurred in this grid, mostly among the ballast stones of the east sector. Elephant tusks, hippopotamus fangs, and coarse ceramics were present in the north of the grid where the depth of the sediment reached 1.90m to the cultural layer. One ivory piece of a board game (probably checkers) and one pewter buckle were the personal belongings found in S9, but another set of navigation dividers was found deeply buried within the timbers. Following this find we can conclude that it is very likely that S9 belongs to the stern section of the ship. (Fig. 10)

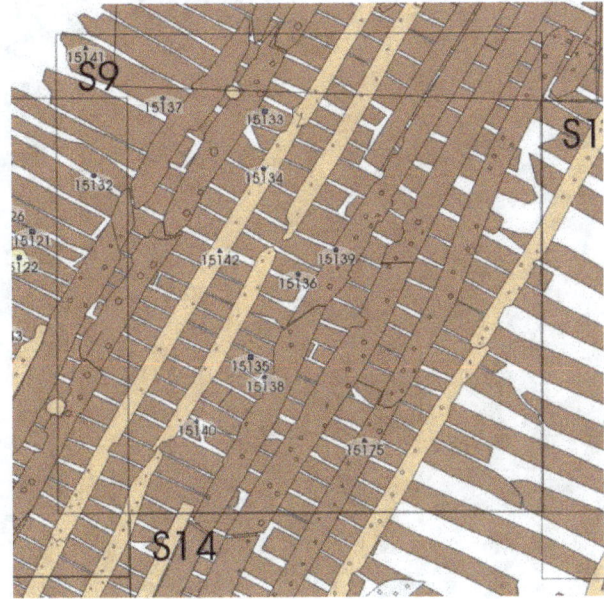

FIG.10

S10 GRID.

Nature of the overburden	⟶	Fine sand/mud and ballast stones
Depth of the overburden	⟶	0.60m
Depth of the cultural layer	⟶	0.70m
Average depth excavated	⟶	0.80m
Artefacts observed	⟶	Wood structure, coarse ceramics
Artefacts recovered	⟶	No artefacts recovered
Excavation status	⟶	Finished

This grid was opened to the north and adjacent to S9 and as a safety measure, overlapped the marks we had left the previous season, in an attempt to ensure that no gaps were left between both grids. The north western sector of the grid was deeper than 1m at the end of the wood structure and although no artefacts were found at this location, some fragments of coarse ceramics were observed. One loose small knee was found almost in the centre of the grid, resting on the stringers, but it was evident that it had moved from its original position in the structure of the hull. A massive concretion located between both stringers was observed, its composition affected by small fragments of burnt wood and coarse ceramics. Traces of burnt wood were also visible at the ends of the frames along the entire grid. (Fig. 11)

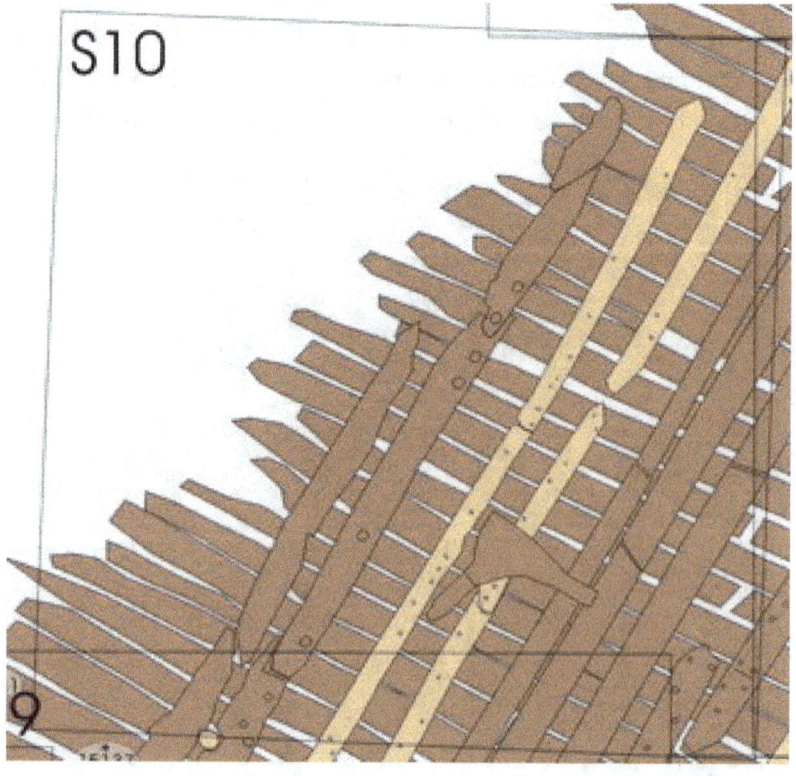

FIG.11

S11 GRID.

Nature of the overburden	——————➤	Fine sand/mud and some shells
Depth of the overburden	——————➤	0.60m
Depth of the cultural layer	——————➤	0.45m
Average depth excavated	——————➤	0.90m
Artefacts observed	——————➤	Wood structure
Artefacts recovered	——————➤	No artefacts recovered
Excavation status	——————➤	Finished

Following the coherence of the wood structure found in S10, the S11 square was opened to the north of S10 but displaced to the east as most of the western sector of the previous square lacked any wreck material. The stringers ended right on the south of the grid and therefore the few surviving frames were not very strongly fixed between the stringers and the planking of the hull. The planking was dislodged from the frames and appeared much deeper than the rest of the structure, following the natural shape of the seabed in that area. The condition of the timbers at this end of the structure was much more degraded than the rest of it, showing signs that this end, uncovered from ballast, had rapidly rotten away after the accident. This part of the structure marks the stern end of the surviving hull and the northern end of the excavation area. (Fig. 12)

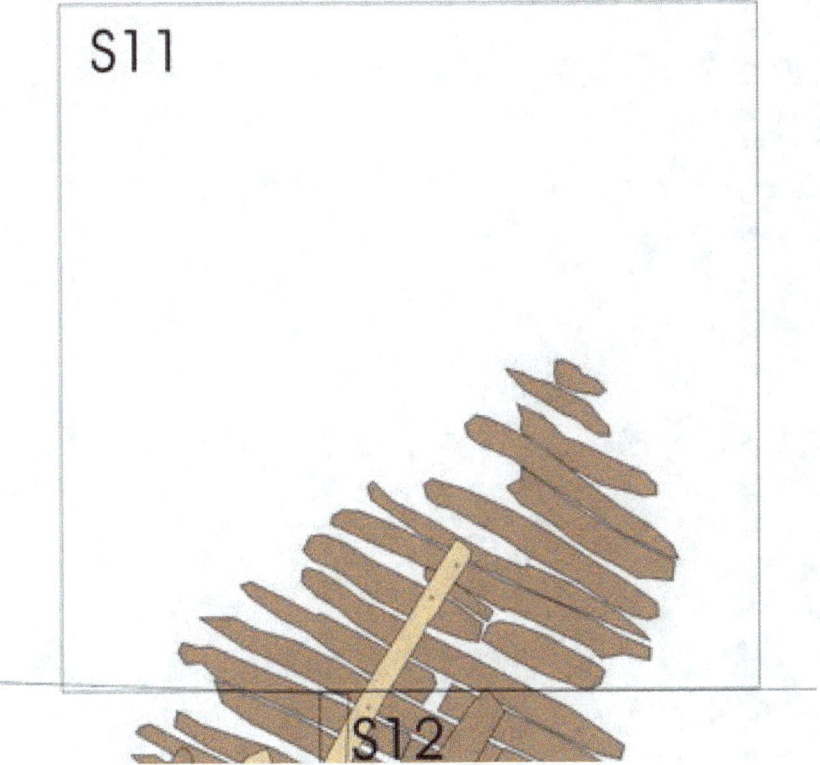

FIG.12

S12 GRID.

Nature of the overburden	⟶	Fine sand/mud, coral head and some shells
Depth of the overburden	⟶	0.60m
Depth of the cultural layer	⟶	0.45m
Average depth excavated	⟶	0.90m
Artefacts observed	⟶	Wood structure
Artefacts recovered	⟶	No artefacts recovered
Excavation status	⟶	Finished

This grid was opened in the south of S11 and adjacent to S10, following the wood structure. A massive coral head was removed from the northeast sector of the grid. It was interesting to note that this formation grew entirely over the remains of the ship indicating that the coral colony was less than 400 years old. The wood structure of this grid showed a better-organized assembly of timbers, with a stringer, a deck clamp and 7 first futtocks being recognizable. No artefacts were observed during the excavation of this grid. (Fig. 13)

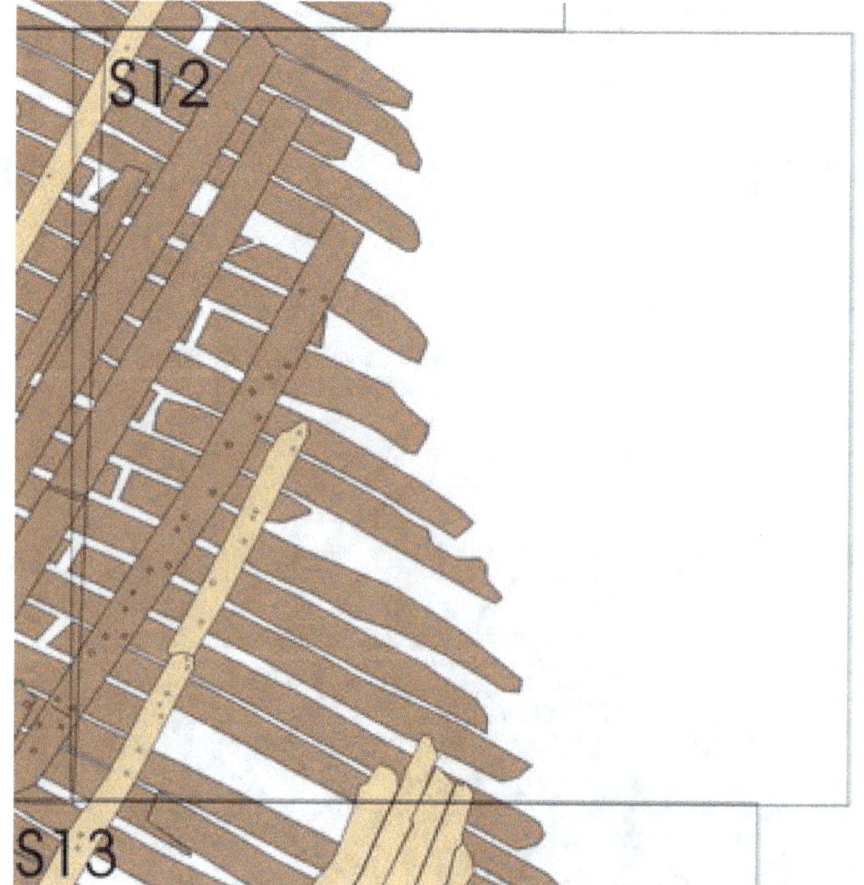

FIG.13

S13 GRID.

Nature of the overburden	————————➤	Fine sand/mud and ballast stones
Depth of the overburden	————————➤	0.70m
Depth of the cultural layer	————————➤	0.45m
Average depth excavated	————————➤	0.90m
Artefacts observed	————————➤	Wood structure
Artefacts recovered	————————➤	No artefacts recovered
Excavation status	————————➤	Finished

The northern edge of the ballast pile started in this grid, increasing in height towards the south. All ballast stones from this grid were removed manually and with great care due to the possibility of finding artefacts among the stones, but this was not the case. The wood structure of this grid, because it was almost completely covered and protected by the ballast stones, appeared in much better condition than the one in the northern grids. There was a recognizable part of the planking of the ceiling amidships as well as 12 first futtocks and the beginning of the surviving part of the keelson. The ceiling planking is made of a different kind of wood to the futtocks, deck clamps and frames previously observed, appearing of a lighter colour and with less resistance to mechanical penetration. (Fig. 14)

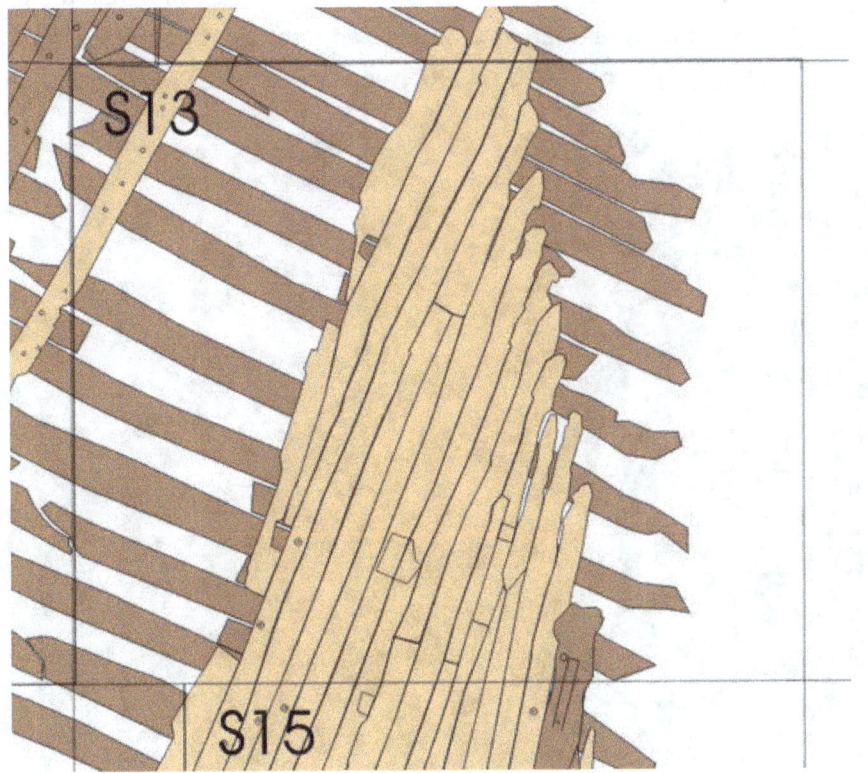

FIG.14

S14 GRID.

Nature of the overburden	⟶	Leaf coral and ballast stones
Depth of the overburden	⟶	1.90m
Depth of the cultural layer	⟶	1.90m
Average depth excavated	⟶	2.10m
Artefacts observed	⟶	Lead ingots, iron frame, cannons
Artefacts recovered	⟶	7 artefacts (106 lead ingots, 1 ceramic lid)
Excavation status	⟶	Finished

This grid was opened to the south of S9 and continued in the direction of the ballast stones which started to be removed in S13. At this portion of the wreck site the ballast mound was at its highest point (along with another 3 grids) and several tons of stones were manually removed to reach the layer where the artefacts and wood structure were present. The most interesting artefacts found in this grid were 106 boat-shaped lead ingots, found within the ballast and without any trace of arrangement, although this can be the result of the turning over of the ship when stranded. Moreover, when the surroundings of cannon G1 were freed of ballast stones we found that there were actually four iron cannons stacked one on top of another, the lowest one touching the timbers of the hull. In this case the storage system was obvious, with the cannons originally tied muzzle-to-muzzle alongside each other to prevent them from sliding with the ship's movements. The three cannons on the top (G1, G2 and G3) are identical, but G4 is slightly larger in dimension. An iron frame, apparently from the rigging was also observed, measured and left *in situ* as it was strongly concreted and its removal would have been compromising. (Fig. 15)

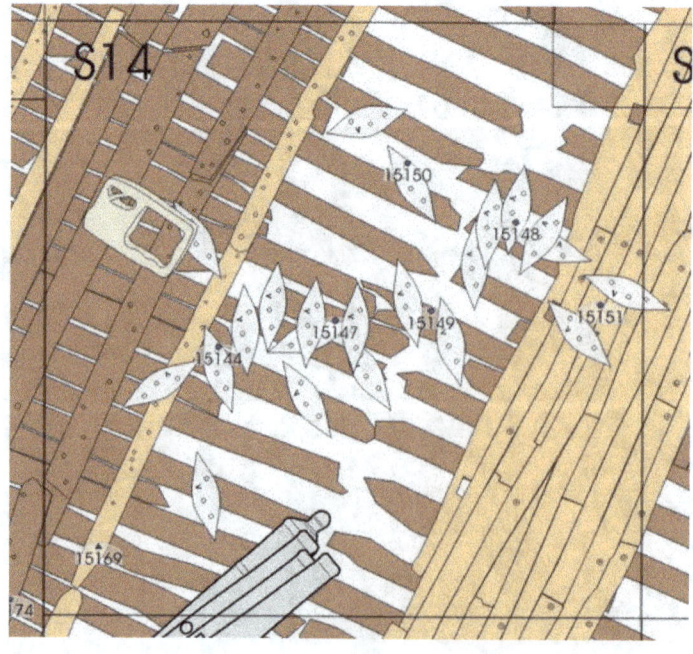

FIG.15

S15 GRID.

Nature of the overburden	⟶	Leaf coral and ballast stones
Depth of the overburden	⟶	1.90m
Depth of the cultural layer	⟶	1.90m
Average depth excavated	⟶	2.10m
Artefacts observed	⟶	Wood structure
Artefacts recovered	⟶	No artefacts recovered
Excavation status	⟶	Finished

This grid was established at the east and adjacent to S14, following the larger timbers in the structure of the hull. The overburden was similar to the one in the previous grid and the ballast removal continued. The wood structure found underneath the ballast was the continuation of the planking of the ceiling amidships, very tightly packed together with no space in between them, but the most interesting feature of the wood structure found here was, without doubt, the mast-step with its braces located either side. No remains of the mast were found inside its mortise, suggesting the manual removal of that piece. Anyhow, some traces of a type of felt were observed attached to its walls, which presumably could have acted as filling for the mast heel. The mast brace in the east was in worse conservation state than the one in the west of the mast-step and was not used for measurements. The entire eastern sector of the grid was free of any wood remains, making it evident that the port side of the ship was left exposed, burnt and consequently disappeared soon after the wreckage. (Fig. 16)

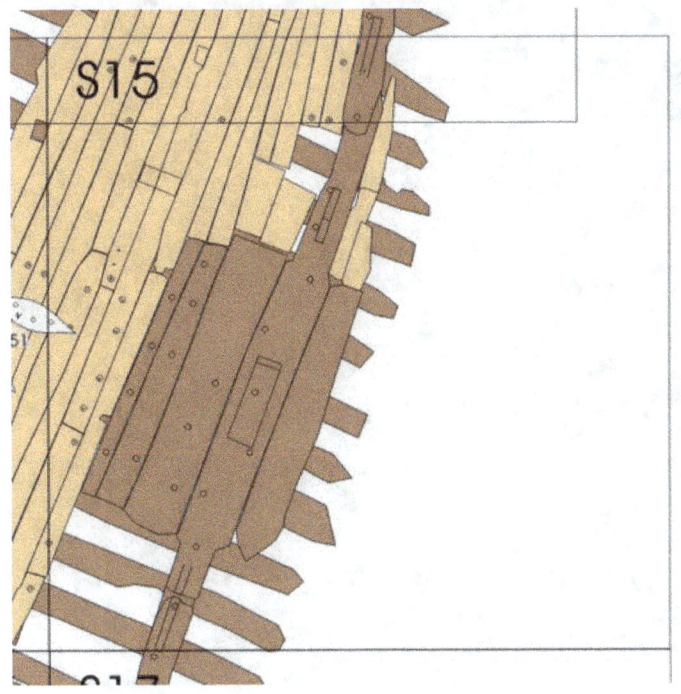

FIG.16

S16 GRID.

Nature of the overburden	———————▶	Leaf coral and ballast stones
Depth of the overburden	———————▶	1.90m
Depth of the cultural layer	———————▶	1.90m
Average depth excavated	———————▶	2.10m
Artefacts observed	———————▶	Wood structure , cannons
Artefacts recovered	———————▶	No artefacts recovered
Excavation status	———————▶	Finished

This grid was deployed at the south and adjacent to S14, following the timbers in the structure of the hull, which continued coherently in that direction. Main excavation target was to remove the ballast stones coverage, which at this point was one of the highest and densest of the wreck site. No artefacts were observed within the ballast stones and excavation ended when the wood structure was reached. In this grid the wood structure was made of the ceiling planking from the first futtocks and floor timbers, as well as a portion of the keelson. It is interesting to note that the fracture of the first futtocks observed in S14 continued here with the same orientation, apparently at the level of the turn of the bilge. In the northeast corner of the grid three floor timbers were observed, arranged with no space in between them, possibly part of the ship's master frame. (Fig. 17)

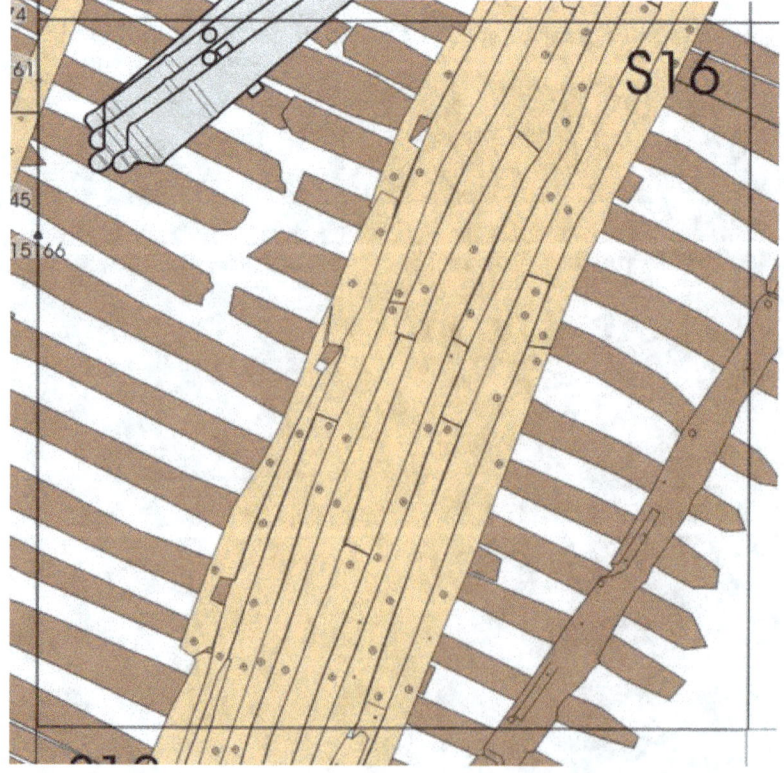

FIG.17

S17 GRID.

Nature of the overburden	⟶	Sand, shells and ballast stones
Depth of the overburden	⟶	1.20m
Depth of the cultural layer	⟶	1.20m
Average depth excavated	⟶	1.30m
Artefacts observed	⟶	Wood structure
Artefacts recovered	⟶	No artefacts recovered
Excavation status	⟶	Finished

This grid was opened to the east and adjacent to S16, in search of the end of the wood structure, which appeared 1.8m in that direction. The wood structures observed in this grid were part of the master frame and the keelson as well as the end of the floor timbers, which appeared burnt and eroded. Going deeper into the sediment after the end of the wood structure it was possible to observe the external planking of the hull underneath it, made of thick strakes, apparently of pine. Only the northwest corner of the grid presented wood structure, the rest was just sediment up to a depth of 1.5m. (Fig. 18)

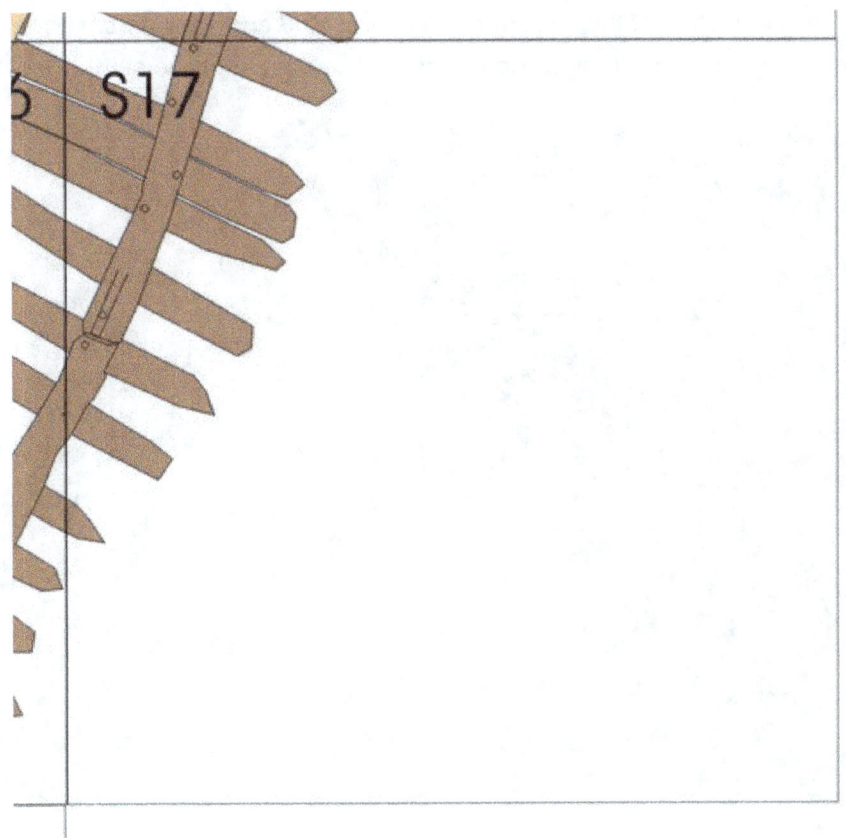

FIG.18

S18 GRID.

Nature of the overburden	————————▶	Sand, shells and ballast stones
Depth of the overburden	————————▶	1.30m
Depth of the cultural layer	————————▶	1.30m
Average depth excavated	————————▶	1.50m
Artefacts observed	————————▶	Wood structure
Artefacts recovered	————————▶	No artefacts recovered
Excavation status	————————▶	Finished

This grid was opened to the south of S16 and adjacent to S4 to the east in search of the end of the wood structure, as in the previous grid. The coverage was almost completely made up of ballast stones. Only one big coral head was removed from the SE sector of the grid, which had grown over the end of the floors. Underneath the southern end of the floor timbers it was possible to observe a piece made of thick timber. We believe it was part of the keel. We also reached the southern end of the ceiling planking in this grid, but it was very eroded and damaged, yet easily recognizable.

With this grid we finished the excavation of the hull structure of IDM-003 and its closest surroundings, uncovering the entire surviving assemblage of timber of the bottom and starboard side of the ship. (Fig. 19)

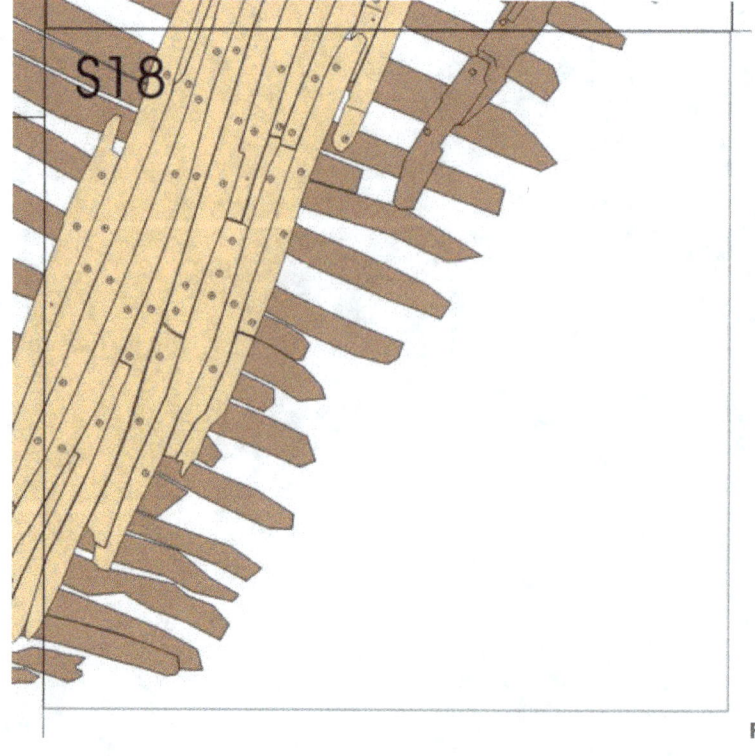

FIG.19

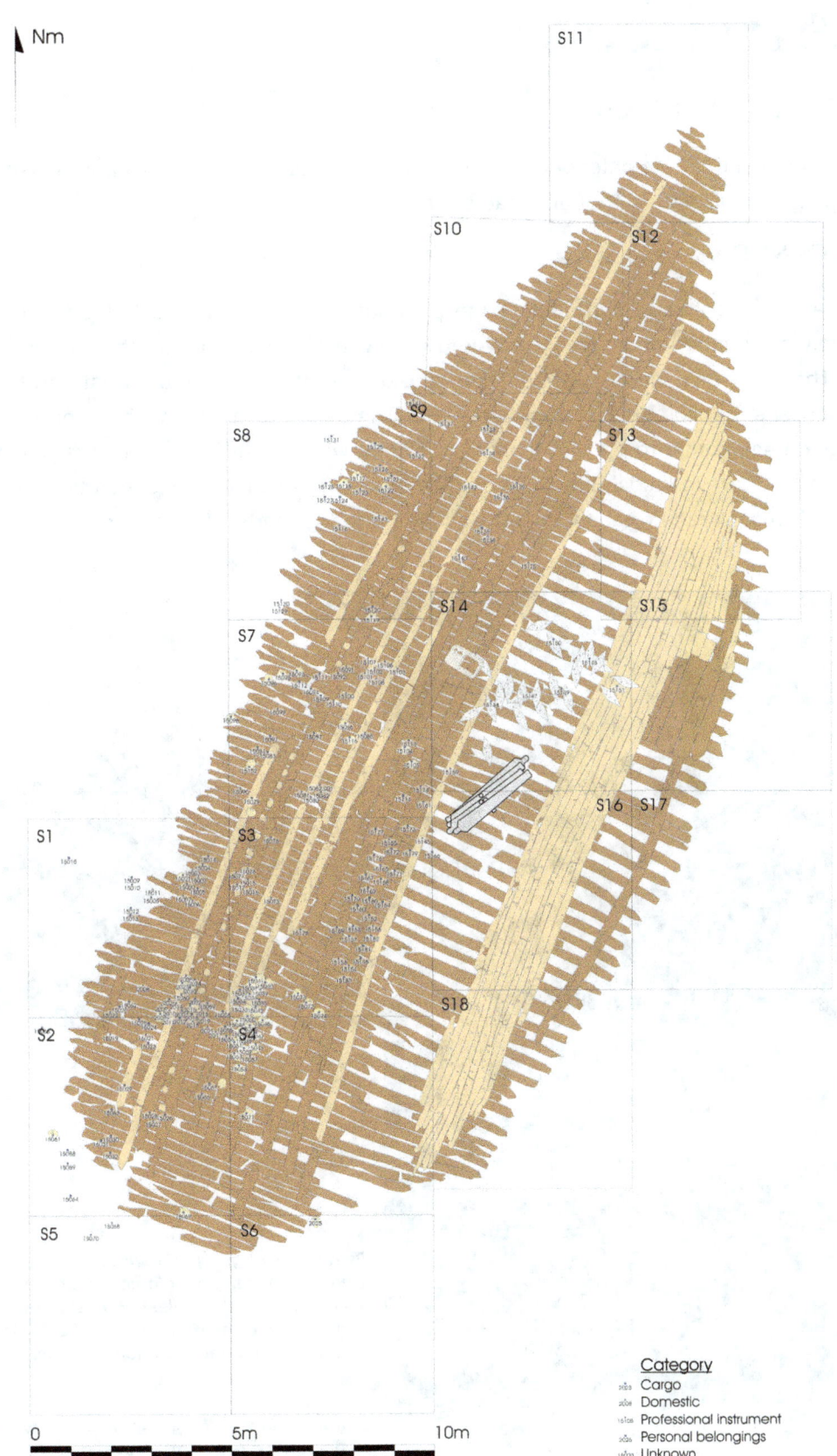

FIG.20
*IDM-003 Site plan
(At the end of
its excavation in
2006).*

Category
Cargo
Domestic
Professional instrument
Personal belongings
Unknown

SECTION 5

The Artefacts

ORDNANCE CATEGORY

The artefacts belonging to this category, observed at the site during the excavation phase were 4 iron cannons, several iron cannon balls, stone shot and lead shot.

THE IRON CANNONS

During excavation, in the area surrounding the previously discovered muzzle loader (G1) (2.5m long), which was completely surrounded and partially covered by ballast stones, another three cannons were found stored underneath. The four iron cannons were stacked one on top of another, the lowest one touching the timbers of the hull. In this case the storage system was evident. The cannons must have been originally tied up muzzle-to-muzzle alongside each other to prevent them from sliding with the ship's movements. The three cannons on the top (G1, G2 and G3) are identical, but G4 is slightly larger in dimension. Deconcretion of one of these cannons was done to allow for proper measurement. Sacrifice anodes made of zinc were installed afterwards to delay corrosion.

FIG.21/22
Two views of group of cannons (G1 to G4). Left photo shows the conglomerate at the time when most of the ballast stones around it were removed and the right picture shows G1 (on top) during its deconcretion process.

FIG.23
Another view of the group of cannons (G1 to G4) showing the original level of the ballast stones and the storage system.

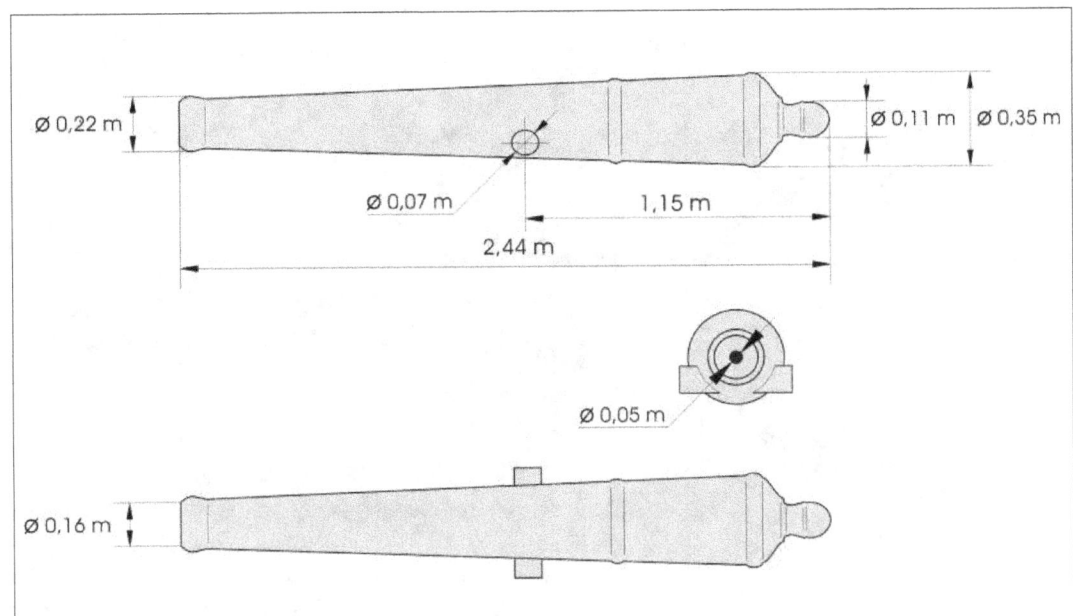

FIG.24
Measurements of cannons G1 to G3.

IRON CANNON BALLS

A large amount of cannon balls were found at the site, mainly on grids S7, S8 and S9, all of them concreted in clumps. They can be catalogued as small ones (2kg or 4.4lbs.), with a diameter of 0.07m. They were probably used with the iron cannon found, as well as others similar to G1.

STONE CANNON BALLS

Four stone shot were observed at the site. They were perfectly spherical and their diameters vary between 0.15m and 0.25m. No piece of ordnance, which could have used these projectiles, was found at the site.

LEAD SHOT

The large amount of lead shot found at grid S8 is all exactly the same type, weighing 35g with a diameter of 18mm. None of these lead shots were fired.

Two interesting concentrations of lead shot were observed between the timbers of the hull, contained between two thinner planks as if this were the original storage location for these items.

CARGO CATEGORY

The types of artefacts found at this site that can be catalogued as cargo are the olive jars, *Martaban* jars, ceramic lids, lead ingots, lead seals and elephant and hippopotamus tusks. This conclusion has been reached because of the large amount of these kinds of artefacts and the traces of arrangement observed among them.

ANIMAL TUSKS

A total of 22 animal tusks were found at the wreck, only 7 of them were recovered and conserved for identification purposes. Four of these tusks apparently belonged to African elephants *(Loxodonta Sp.)* and three to hippopotamus *(Hippopotamus amphibious).* (Fig. 25)(Fig. 26)(Fig. 27)

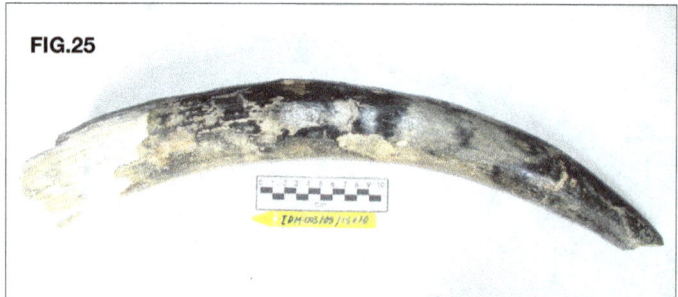

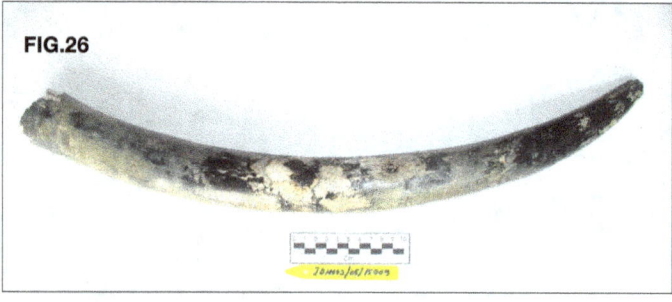

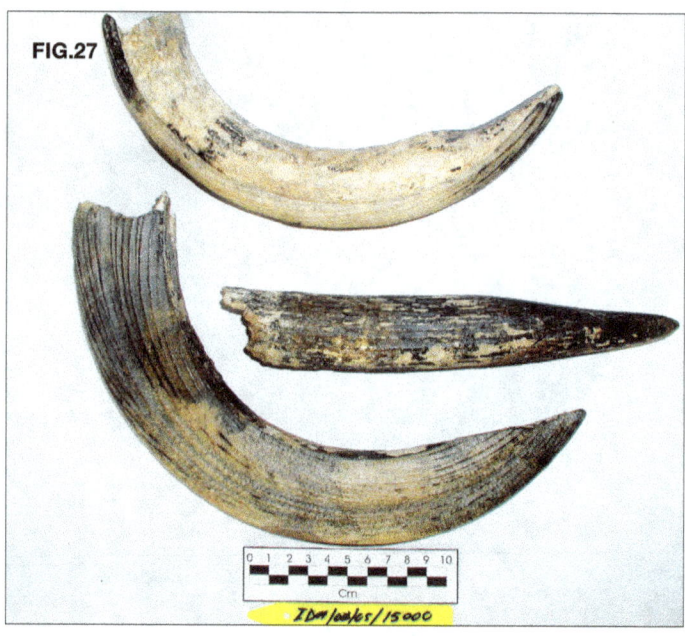

FIG.25/26/27
Two elephant tusks (Art. 15009 and 15010) left, and hippopotamus fangs on the right (Art. 15000).

The animal tusks were observed scattered mostly on grids S7, S8 and S9, but in two cases (west sector of S8 and north sector of S9) these objects were found close to fragments of a thick *Martaban* jar. The tusks found in the west of S8 were arranged inside the remains of the jar. This probably indicates that in at least two cases the tusks were transported inside these ceramic containers, which were otherwise mainly used for pepper and other spices.

All the pieces of tusks observed were in reasonably good condition, with little degradation due to the scarcity of oxygen and bacterial action deep under the sediment.

The remaining tusks observed at the wreck site and not recovered, were relocated and buried in the southern sector of S9 after having been measured and photographed, exactly on the edge of the stone ballast pile.

OLIVE JARS

This type of artefact was found in almost every grid along the wreck site, with an important concentration between grids S1, S2, S3 and S4, where some form of storage arrangement was observed. (Fig. 28)

FIG.28
In situ olive jars resting on the hull's timbers on the northwest section of grid S4.

Large containers, these olive jars transported a variety of contents, including bullets, capers, beans, chick peas, lard, tar, wine, olives in brine, and olive oil *(Goggin 1960:6)*. These are jars for shipping and storage, with three general shapes. Goggin (1960) established a basic typology still in use, designating the oblong shape as **Type A**, the globular form as **Type B**, and the tapering "carrot-shape" as **Type C** (*Hurst et al.* 1986:66). All have a constricted neck and a thick rim, some of which have been found with pitch-covered corks still in place.

Volume measurements of examples from shipwrecks imply Type A oblong jars were used to hold the Castilian wine arroba of 4.26 gallons, although two 1695 examples seem to be for the Castilian oil arroba of 3.31 gallons (*Marken* 1994:127). Late 16th century Type B globular jars appear to be half of an oil arroba (1.65 gallons), but early 17th century samples showed an average volume of about 1.56 gallons. Type C carrot-shaped jars had an average volume of about 0.57 gallons (*Marken* 1994:123).

In total, 51 olive jars were found at this wreck site and although they are all different in terms of their shapes and the material used to make them, it is still possible to catalogue them in three essentially different groups.

TYPE A

Only 4 olive jars from this wreck site were described as Type A (oblong shape) due to their shape, but with the difference that, in our case, the volume of these items is of 6 litres (1.65 gallons or ½ oil arroba), more similar to the volume described for Type B in the early 18th century. (Fig. 29)

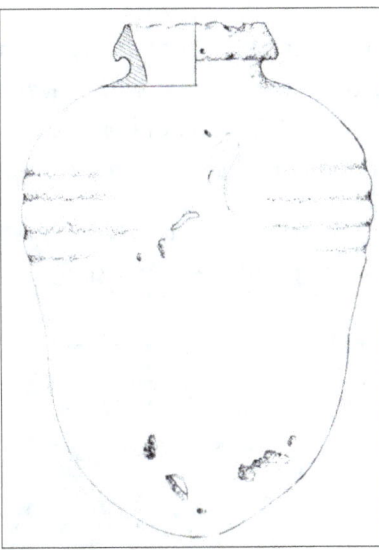

FIG.29
Two samples of Type A olive jars (Art. 15004 left and Art. 15098 right) and drawing of Art. 15098.

These items are light sand in colour with no trace of glaze neither on the inside nor the outside. They are made of a thick material with coarse sand and with large air pockets in the mass.

TYPE B

This type was the one with the largest number of samples found: 46 artefacts. They are quite similar in shape if we disregard the deformations produced during the process in the kiln. They are all of the same volume (6 litres / 1.65 gallons) although the material is different. Some of them show traces of green or grey glazed both in the interior and on the exterior, mainly around the neck and other protected areas. (Fig. 30)

FIG.30
Typical sample of Type B olive jar (Art. 15051) and its drawing.

TYPE B WITH A FLATTENED BASE

Only one olive jar of this type was found at this wreck. It is of the same volume (6 litres / 1.65 gallons) as the large group described above. Nevertheless, the feature of the flat base and the fact that it was found in the western sector of S2, completely isolated and far from the main concentration of olive jars, lead us to believe that it had a domestic function on the ship rather than being part of the cargo.

It is made of reddish-brown clay with large air pockets in its material, partially cracked and with a small fragment missing. The base is slightly concave and has a thick wall.

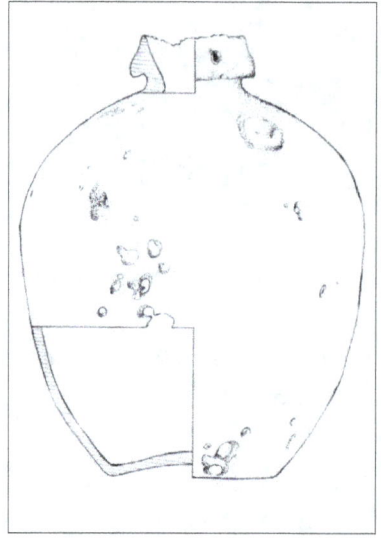

FIG.31
Type B olive jar with a flattened base (Art. 15061) and its drawing.

CERAMIC LIDS

A group of 8 ceramic lids belonging to the ship's cargo were found close to the olive jars. Due to this and because of their diameter (84 to 88mm) and shape, which perfectly matches the mouth of the olive jars, we believe that they may have been used to close the olive jars over the cork. (Fig.32)

FIG.32
Example of a ceramic lid in relation to an olive jar, both in-situ, suggesting a closing function.

In all cases these ceramic lids present traces of having been glazed both on the interior and exterior sides. Seven of them are greenish in colour and one of them is dark grey. (Fig.33)

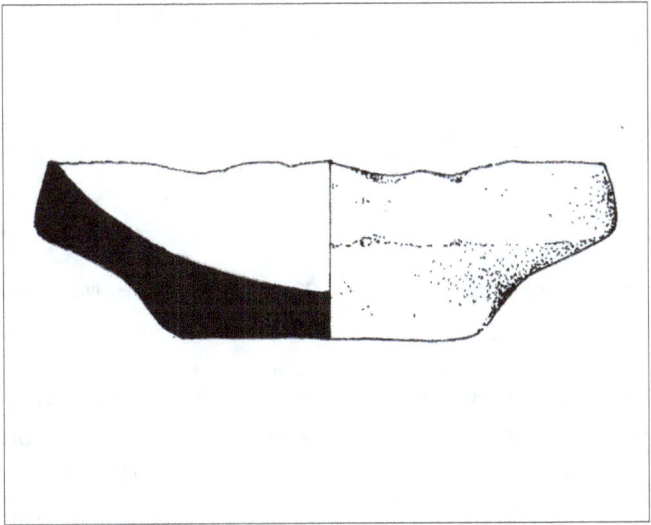

FIG.33
Ceramic lid and its drawing (Art. 15084) showing clear traces of glaze on its interior and rim.

MARTABAN JARS AND OTHER CONTAINERS

This group comprises a wide variety of large ceramic containers or fragments of them, which were found on the wreck site.

The *Martaban* is a large earthenware jar, usually glazed (to prevent liquid contents leaking), bearing circular lugs on the upper shoulders. Made since the Tang dynasty (618 to 906AD), and possibly earlier, their original purpose was to store liquids, especially water, on long voyages. However, they were also used for storing other things such as food, pickles, spices and even breakable porcelain. Made in South China, they were exported in large numbers for at least 1,000 years to the Philippines, Indonesia and other parts of South East Asia.

Although some of the fragments are of varying thickness and the partially complete artefacts are of different sizes, we grouped them according to the kind of glaze, the flat base and the presence of lugs or "ears". The reason for this is that we really know very little about these huge jars. They are notoriously hard to date. Moreover, they are all called *"Martabans"* despite the fact that many of these jars could actually have been made throughout Asia and may have remained practically unchanged from the 13th/14th to the 19th century. (*Vihn*, pers. comm.) (Fig.34)

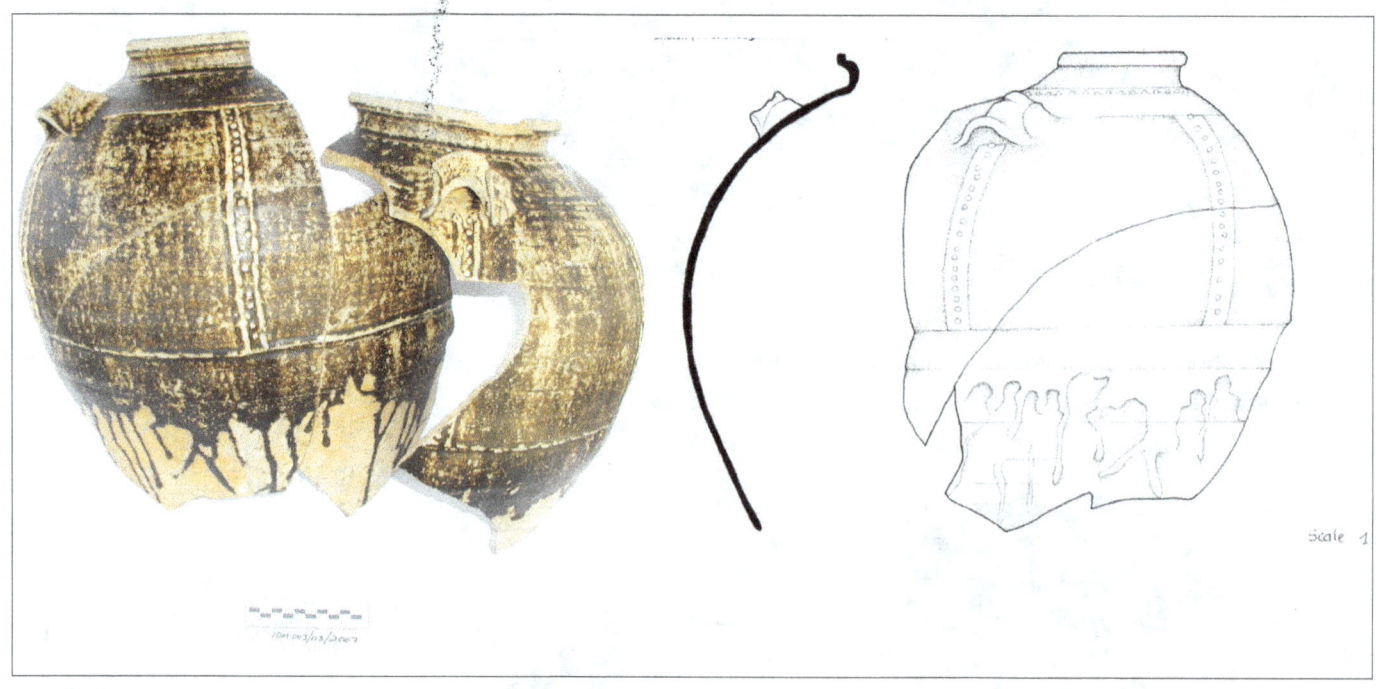

FIG.34
Fragmented Martaban jar (Art. 2007) and its drawing. Note the marks of the tar used to close and seal the mouth of the jar.

There are undoubtedly two kinds of jars. The first kind includes ones that are undecorated or decorated with common motifs (dragons, flowers, symbols and emblems) and clearly made for usage. The second kind includes high quality fine jars, glazed in several different colours (up to five). These were also for usage, but probably only inside homes serving simultaneously as decorative pieces or as urns. The most common decoration of our artefacts is the one showed above and below, with simple strips and dots. This simulating reinforcement in the material suggests a clear use for storage rather than a purely decorative use. (Fig.35)

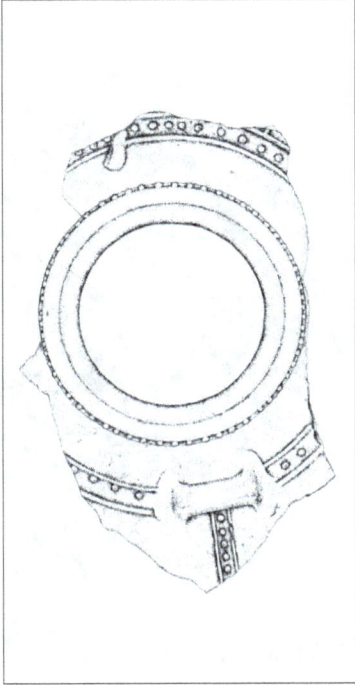

FIG.35
Two views of another fragment of a Martaban jar (Art. 15088) showing the same decoration.

The variety of sizes, thickness and colours of the material used to make these jars is in fact interesting. The team found several fragments of different *Martabans* at the wreck site and none of them were identical to another. It is also curious that most of the animal tusks seen during the excavation were found in close contact to the largest *Martaban* fragments, suggesting that they were transported inside them. However, no description has been found indicating that these jars could have been used mainly for this purpose. (Fig.36)

FIG.36
Examples of the different characteristics of the material and manufacture of Martaban jars found at the wreck (Arts. 15015, 15017 and 15089 on the right).

The team also found another type of storage container (Artefact No. 15092). It is smaller in size but very similar in shape to the bigger *Martaban* jars, with a flat base and glazed. The main difference is that it has no lugs. Part of the rim is missing and we can see some faint traces of tar running down the body up to about 0.05m from the base. (Fig.37)

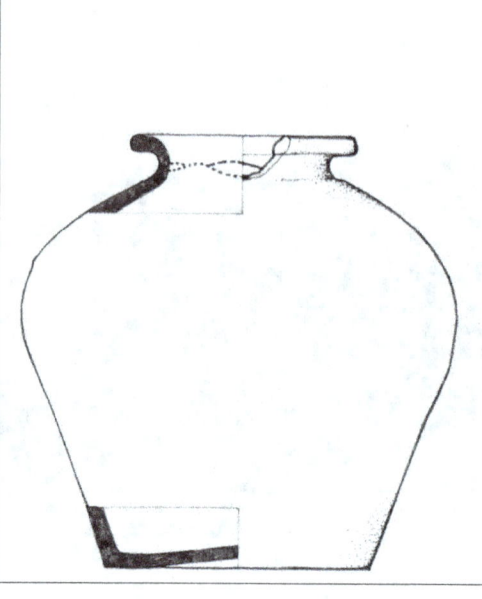

FIG.37
Artefact No. 15092 and technical drawing. A similar jar was found at the site but was left in-situ as it was strongly attached to a coral colony.

LEAD INGOTS

In total 106 lead ingots were found at the wreck. These ingots are boat-shaped with a triangular transversal section and narrower towards the ends for easier handling. On the flat upper face they show circular marks, probably indicating the ownership of these objects. The weight of each ingot is approximately 50kg and the length is 650mm. (Fig.38)

FIG.38
Lead ingot (Artefact No. 133) and a close up of one of the stamps.

FIG.39
Views of the cargo of lead ingots as found during excavation and prepared to be lifted to the ship.

The concentration of lead ingots in Grid S14 and some small round timbers observed in their vicinity suggests that they were stored directly on top of the planking of the ceiling. It seems that some sort of wooden "corral" was built around them, but got destroyed by their weight when the ship turned over starboard side and the cargo of ingots slid.

LEAD SEALS

In total 49 lead seals were found during excavation, most of them agglomerated inside an iron concretion at the level of the first deck clamp and the bow tail frame. These lead seals are basically shaped in two different ways, the first one is the one formed by two lead discs attached by a lead strip, allowing to press and close both discs **(Type A)**. The second shape is a flattened octagonal cylinder with small stamps on both flat faces **(Type B)** and although this type does not seem to be a proper "seal", as it has no apparent sealing function, we included it in this group because of the material and the spatial relationship with the former group.

TYPE A

This group of lead seals presents four different pairs of symbols. The most common is the one depicting the Portuguese symbol *"Esfera Armilar"*. This image was the personal emblem of King D. Manuel I, even before he became King, when he was still the Duke of Beja. It represents the Portuguese navigational epic. This seal could confirm that the ship was transporting official cargo to India from the Portuguese King. Strangely, the symbol on the back face was unrecognizable in all of the lead seals of this subgroup, although it was evidently some sort of coat of arms or blazon. (Fig.40)

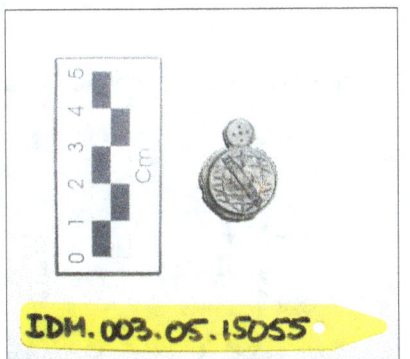

FIG.40
The lead seal in the shape of the Portuguese "Esfera Armilar" (Artefact No. 15055).The finding of this artefact strongly reinforces the hypothesis of the Portuguese origin of this ship.

The second most commonly found were the seals with a *"Fleur de Lis"* on one face and an unidentified coat of arms on the other. The artefacts that are part of this group were the smallest of all the lead seals found. (Fig.41)

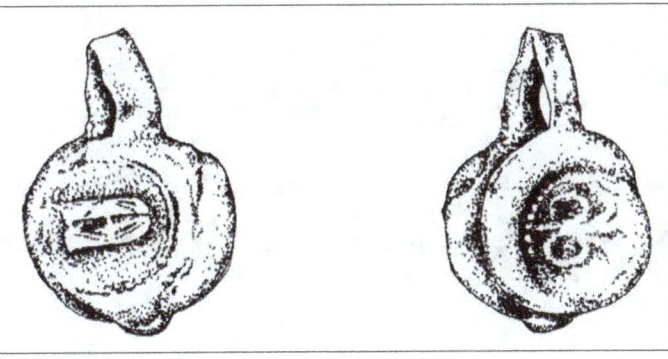

FIG.41

The third group, with only four occurrences, is composed of seals depicting a stylized horse with a pole and a flag on one face and an unidentified figure on the back face. (Fig.42)

 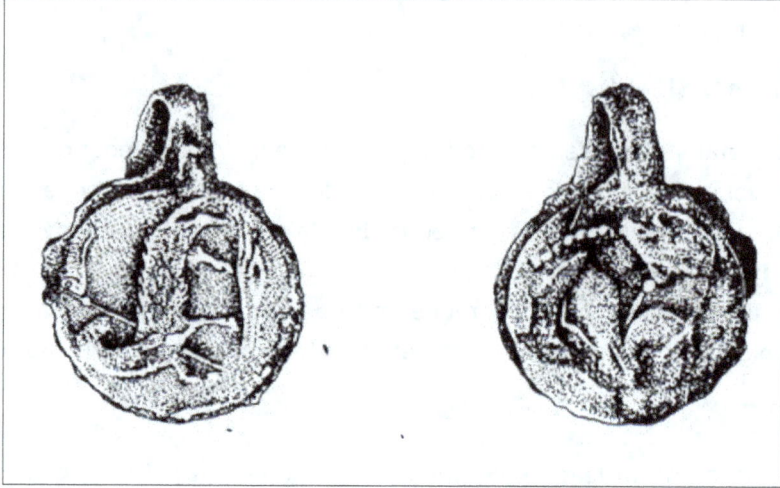

FIG.42

The "horse with a pole" in the description is probably an *"agnus dei"* - a traditional symbolization of Jesus Christ. On primitive (and very small) lead seals - which are hit sloppily just to make sure that the bail of cloth is secure - the real image of the "Lamb of God" holding a banner on one of its legs can easily lose its lamb characteristics and turn into a horse and the banner into a pole. We had observed this phenomenon on another occasion - not with a lead seal but with a wax pilgrim's token in Germany.

The last group of lead seals, **Type A**, is represented by only two artefacts with a letter "A" and two linked "C"s under it in one face and apparently no figure on the back. (Fig.43)

 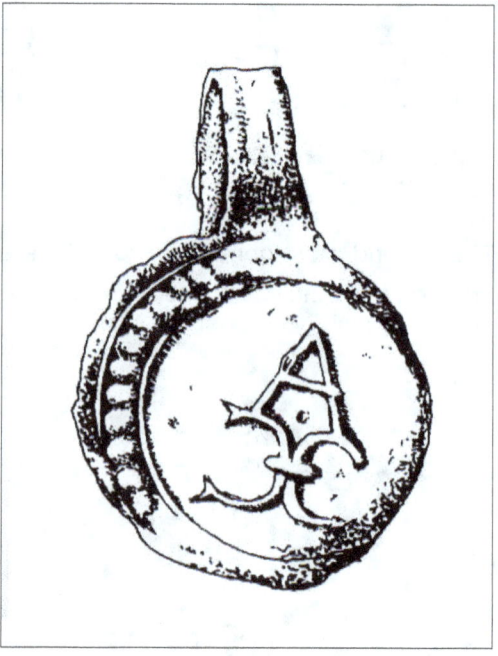

FIG.43

TYPE B

The lead artefacts included in this group are only two octagonal cylinders with marks on both faces, probably used as stamps rather than seals. The doubt regarding this use is the fact that the "R" depicted on one of them is in the correct position rather than a "mirror reflection", as it would be on a stamp. (Fig.44)

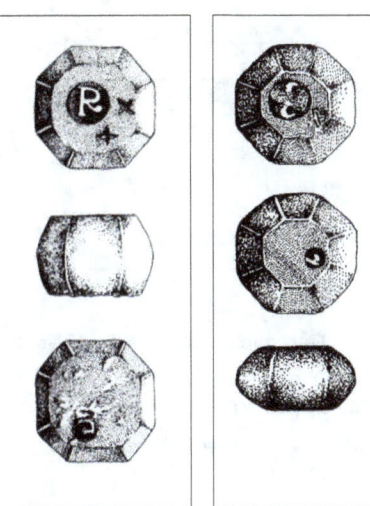

FIG.44

DOMESTIC CATEGORY

The types of artefacts found at this site that can be catalogued as domestic are: pottery containers, glass vessels, Chinese porcelain, glazed ceramics, pewter tableware, copper kitchenware and pewter tops. Due to the diversity of artefacts, these will be described below according to the material they are made of.

POTTERY

An interesting group of small and delicate flasks, bowls and cups was found in the intersections of grids S1 and S2, lying between the timbers. The flasks are decorated with leaves' motifs around the globular part of the body. They seem to have been manufactured in India and used for fine oil or other precious liquids as in both cases the outlet orifice is very narrow. (Fig.45a/45b)

FIG.45a

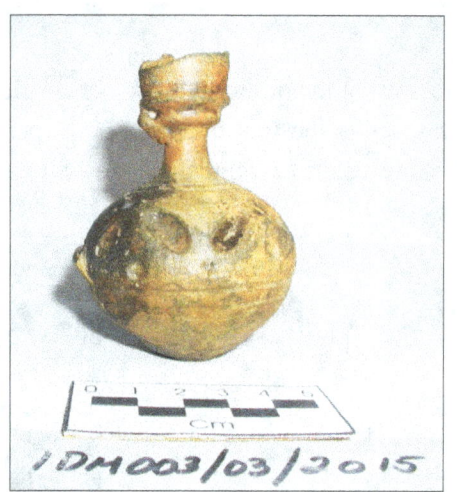 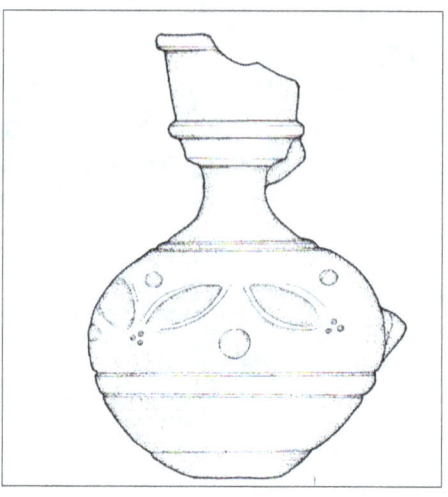

FIG.45b

FIG.45a/45b
Ceramic flasks (Artefacts No. 2009 and 2015) and technical drawings.

A small dispenser, apparently used for salt or pepper and found with the previous flasks and a small cup, both made of the same fine grain earthenware, are also interesting artefacts. (Fig.46)

 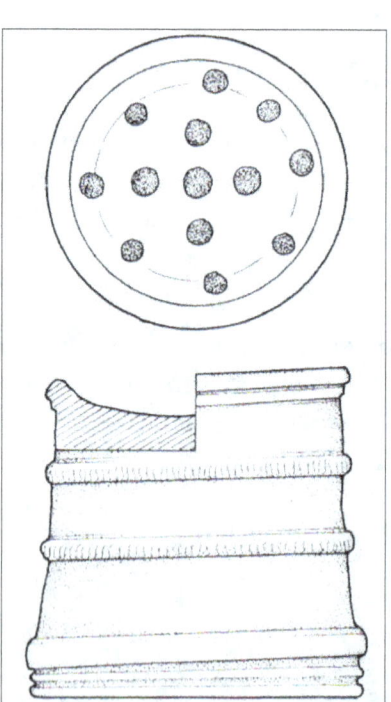 

FIG.46
Ceramic dispenser and cup (Artefacts No. 2017 and 2011).

Together with these small and delicate objects, the team found a stack of four earthenware bowls, as originally stored. These objects were supposedly used in everyday life on board as no packing material was found between them, potentially indicating long-term storage. (Fig.47)

FIG.47
Stack of bowls as was found, bowls displayed and drawing of one of them (Artefact No. 2019).

Various pottery vessels, part of daily life on the ship were also found. The wider ones were used for thicker liquids (such as honey) and the narrower ones for wine, water, etc. (Fig.48)

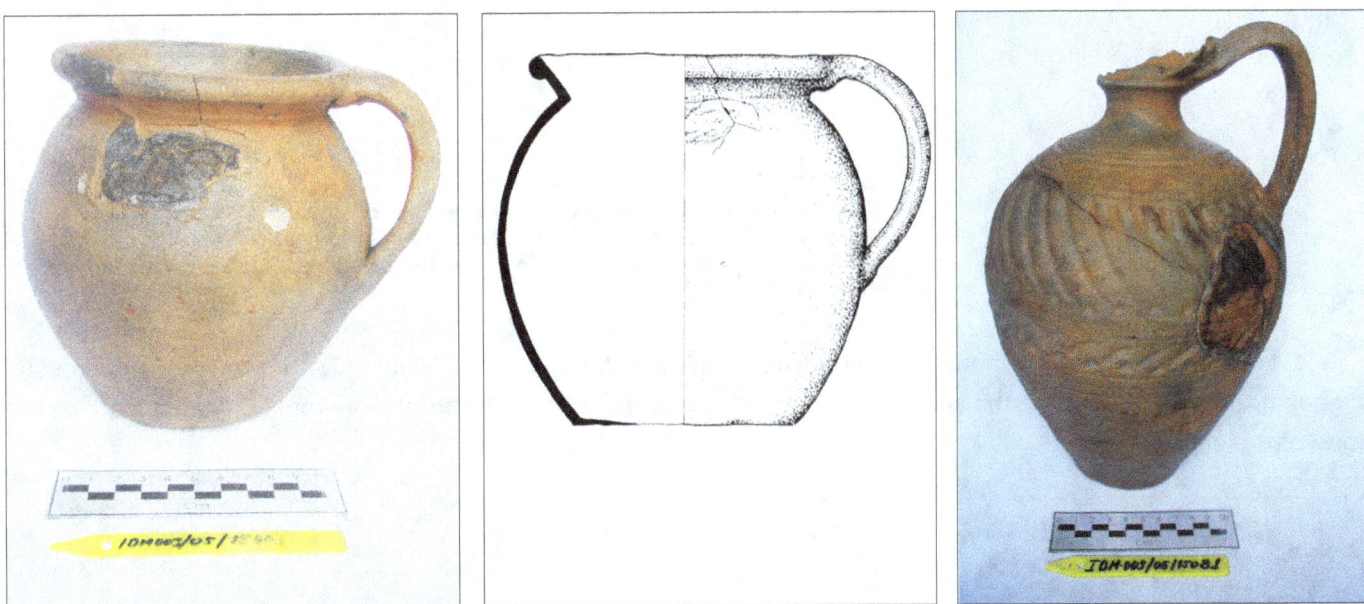

FIG.48
Pottery vessels. Art No. 15003 and drawing (left and center) and Artefact No. 15081.

Two earthenware pots, apparently of African origin, were found at the site, one partially cracked and concreted to a cannon ball and the other one intact. They are both of a very dark tone of brown and very porous material, the result of a relatively low firing temperature.

Artefact 15080 is decorated around the wider part of the bulge with a design of "hills" filled with a very symmetrical pattern of dots arranged in diagonal and parallel lines. It shows a smaller belt around the base of the neck with crossed lines, both deeply carved in the paste. (Fig.49)

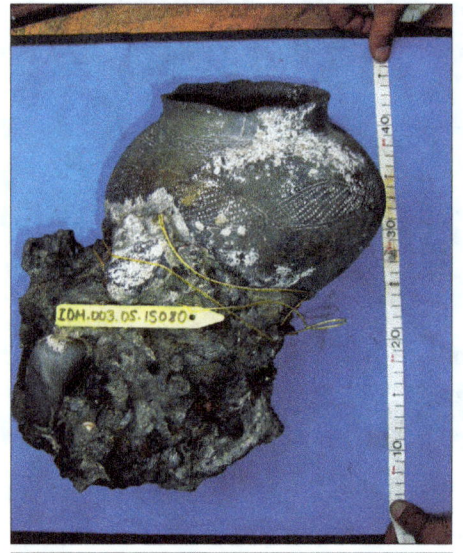

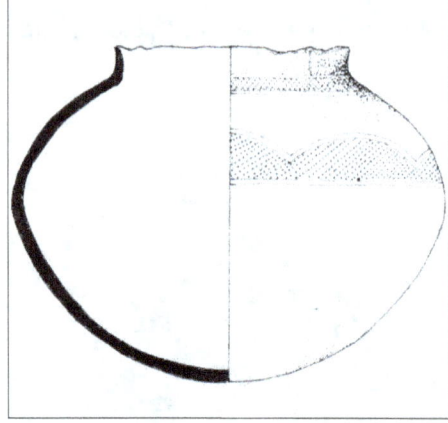

FIG.49
Different stages of the conservation and restoration process of Art. No. 15080. Above left, when found and still attached to the cannon ball. Above center during the reconstruction works and above right after restoration. Technical drawing of the artefact on the left.

Artefact 15102 is of the same manufacture but with much simpler decoration, with only shallow marks of crossed diagonal lines on the rim. It is the shape of a bowl with an acute concave bottom. It presents the same dark brown tone of the clay. (Fig.50)

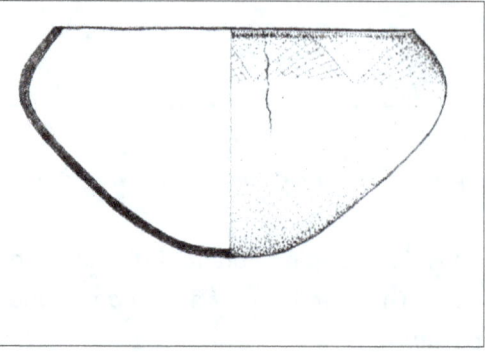

FIG.50
Earthenware bowl, Art. No. 15102 and technical drawing.

GLASS

As expected in a wreck from such an early period, very few fragments of glass had survived. During excavation we observed different typologies of glass, varying from flat transparent fragments (possibly from lanterns) of very fine glass to a thick "sodium glass" found in the only intact glass artefact of the wreck. (Fig.51)

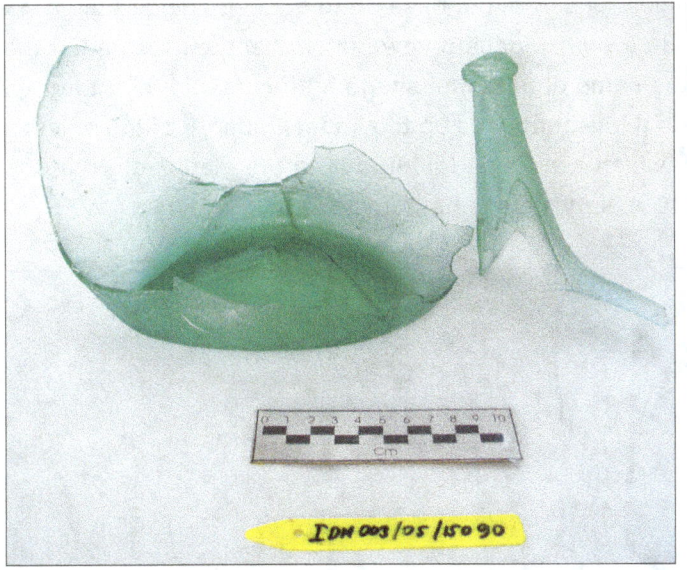 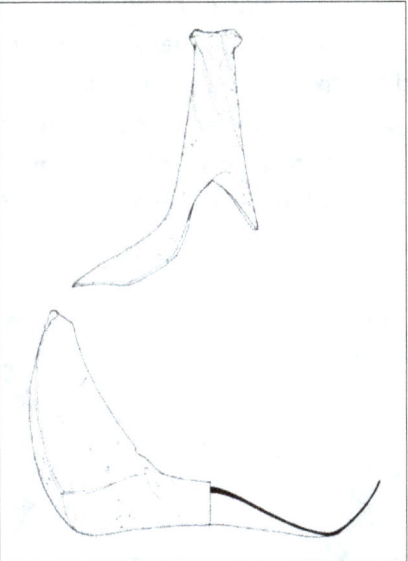

FIG.51
Fragmented blue glass bottle (Art No. 15090) and drawing. Made of blown glass.

 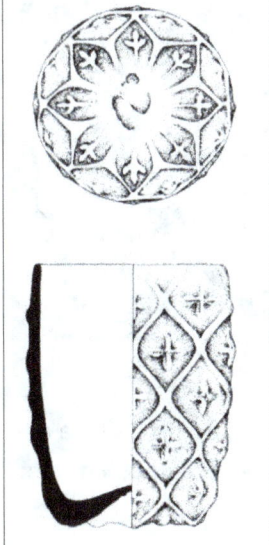 

FIG.52
Intact drinking glass (Art No. 15091) and detail of the ornamental design on the bottom. Soda glass.

The drinking glass is nicely ornamented with four *"Fleur de Lis"* petals around its body and on the bottom, which is concave and presents a shallow "thieve" with the mark of the blowing stem in the centre.

This sodium silicate, or soda glass, is a vitreous substance and although it is not colourless and transparent, it may be considered a glass for general use. Although glass is said to be a silicate of one of the basic metals and thus we speak of sodium glass, potassium glass, lead glass, etc., in practice this is never the case. Each glass is actually a mixture of these different silicates in varying proportions. The silicate of the metal from which the glass is named is predominant or usually imparts some particular characteristic on the glass. Every glass fragment found on the wreck shows bubbles inside the material.

The most striking find within the ballast stones was probably a blue delicate glass flask. Although it had been trapped in such an aggressive environment with heavy stones, the glass was, incredibly, still intact. This flask has a globular body decorated with strips of chained ovals, which runs from the base up to the beginning of the neck like meridians on the earth's globe. The neck is shaped like a swirl widening upwards and ends truncated at the top, apparently to hold the missing top. The spout has the same ornamental shape and ends as if cut, after an acute gooseneck. The circular base of this flask has a deep thieve that goes up to almost a quarter of the object's height. The handle is an elaborate figure of blown glass, which was added later, during the manufacture of the flask. The glass is bluish in colour and only a few air bubbles are visible in its body. (Fig.53)

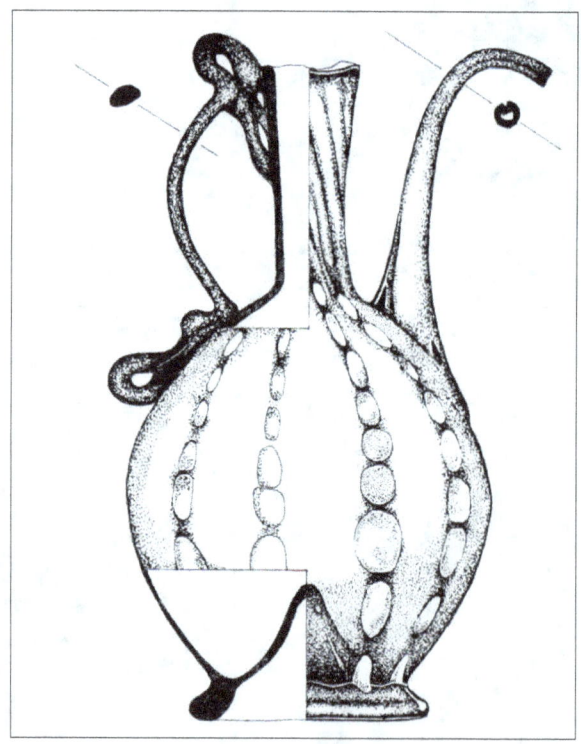

FIG.53

The function of this beautiful flask can only be deduced based on its size and the narrowness of its spout, which suggests that it was used to drop fine oil, perfume or other precious liquids.

CHINESE PORCELAIN

Only two artefacts made of Chinese porcelain were found during the excavation (a plate and a *Kendi*), although some fragments were observed in grids S7, S8 and S9. These were not in sufficient quantity to be considered cargo, therefore the Chinese porcelain objects of this wreck have been catalogued as domestic items.

The plate was found in twelve fragments scattered all along grid S7 and was put together during the conservation process in the laboratory. The deer's landscape motifs are very common in "Kraak" porcelain, the Chinese export porcelain typical of the 1580-1640s period. It is characterized by shapes seemingly related to metal and by its dense decoration, mostly organized in radiating panels. Portuguese traders, who in the 16th century began to import late Ming dynasty blue and white porcelain into Europe, introduced Kraak porcelain to the west. It is generally believed that the name "kraak" came from the Portuguese ships, called carracks, in which the porcelain was transported.

FIG.54
Deer plate (Art. 15107) as found before and after conservation. No stamp was placed on the back.

The *Kendi* (also called "nose drinking cup") was found in the centre of grid S7, heavily attached to an iron bolt, with a crack at the base of the stem. It was restored in the lab during the conservation process.

This particular artefact is made of white porcelain with blue cobalt decoration under the glaze, showing a circular bulge, a long straight stem and a very prominent spout. It is decorated with a scroll of stylized lotus around the bulge as well as curled and straight leafs around the stem. The base shows a mark depicting a white hare in front of a blue rock. This form is typically found in late 16th century Ming porcelain, most probably from the Wanli period (1573-1619). *(Pinto de Matos,* pers. comm.)

A *Kendi* is a pouring vessel with a spout on the side but without a handle. While pouring, the pot is held around its neck. Pouring vessels of this kind were not available in China before the Song dynasty. The earliest types seem to have been straight spouted vessels, with a Southern Chinese brown-black *Jian* type glaze. (Fig.55)

FIG.55
Kendi (Art. 15085) after conservation (left) and still attached to the iron bolt. Detail of the stamp, a hare against a blue rock, is located on the bottom.

In South East Asia *Kendis* were used whenever a pouring vessel with a spout could possibly be practical; from administering medication to drinking and from washing to sacrificial blessing. Its main use seems to have been as a water drinking vessel, as several people could share one water bottle hygienically and without using any cups, by tilting the kendi and drinking directly from the stream coming from its spout.

It might also be that a *Kendi* is the vessel referred to in *Jingdezhen Tao Lu* as translated by G. R. Sayer in 1951. The following entry #65 on page 90, says: *"Southerners practice nose-drinking. They have pottery vessels like cups or bowls with a small tube like the lip of a bottle fixed at the side ..."* The source, Tao Lu, cites a *Treatise on the Geography and Natural History of the South of China*, dated the 11th century (mid Northern Song dynasty).

Contemporary paintings, literary or archaeological evidence has so far not confirmed that anybody ever "drank through their nose". The original name mentioned in the Northern Song source above might instead have been *spout drinking* vessel instead of *nose drinking*, since the protruding spout even today is sometimes called the "nose" of a vessel. The *Kendi* was unique because one was actually supposed to drink directly from the spout. The 'nose drinking cup' in the Northern Song source above might therefore have been a *Kendi*. *Kendis* come in all sizes from very large to miniature ones, possibly used as water droppers. Some medium-sized to small *Kendis* were used for medication. Whether or not some of the drugs could have been administered through the nostrils at some point will probably remain an open question. (*Vihn,* pers. comm.)

GLAZED CERAMICS

A few fragments of glazed ceramics, both of European and Asian origin were found during the excavation of this site. The fragments identified as European are of the *Majolica* type, a tin-glazed earthenware. Tin enamel is a form of glaze, containing a tin oxide, with which earthenware is coated before being painted with colours. When fired, the glaze and the pigments fuse, producing a bright and glowing appearance. (Fig.56)

FIG.56
Two views of Art. 15142 one of the few fragments of Majolica found at the wreck.

Majolica, the first tin-glazed earthenware seen in Europe, reached Italy in the 14th century when the painters of the region were moving into the heady excitement of the Renaissance. In about 1400, merchants from Majorca exported them from Spain to Italy. They become known to the Italians as Majorca-ware, or *majolica*.

The only complete artefact of this kind is one of the two lids found in grid S2, all fragmented but with all fragments present. The artefact was later conserved and restored, in the conservation laboratory, to its original form. (Fig.57)

  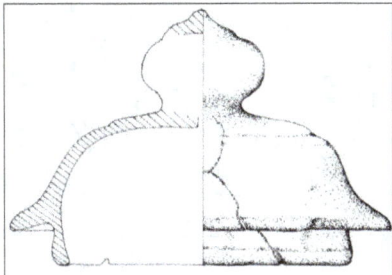 

FIG.57
Artefact 15027 as found in grid S2 (upper left), during its restoration process (above, centre), technical drawing after the pieces were put together (upper right) and after completion of its conservation and restoration (right).

One interesting glazed ceramic fragment was found on grid S7, with leaves motifs, but also depicting a swastika. At this phase of the study we have not yet determined whether it is of Chinese or Indian origin.

The swastika is an ancient symbol that has been used for over 3,000 years (it even predates the ancient Egyptian symbol, the Ankh). Artefacts such as pottery and coins from ancient Troy show that the swastika was a commonly used symbol going back as far as 1000 BCE.

During the thousand years that followed, the image of the swastika was used by many cultures around the world, including in China *(wan)*, Japan, India *(swastika)*, and southern Europe. By the Middle Ages, the swastika was a well known, if not commonly used, symbol but had different names in different countries such as in England *(fylfot)*, Germany *(Hakenkreuz)* and Greece *(tetraskelion and gammadion)*. In general the swastika has been used by many cultures throughout the past 3,000 years to represent life, sun, power, strength, and good luck. (Fig.58)

 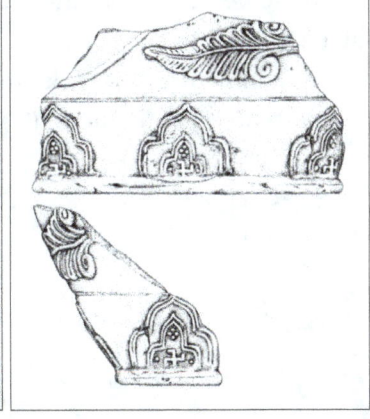

FIG.58
Artefact 15126. Almost the entire glaze is presently missing, with only a few traces of green in the upper right corner. Note the swastika motifs around the base.

PEWTER

The team found various artefacts made of pewter, from tableware to medicine bottle tops and catalogued them as domestic. The pewter artefacts found had marks of the provenience or quality of the material as is common, leading us to believe that they were utilitarian objects with no ornamental function. (Fig.59)

 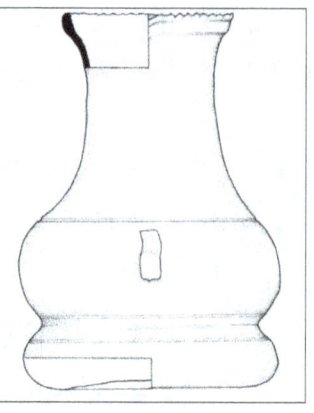 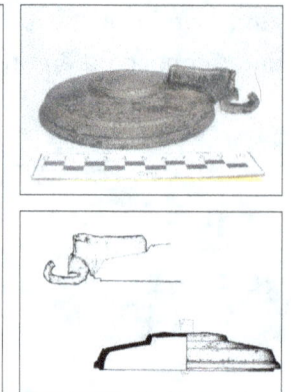

FIG.59
A pewter jar (Artefact 2008) found in grid S1 and a pewter lid (Artefact 15011) found in grid S1 but 4m to the north. Due to the measurements and characteristics of these artefacts, we think they belonged together.

Two plates made of very fine pewter were also found, heavily concreted with iron pieces and cannon balls in grid S7. One of these plates was partially cracked along the rim and was restored in the laboratory. (Fig.60)

 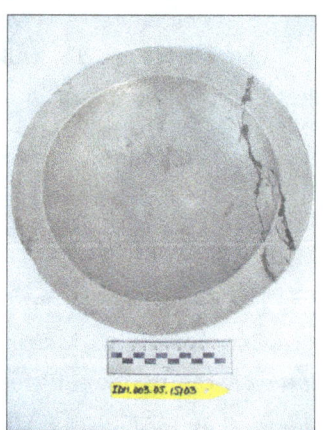 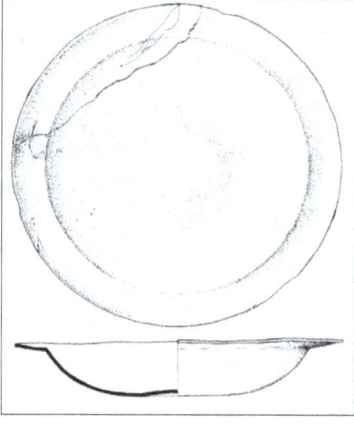

FIG.60
A pewter plate (Artefact 15103) found in grid S7 during the restoration process and in its final condition. Technical drawing on the right.

The bottle tops recovered (5) are all of a similar type, with two parts, one with an outer thread and the other one with an inner thread and an attaching ring on the top. The lower part was attached to the rim of a green glass bottle as evidenced by some remains of this material still attached to the body and the upper part screwed to the latter. As observed on some marks on the sediment in the vicinity of these finds, the container bottle might have been of a flat base, like the ones used for medicine on board ships at the time. (Fig.61)

  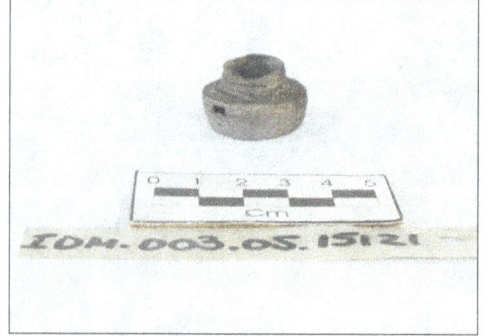

FIG.61
Samples of pewter bottle tops (Artefacts 15097 and 15121) after conservation. Note that 15121 had a missing top - the thread where the upper part was attached was clearly visible.

COPPER

The sample of the domestic artefacts made of copper comprises mainly kitchenware: a frying pan and an unidentified object. Both were found close to fragments of the handle of a larger copper pot and pottery coarse ware, most probably belonging to the ship's galley. (Fig.62)

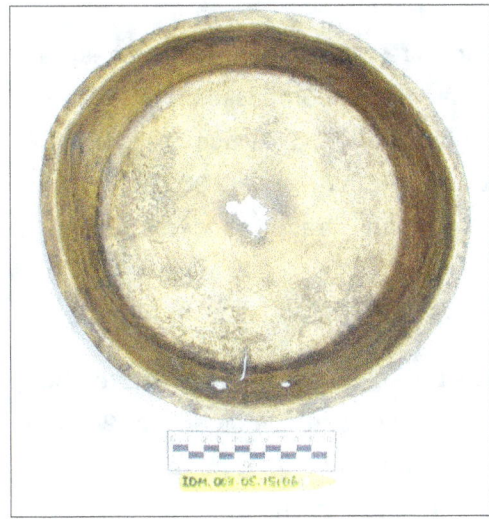 

FIG.62
Above the surviving part of the frying pan (Art. 15106) and the object of unknown function (Art. 15012), but presumably from the kitchen.

A large group of artefacts of various shapes but apparently with the same function was found inside the iron concretion on the deck clamp of the first deck (orlop deck). These consist of a variety of copper sheaths with some ornamentation and fixing holes on their bases, in some cases with the rivets still in place. The upper and narrower end of these sheaths is slightly bent inwards ending in a dented elbow, which might have served as an attachment to something. These ornamented but functional pieces were apparently part of a lamp, leather book cover's binding pieces or some other part of the ship's furniture. (Fig.63)

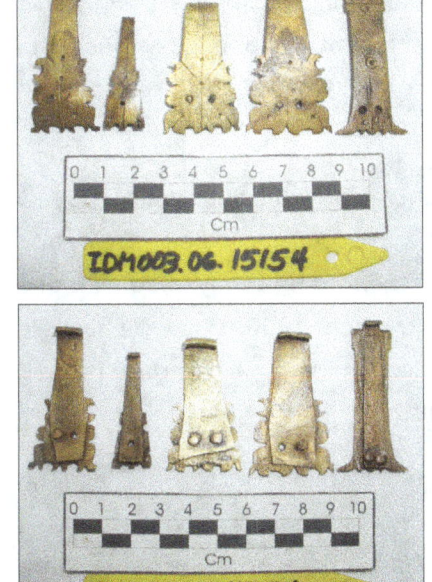 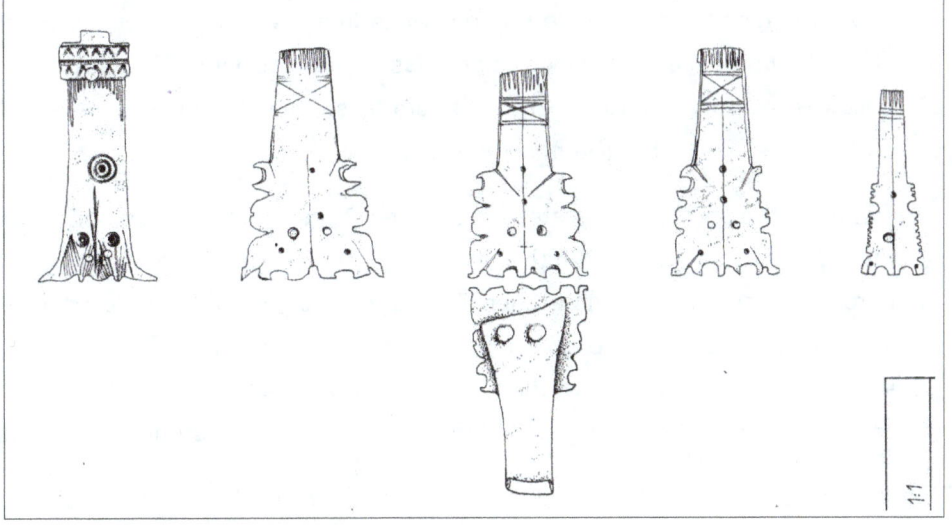

FIG.63

PROFESSIONAL INSTRUMENTS CATEGORY

The artefacts belonging to this category found at the site during this phase of excavation were: 5 navigation dividers, 1 ruler and a sail maker's palm. The sample of navigational instruments of this wreck is impressive due to the remarkable conservation condition of some of the dividers and the ruler.

Dividers, called "compasses" in those days, are frequently found at shipwreck sites, testifying to their widespread use in maritime navigation. Artisans, carpenters, engineers and navigators used plain compasses for marking off distances, measuring scales, dividing measurements into equal parts, and for copying drawings and charts. As part of a typical set of drafting instruments, dividers are used for measuring lengths (*Turner* 1980:55). A basic compass is easily described. Made of brass, the instrument consists of two long, straight pieces attached by a central joint. Due to later innovations, this basic type is commonly referred to as "simple" or "plain" dividers (*Turner* 1980:56).

Dividers or compasses were especially helpful if the navigator had to estimate the ship's position. When attempting to sail along a latitude, that is to say east-west or west-east, the navigator would take two sightings, 24 hours apart. Hopefully, the two readings would be the same. If they were not, he could use two dividers to estimate the position of the vessel placing one leg on the point where he thought the ship was and the other on the course he thought he had sailed. The second compass would be placed as well, with one leg on the latitude scale of his observed latitude and the other leg on the east-west line where the course met the latitude scale. He would draw the two innermost legs of the compasses together and where they crossed was his estimated position (*Waters* 1958:76).

By the 16th century, instrument makers had designed a wide variety of compasses for a variety of purposes. The first innovation involved cutting the ends off the legs and adding a joint so other attachments could be used. These bronze compasses with interchangeable steel legs often included extra steel points so the attachments could be changed. Some deluxe compass kits included inking nibs or pencil holders. A compass using these attachments was called a "drawing compass." Kits also included another attachment to append a wheel with small spikes radiating out to the end of a compass. This attachment, called a "dotting wheel," was used to make punctuated lines on charts (*Hambly* 1988:69).

In addition to the straight, plain steel legs, compasses came in other, non-straight leg designs for other purposes. A charting compass has legs that are curved. The legs begin closer together widen out into a near circle, and then are bent back toward each other. The large, circular configuration allowed them to be easily used with one hand. A final type, called a "proportional compass," was developed by Jost Bürgi about 1600. This type has two arms and a pivot part way down the leg so the ends open at different lengths, usually 2:1. This compass is used to create distances that are twice the length of the original distance (*Turner* 1980:56).

Our compasses are made of copper along the entire body, without the removable steel points of the legs, so common in other early dividers. Four of these instruments are of the One Hand Divider type, showing the top part of the legs curved so that they can be opened and closed with only one hand whilst working on the nautical chart. The other divider is of a straight pattern type. (Fig.64)

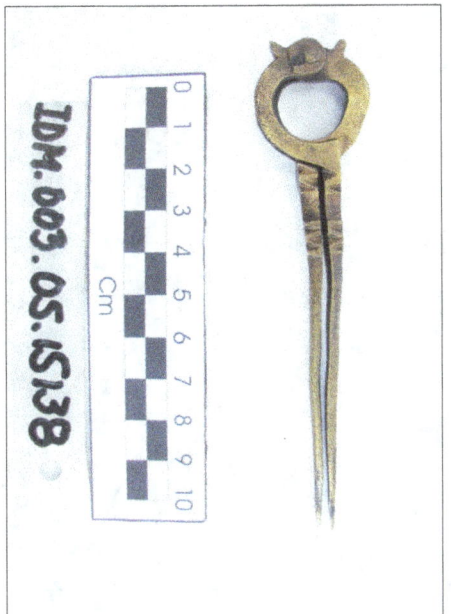
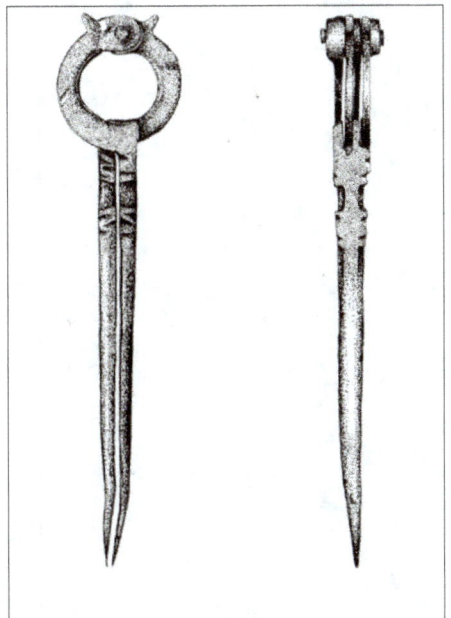

FIG.64
One hand navigational divider (Art. 15138) and drawing of Art. 15140.

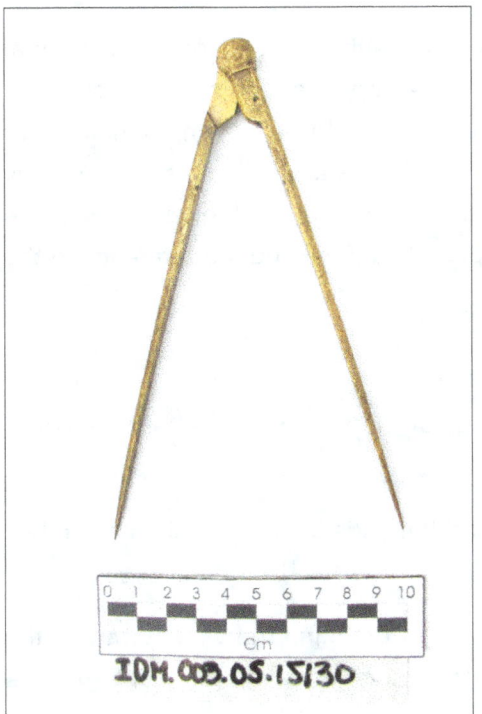
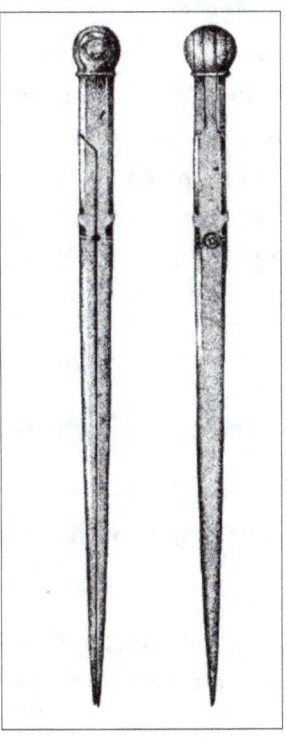

FIG.65
Straight pattern navigational divider (Art. 15130) and drawing.

The ruler is made of copper and presents different scales on both faces and a flattened wider end on the top for easier grip. Each of the scales increases the size of the divisions when approaching the lower end of the stem. The divisions are very close together on the upper part of the ruler and wide apart on the lower end. (Fig.66)

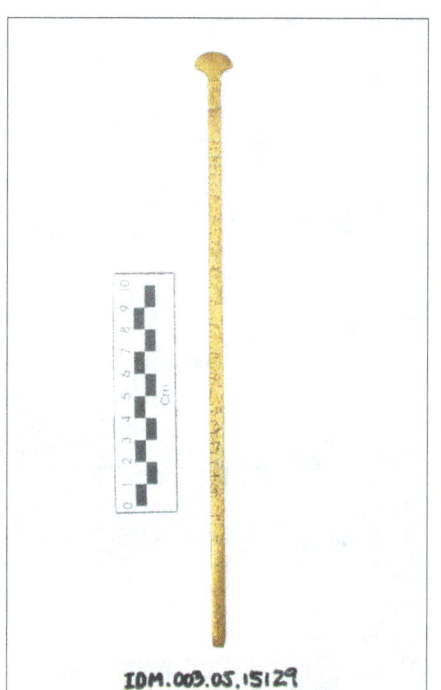
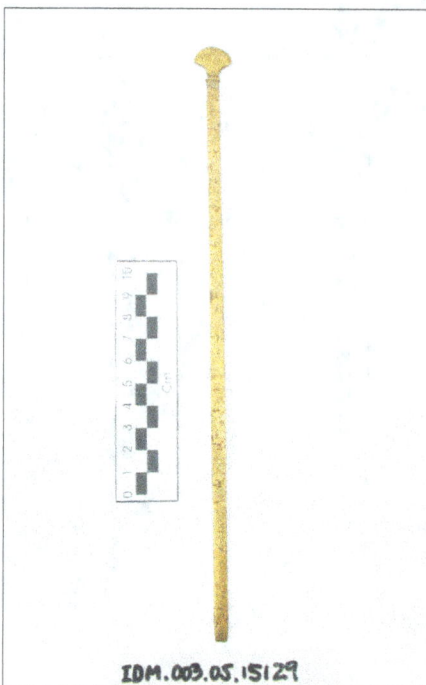
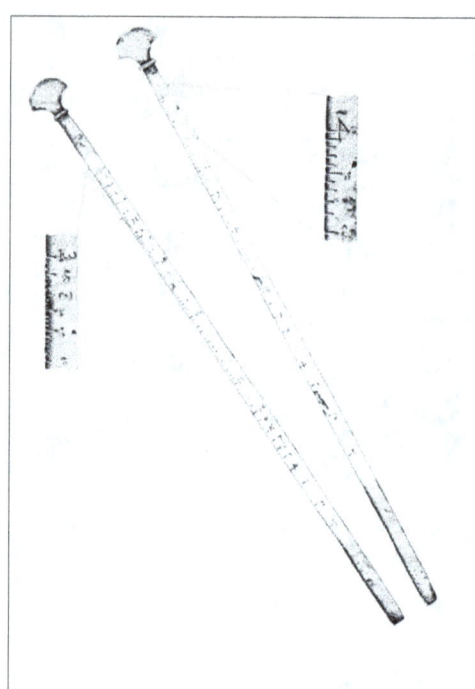

FIG.66
Both sides of the ruler (Art. 15129) and drawing showing details of the scales.

The graduation of the scale on one side is from 1 to 4, repeated three times, and although it is not clearly visible, it seems to have the "degree" symbol (°) over the numbers. The scale on the opposite side of the ruler is not clearly defined but maintains the pattern of variable division sizes. This ruler seems to be part of an instrument to measure arcs or angular distances and needs further research to determine if it is an example of a very early navigational instrument or any other measuring tool. One specialist in artillery, contacted by the author, is of the opinion that this instrument is a gauge to measure calibres of different types of cannons, but no reference in the written sources has been found yet confirming this idea.

SAIL MAKER'S PALM

This artefact was also found within the timbers of the hull, apparently part of the tool box of a carpenter or a sailor on board.

This is a device used by sailors to repair sails and sometimes to whip or bind the ends of ropes or sheets, as they are more commonly known by the initiated.

The small device consists of a loop of leather with a hole for the thumb to go through. The widest part of the leather sits across the palm of the hand and includes a dimpled metal plate to accommodate the blunt end of a needle.

Sail maker's needles are necessarily tough and big enough to take the heavy thread and the plate, held in place across the palm and used to force the needle and thread through the tough material of the sail.

In our case the leather loop had disappeared completely after almost four centuries of immersion but the metal plate (used as a thimble) survived, with its fixing holes conserved. (Fig.67)

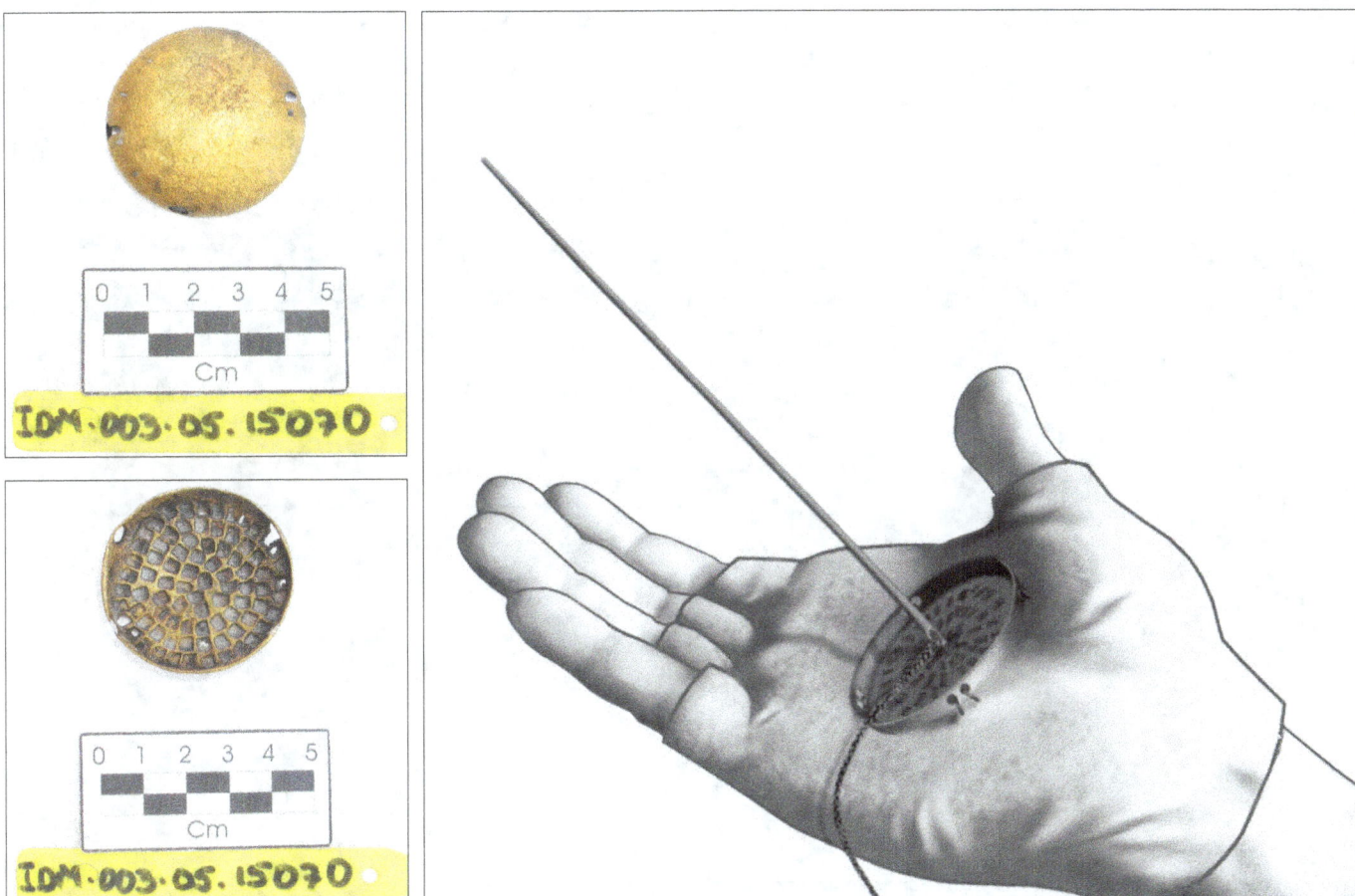

FIG.67
Both sides of Artefact 15070. Note the attaching holes in the rim.
Representative drawing of its function. The leather loop has been omitted in the drawing in order to show the full plate and fixing system.

PERSONAL BELONGINGS CATEGORY

This group includes a large variety of artefacts that were presumably used by the crew, officials and passengers of the ship. As expected, they are of many different materials and uses and therefore here we will describe the most interesting ones or those that could shed more light on the provenance of the ship and its crew.

SILVER COINS

A total of 37 silver coins were found on this site, either concreted in small clumps or loose. They appeared in almost every grid, but with a higher concentration in grids S1 and S2, where most of the personal belongings were found. In general the condition of these kinds of artefacts is very poor. It was often the case, that when the concretion was cleaned no silver nucleus was found inside. In the case of the concretions, which still had some part of the coin surviving, these were in such a bad condition that it was almost impossible to gather any information on them. The only visible information found so far on most of the coins is that they were minted in Mexico and Potosi. An assayer mark on one of the Mexican coins, an **F**, was hardly visible. It was possibly Francisco de Morales who worked at the Mexican mint house from 1589 to 1608. (Fig.68)

FIG.68
Silver coins from Artefact 15020, the better conserved sample of coins from the wreck.

This unusual degradation of the silver might have been produced by the close contact with decaying organic material, in their vicinity, for almost four centuries. The load of spices carried on this ship as suggested by the remains of *Martabans* and big jars might have been the source of the nitric acid that damaged the silver so intensely.

BEADS AND PENDANTS

During excavation in grid S2 the team found three ornamental beads, apparently from a necklace or a bracelet. These beads are made of a light material of very dark black colour, possibly ebony or lignite (a soft coal) and are carved on the front face with a four petal flower and diagonal lines creating a frame around it. They present two longitudinal perforations drilled through the body presumably for the string, which linked them together. (Fig.69)

FIG.69
Ornamental bead, Artefact 15064 and drawing showing the perforations.

Two pendants of the same material but in the shape of a hand were also found in grid S2. These pendants represent the *"mano fico"*, also called *figa*, which is an Italian amulet of ancient origin. It represents a hand gesture in which the thumb is thrust between the curled index and middle fingers in obvious imitation of heterosexual intercourse. Examples have been found from the Roman era, but the Etruscans also used it. *Mano* means "hand" and *fico* or *figa* means "fig," with the idiomatic slang connotation of a woman's genitals. (Fig.70)

 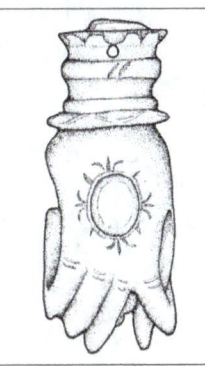 

FIG.70
Two views of one of the "Mano fico" amulets, Artefact 2012, and drawing.

Whether made as an apotropaic gesture or worn as an amulet, the *"mano fico"* is used for magical protection against the evil eye to this day. It resembles other hand gestures and hand images that ward off evil, including the hamsa hand, the *eye-in-hand,* the *mano cornuta* (horned hand) and the interlocked thumb gesture. This popular amulet is present in many cultures up to this day and is has been well known among the Portuguese since the time before the Portuguese India Run. It is also believed that it had the function of protecting one against infertility.

RELIGIOUS ICONS

An interesting artefact of this category was found in the centre of grid S7 lying between two timbers of the hull and close to a silver coin. It is a small statue showing Jesus Christ in the crucifixion position with spread arms, palms up and crossed legs. The cross is missing as it was most likely made of wood, but the nails in both hands are still in-situ. The nail from the legs is also missing. The statue is made of pewter which is a metal alloy, traditionally 85-99% tin and 1- 4% copper acting as a hardener, with the addition of lead for the lower grades of pewter and a bluish tint. There were three grades: *Fine*, for eating ware, with 96- 99% tin, and 1- 4 % copper; *Trifle*, also for eating and drinking utensils but duller in appearance, with 92 % tin, 1- 4% copper, and up to 4% lead; and *Lay* or *Ley metal,* not for eating or drinking utensils, which could contain up to 15% lead. (Fig.71)

FIG.71
The statue of Jesus (Art. 15094) as found, after conservation and technical drawing.

From the appearance and weight of this particular artefact we believe that is made of *Ley metal,* which would have a higher content of lead, making it heavier. It is interesting to note that the statue is incredibly detailed, even on the back part of the figure, which would have been covered by the cross and therefore hardly visible. (Fig.72)

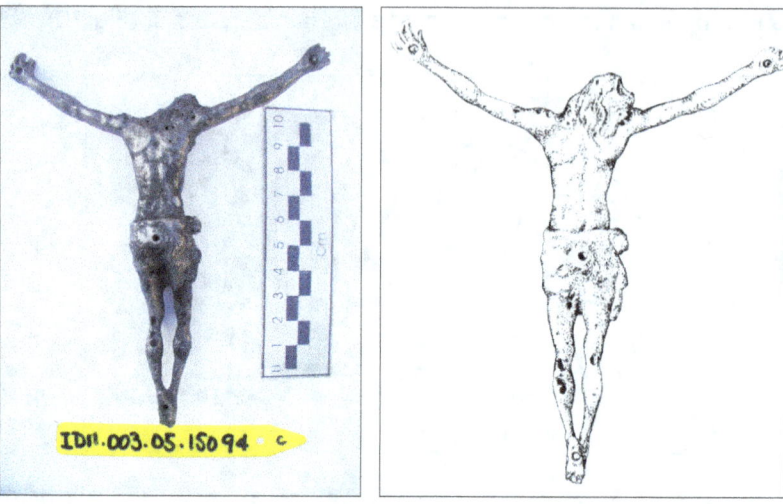

FIG.72
Back side of the statue of Jesus (Art. 15094) showing the details of its construction.

BALLAST STONES

This was the site with the smallest ballast stones found so far in our area of study. The stones are a maximum of 20cm in diameter but most are between 5 and 10cm. They are regular and rounded with a smooth surface. Their colour is mostly light grey in most pieces, without lines or patterns on their surface. All the stones were concentrated in a huge mound surrounded by a deep layer of sand and only after full excavation was finished were we able to appreciate the extent of the ballast in terms of quantity. (Fig.73)

A total of approximately 250 tons of ballast stones were removed from the wreck and relocated in the surrounding area. This calculation was made based on the amount of times that 500kg lifting bags were loaded. The system to remove the ballast from the site was to fill up a squared net of 2 x 2m, then lift it, one bag at a time, at its limit of lifting power, giving us an approximate weight of ballast removed each time. During the 2005 and 2006 seasons, a total of 412 lifting bags were filled and removed, with a total approximate weight of 206,000kg. Some ballast was removed manually in small plastic crates simultaneously, so it is possible to estimate the total weight of ballast in the vicinity, at 250t. (Fig.74)

FIG.74
Two views of part of the ballast stones piles relocated around the wreck site during excavation.

SECTION 6

The Wood Structure

After archaeological excavation and the removal of approximately 200 tons of ballast stones, part of the wood structure of the hull of the ship was discovered, having survived due to the protection of the ballast.

Below is the description of the surviving part of the hull and a preliminary study of its structure, based on measurements, photographs, drawings and observation of the pieces *in-situ*. No dismantling of individual pieces was done at this stage; therefore the information on the assemblage of structural parts is limited to the loose pieces found. To help in the interpretation task, a photo mosaic of the entire remaining structure was completed. For this we used 158 photos with an area of 4m^2 each (2m x 2m) from the total of 731 photos taken.

GENERAL DESCRIPTION OF THE HULL'S REMAINS

The surviving part of the hull is orientated at 35° to the magnetic north and it has an overall length of 32.5m along the clamp of the second deck and a width of 12.9m at the level of the master frame. This indicates that the preserved portion of the hull includes part of the bottom amidships and part of the starboard side up to a level further above the upper twin deck. A single piece of timber, apparently part of the deck clamp of a third deck (or gun deck) was found, suggesting the position of that deck. However, as no deck beams related to it were preserved, the resulting measurements and analysis should be taken with great caution.

The pieces forming the assemblage are the **keelson** (*sobrequilla* - including the mast-step), **45 floor timbers** (*varengas*), **65 strakes of the ceiling planking** (*plan* - between the keelson and Stringer # 1), **60 first futtocks** (*primeras ligazones*), **59 second futtocks** (*segundas ligazones*), **5 stringers** (*palmejares*), **2 deck clamps** (*durmientes*) (and remains of a third), **2 waterways** (*trancaniles*), **2 spirketings** (*sobretrancaniles*) **4 fragments of baulks** (*puntales*), **1 small knee** (*curvaton*), **25 deck beams** (*baos o cabezas de curva valona*) and **136 frames** (*cuadernas*).

The hull's external planking is barely visible between some of the floor timbers and frames and therefore counting it would be very inaccurate, if not impossible, without disassembling the structure. At the western end of the structure, we observed that the hull is sheathed with lead. Only an average of 0.5m in length of the floor timbers to the port side of the ship has survived, most probably due to the collapse of the side exposed over the water.

DESCRIPTION OF THE STRUCTURE'S PIECES

KEEL *(QUILLA)*

Following the decision not to dismantle the timbers of the structure, very little has been seen of the keel of this ship as most of it is still buried under more than 1.7m of sand and ballast stones. However, a part of it that was visible under floor timber V-1, allowed for some measurements to be taken. The width of this timber is 0.28m and due to various small sondages performed along the keelson it was possible to observe that the keel continues until, at least under floor timber V-33, for a length of 20.55m. Its depth hasn't been preserved.

We were not able to observe how many pieces make up the keel, but if we take into account the appearance and strength of the wood we can assume that it is made of the same wood as the floor timbers, keelson, first futtocks, second futtocks, deck clamps and frames.

At the first floor timbers (V-1 to V8) it was possible to observe square scarfs attaching the floors to the keel.

KEELSON *(SOBREQUILLA)*

The keelson has an overall length of 12.95m, including the mast-step, a width that varies between 0.21m and 0.24m, approximately 1 *palmo de goa* (0.256m), except at the area of the mast-step where the width reaches 0.39m and an average depth of 0.34m. It is formed by 5 pieces, assembled using swallow-tail scarfs between them and fixed to the floor timbers underneath with square scarfs. The height over the floor timbers varies towards the south (the only place where it was possible to take measurements), from 0.21m to 0.29m.

In the upper face of the keelson, 6 channelled-shaped rabbets are present. In their interior we observed remains of wooden wedges made of a different kind of timber to the one used to build the keelson. These rabbets have a slanted longitudinal section going from the upper face of the timber until a depth of 0.06m at the other end in most cases. These slanted channels, together with the wooden wedges fitted inside them create a kind of small mortises, presumably used to tighten baulks to support the orlop deck.

The team identified 32 perforations along the keelson (Table 1), which can be grouped into three different types: the first of circular transversal section and a diameter of 0.03m (keel bolts), the second with a square transversal section and measuring 0.02m on the sides, and the third type (always in relation to the slanted rabbets), also a square section but measuring 0.01m on the sides (iron spikes). Additionally, we observed fragments of these bolts, but if we consider the rust remains inside the perforations we can conclude that they were made of iron. No copper fastening was found on the wreck.

The buttresses, made of very thick timber, are located on either side of the mast-step. The one to the east of the keelson is badly corroded and we were only able to gather very little information from its observation. The one in the west was in much better condition. This buttress was very similar and will therefore be used later on to document a detailed description, independent from the other pieces of the keelson.

For description and study purposes the pieces which include the keelson were numbered from K1 to K5 in north-south direction, the same way as the rabbets, bolt and spike perforations, which will be referenced in that direction and in consecutive order. (Fig.75)

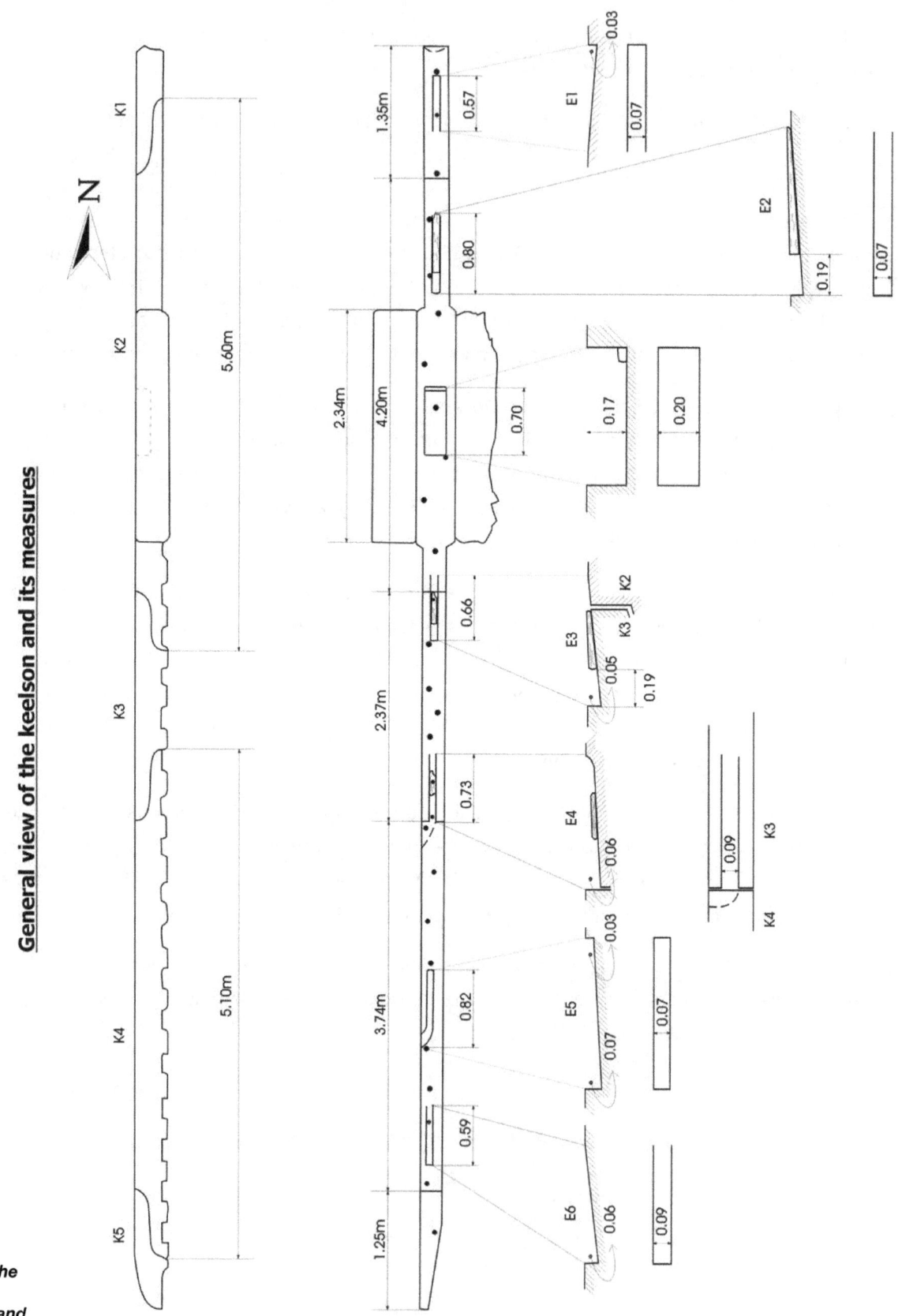

General view of the keelson and its measures

FIG.75
Representation of the keelson, its structural parts and measurements.

K1

This is the first piece to the north, with a total length of 1.35m, a maximum width of 0.23m and a maximum height over the floor timber of 0.30m. At its southern end it connects in a wedge scarf over K2.

This piece is in its original position but disassembled from K2 and more heeled to the west than the rest of the keelson. The condition of this piece is poor. It is deteriorating at its northern end through the action of the *Teredo* worm and other macro-biological organisms. (Fig.76)

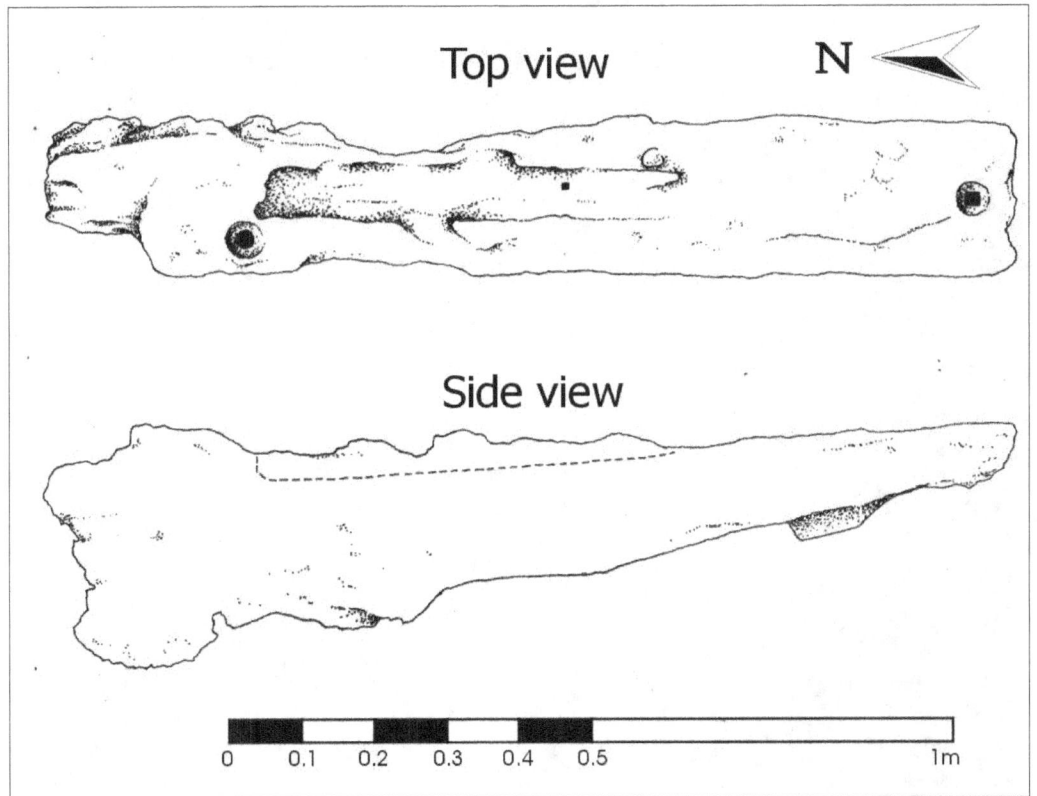

FIG.76
K1.

RABBETS AND SCARFS

There is one slanted rabbet on its upper face (E1) along the axis of a piece that is 0.57m long, with a width of 0.07m. Its deeper end is located towards the north of the piece and has a depth of 0.04m. This rabbet is located at the centre of K1 at 0.31m from the northern end and finishes at the surface, at a distance of 0.89m from the southern end.

It also presents square scarfs under the lower flat of the wedge that joins it to K2.

JOINERY

K1 has four perforations. The measurements are listed in Table 1. We found that p1 fixed over the floor timber has the deepest penetration of the entire structure: 1.03m. It evidently reached beyond the body of the floor timber, most probably fitting into the keel. In the case of p2 it fixed the wedge inside E1 against the body of the keelson and p3 and p4 fitted the join over K2 and the floor timber underneath.

K2

K2 has an overall length of 5.60m, showing only 4.20m of this length on the upper side due to the scarfs that attach it from below to the adjacent pieces K1 and K3. The width of the timber is between 0.21m and 0.23m, exceeding this amount only in the area of the mortise for the main mast, where it is 0.39m. The maximum height over the floor timbers in the southern edge of the mast-step brace is 0.39m, but in the northern and southern edges of the mast-step this height is 0.21m and 0.29m respectively. The depth of K2 in the space between the floor timbers is 0.34m. Therefore we can deduce that the minimum thickness of the timber from which the mast-step was made was 0.39m, squared to achieve a transversal section of 0.40m.

K2 was in very good conservation condition, thanks to the thickness of the timber and to its sheltered position in the hull, compared to the other structural parts. (Fig.77)

FIG.77
K2 in-situ seen from the south. Note the buttress to the west in much better condition.

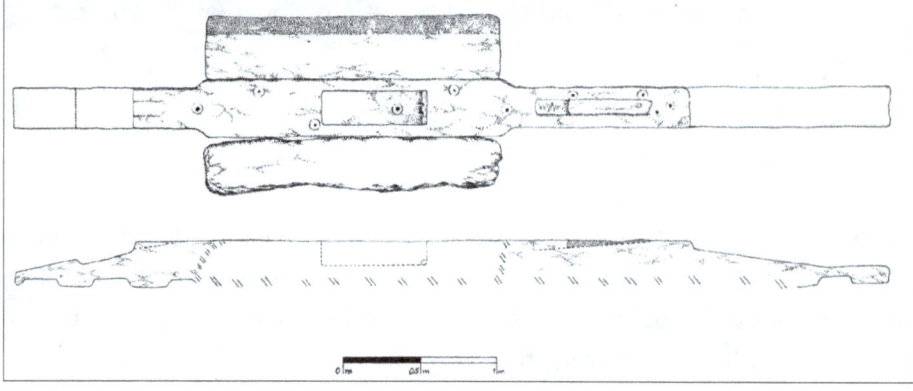

FIG.77a
K2.

This piece joins at its northern end below K1 in a slanted scarf of 0.82m in length and to the south with K3 in the same way along a length of 0.58m.

It is worth mentioning that within the scarfs that join these parts of the keelson and in the flats of the squared scarfs over the floor timbers, a kind of "filling" to fix these joins is visible. This could be a mass of caulker with presence of tar or pitch. (Fig.78)

FIG.78
Scarp joining K2 with K3 as seen from the east. Note the filling mass between both pieces in a lighter colour.

RABBETS AND SCARFS

K2 presents two perfectly recognizable rabbets on its upper face and part of a third one (approx. 25%) that will be commented in the description of K3. Its first rabbet (E2) is also channelled and slanted with a length of 0.80m, a width of 0.07m and a maximum depth in its southern end of 0.06m. Measured from the north of the piece, it starts at 0.37m and ends at 1.17m.

E2 has a particularity as it still holds most of the fitting wooden wedge, which grows in thickness in the same proportion of the depth of the channel without reaching its end, leaving a mortised space of 0.19m. This wedge has a length of 0.61m and is made of a different type of wood. It is lighter in colour and with more fibrous texture than the wood the keelson is made of.

FIG.79
Rabbet E2 on the northern sector of K2. Note the wooden wedge still in-situ and the mortised space in the right side.

The second rabbet, which is not included in the ones named E1, E2, etc, due to the uniqueness of its nature, is the mortise of the mast-step or the base of the main mast. It is located at the centre of the piece and it has a length of 0.70m, a width of 0.23m and a depth of 0.17m. On its seat there is one bolt perforation and cracks filled with apparently the same filling mass mentioned before. A slight narrowing is also visible at the northern end, in the interior width (going down to 0.20m) with carved imprints running down the walls, ending in trammels of 0.05m of length, 0.01-0.02m width and up to 0.02m height over the seat, that run from side to side of the mortise.

It is also interesting to notice that not a trace of the mast-heel survived. Clearly the mast had been manually removed; proof that the vessel had been extensively salvaged after it struck.

JOINERY

We observed eight perforations on the surface of K2 (Table 1). There is a ninth perforation that is not registered in the table and deserves a side comment: this perforation appears in the scarf that joins K1 with K2, that is to say, under the former. It was observed because both pieces were loose. When checking the numbers of perforations of K1, we realized that in K2 there was one more than expected. A detailed observation revealed that the bolt was placed to fix K2 to the floor timber before mounting and closing the join with K1. (Fig.80) (Fig.81)

FIG.80/81
Circular and squared section perforations on K2. Both present countersink holes for the bolt or spike not to protrude out of the surface.

K3

The third piece of the keelson has a total length of 2.37m. When fixed by slanted scarfs to the pieces K2 to the north and K4 to the south, in both cases the scarf overlaps the adjacent piece. This is exactly the contrary of what happened in K2. The maximum width of this piece is 0.24m, the maximum height over the floor timbers is 0.28m and its maximum depth (between floor timbers) is 0.31m. K3 rests on the master frame.

The condition of this piece is reasonably good, although some natural erosion is visible in its lower part and the scarfs over the floor timbers. (Fig.82)

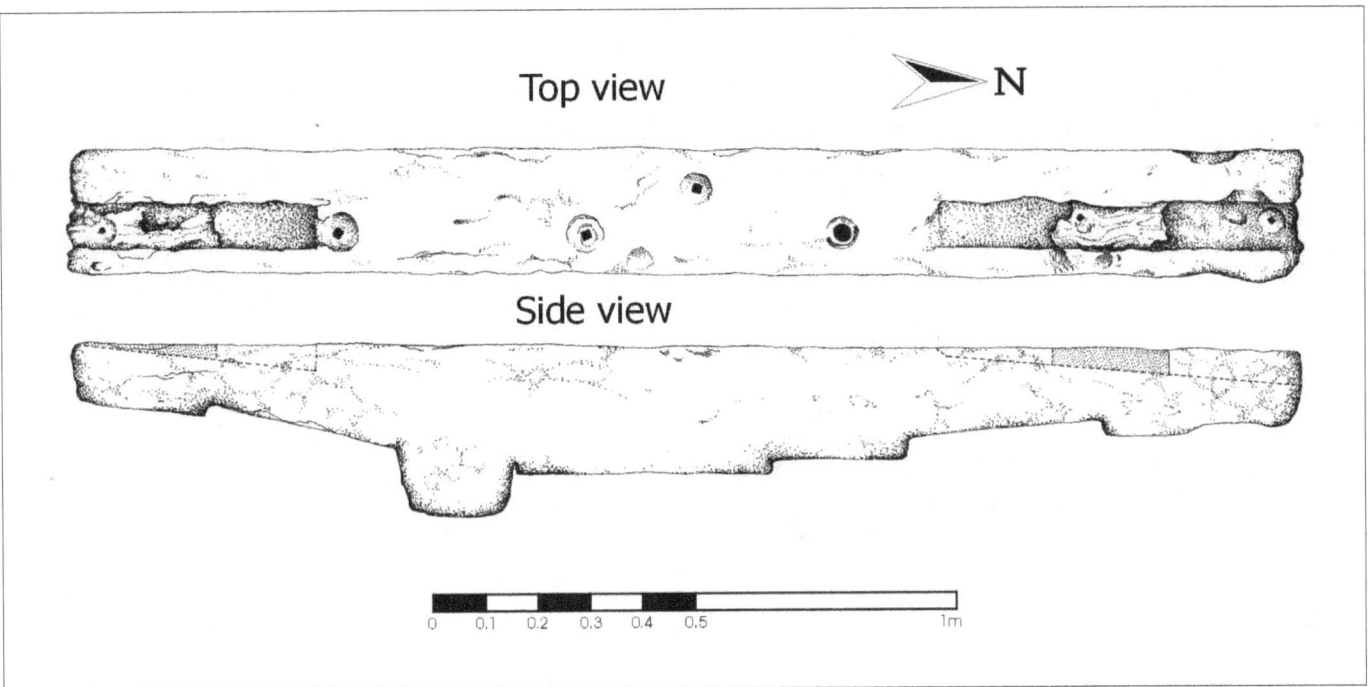

FIG.82
K3.

RABBETS AND SCARFS

Two channelled rabbets are present on the upper face. The first (E3) starts opening on the southern end of K2, runs over the union of both pieces, and ends at 0.45m from the north end of K3, for a total length of 0.66m. E3 has a width of 0.07m and its deeper end to the south has a depth of 0.05m. This rabbet also holds remains of the fitting wooden wedge, leaving a mortised space of 0.19m.

E4 is the second rabbet over K3, located at 1.64m from the northern end and growing deeper as it goes south. It opens at the end in the join with K4 at a depth of 0.06m and with a width of the channel of 0.09m. We were not able to observe if E3 originally continued over K4 because the northern end of that piece is badly corroded and no trace of any rabbet is visible. That is probably why E3 ends open, contrary to the rest of the observed rabbets. In the joins with K2 and K4 this piece also has squared scarfs to fix it over the floor timbers.

JOINERY

Presents seven perforations from which p14 and p19 fixed the wooden wedges inside rabbets E3 and E4 respectively and p20, despite being inside the southern end of E4, probably reinforced the join of K3 with K4 and to the floor timber. The rest of the perforations coincide in their directions with the underlying floor timbers, including p15 of the type of circular section.

K4

This is the second piece in terms of dimension, after K2, with a total length of 5.28m and a visible length of 3.74m in its upper face. The maximum height over the floor timbers is 0.29m and the maximum depth of the timber is also 0.29m. The width varies between 0.22m and 0.24m.

Its condition is generally good but it presents abrasion in the first third of its surface, more damaged in the area of the join with K3. Furthermore, the surface of the latter is 0.06m higher than K4, but it is not produced by vertical displacement. K4 joins under K3 with flat scarfs to the north and K5 to the south, and its lower face rests over 11 floor timbers. (Fig.83)

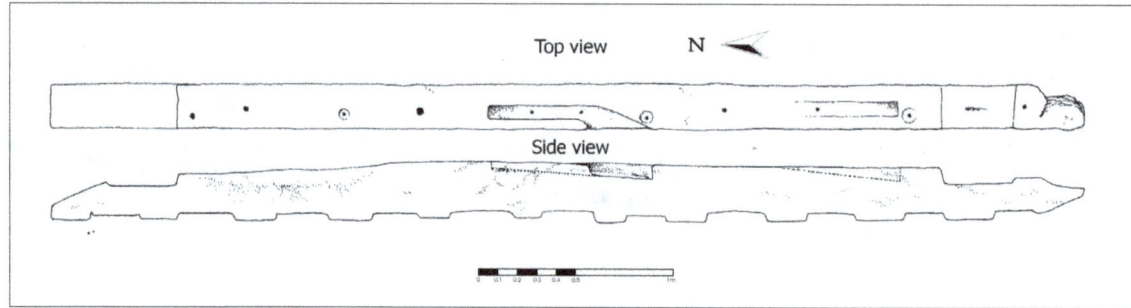

FIG.83
K4.

RABBETS AND SCARFS

It has two slanted rabbets (E5 and E6), two flat scarfs joining the piece with its adjacent (K3 and K5) and eleven squared scarfs for the floor timbers.

E5 is located at 1.50m from its northern edge, with a length of 0.82m and a width of 0.07m. This rabbet is different to the others, where the channel curves at its southern end up to the western edge of the piece, leaving it open at a depth of 0.07m. (Fig.84)

FIG.84
E5.

E6 is located at 2.38m, running along the piece for a length of 0.59m, with a width of 0.09m. The deeper end is at a depth of 0.07m in the south.

The flat scarfs that join this piece with K3 and K5 have a length of 0.78m and 0.76m respectively. This scarf (under K5) can be observed in detail because just like K1 in the north, K5 appears loose and, in this case, out of its original position.

The 11 remaining squared scarfs are holding K4 to the floor timbers and in some cases they appear abraded by the mechanical action of the ballast stones, very compact in that area.

JOINERY

K4 has 10 perforations, all coinciding with the floor timbers underneath. An exception is p28, smaller in size and fixing the wooden wedge inside E6. The circular sections p21 and p24 were bolted very deeply into the floor timbers. Maybe even further, because in spite of the sedimentation, we were able to measure the depth of p21: 0.53m.

K5

This piece appears in the southern end of the keelson, completely loose from the union with K4. The timber is extremely deteriorated. It is incomplete in the southern section and its surface had become blunt to the centre-north, losing more material from the east side towards the south, where it has an almost triangular transversal section. Everything points to the possibility that the piece was under strong mechanical tension during the wreckage or immediately afterwards, and later remained exposed to marine activity.

K5 has a total length of 1.25m and a maximum width in the northern section of 0.23m. (Fig.85)

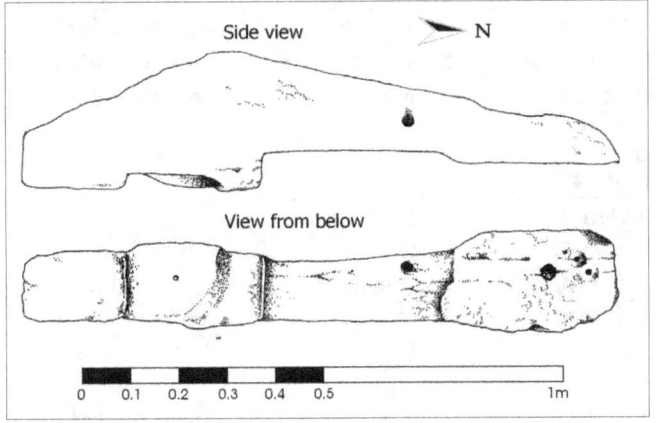

**FIG.85
K5.**

RABBETS AND SCARFS

There are no visible rabbets and the only two remaining scarfs are the ones that join the piece to K4 and a very faint one, squared, that belonged to one of the floor timbers in its lower face.

JOINERY

Two perforations were observed. One (p31) was hidden under the concretion, produced by the bolt in the northern end of the piece and p32 with a circular section.

TABLE 1

PIECE	ID	LOCATION (FROM N END)	COUNTERSINK	SECTION AND MEASUREMENT	DEPTH	OBS.
K1	p1	0.029m 0.05m W	ø = 0.06m	Circular ø = 0.03m	1.30m	
	p2	0.72m, centre of E1	No	Square, 0.01m	0.12m	
	p3	0.51m at centre and end of E1	ø = 0.05m	Square, 0.02m		Covered by concretion
	p4	1.33m at centre of the piece	ø = 0.05m	Square 0.02m		
K2	p5	0.42m, 0.03m W	ø = 0.07m	Square, 0.02m	0.42m	
	p6	0.75m on the wedge of E2	No	Square 0.01m		
	p7	0.94m, 0.03m W	ø = 0.06m	Square, 0.02m		
	p8	1.37m at centre of the timber	ø = 0.06m	Circular ø = 0.03m		
	p9	1.86m, 0.10m W	ø = 0.06m	Square, 0.02m		
	p10	2.34m inside the mortise	ø = 0.05m	Circular ø = 0.03m	0.47m	At centre 0.19m from N end
	p11	2.87m 0.09m E	No	Squared 0.02m		0.02m NE end of mortise
	p12	3.34m 0.10m W	ø = 0.06m	Square 0.02m		0.86m from southern end
	p13	3.78m at centre of the piece	ø = 0.06m	Circular ø = 0.03m	0.49m	
K3	p14	0.06m at centre of E3	No	Square 0.01m		On the wooden wedge remains
	p15	0.50m 0.07m W	ø = 0.06m	Circular ø = 0.03m		
	p16	0.98m, 0.07m W	ø = 0.06m	Square, 0.02m		
	p17	1.21m, 0.06m E	ø = 0.05m	Square, 0.02m	0.50m	
	p18	1.49m, 0.07m W	ø = 0.07m	Square, 0.02m		
	p19	1.95m at centre North of E4	No	Square, 0.01m		0.42m from southern end
	p20	2.32m at centre South of E4	No	Square, 0.01m		0.05m from southern end
K4	p21	0.07m, 0.06m W	No	Circular ø = 0.03m	0.57m	
	p22	0.51m, 0.10m E	No	Square, 0.02m		
	p23	1.02m, 0.08m W	ø = 0.05m	Square, 0.02m		
	p24	1.44m, 0.12m E	No	Circular ø = 0.03m		
	p25	1.88m, 0.05m E	No	Square, 0.02m	0.33m	Inside the rabbet
	p26	2.30m, 0.05 W	ø = 0.05m	Square, 0.02m		
	p27	2.71m, 0.10m W	ø = 0.06m	Square, 0.02m	0.53m	
	p28	3.03m at centre of the rabbet	No	Square, 0.01m	0.09m	0.71m from southern end
	p29	3.18m, 0.07m E	No	Square, 0.02m		Inside the rabbet
	p30	3.66m, 0.06m W	ø = 0.06m	Square, 0.02m		0.08m from S end
K5	p31	0.08m, 0.07m E	ø = 0.05m	Square, 0.02m		Covered by concretion
	p32	0.42m and app. 0.03m W	No	Circular ø = 0.03m		Covered by concretion

MAST STEP BUTTRESSES

These pieces are located at both sides of the mast step, but the following description refers only to the west piece for it is more conserved. It is a piece 2.34m long, approximately 0.40m high and 0.39m wide. This brace has a trapezoidal transversal section due to a longitudinal bevel, creating a slanted surface that allowed for the fixation of the spikes that hold this piece against the western side of the mast step.

No rabbets or scarfs were observed in this piece, only 8 spike perforations that are described in Table 2.

TABLE 2

PIECE	ID	LOCATION (FROM N END)	COUNTERSINK	SECTION AND MEASURE	DEPTH	OBS.
WEST BRACE OF THE MAST STEP	p1	0.18m, 0.17m W	ø = 0.06m	Square 0.02m	0.32m	Brace / Step
	p2	0.43m, 0.17m E	ø = 0.06m	Square 0.02m		Brace / Step
	p3	0.64m, 0.19m W	ø = 0.05m	Square 0.02m	0.31m	Brace / Step
	p4	0.97m, 0.11m E	ø = 0.06m	Square 0.02m		Brace / Step
	p5	1.38m, 0.20m E	ø = 0.05m	Square 0.02m		Brace / Step
	p6	1.53m, 0.19m W	ø = 0.06m	Square 0.02m	0.39m	Brace / Step
	p7	1.88m, 0.15m W	ø = 0.05m	Square 0.02m	0.58m	Brace / Step
	p8		ø = 0.06m	Square 0.02m	0.29m	Brace / Step

FLOOR TIMBERS *(VARENGAS)*

In the assemblage of timbers that make up the wood structure of IDM-003 we identified 45 floor timbers. These seem to make up the entire central section of the starboard side of the ship. These floor timbers include the Master frame *(Cuaderna Maestra)*, the stern Tailframe *(Almogama de popa)* and the bow Tailframe *(Almogama de proa)*.

The master frame is made of 3 flat timbers of the same width (0.24m) placed together without any space between them, for a total width of 0.72m. The height of these timbers over the keel is the lowest recorded of all floor timbers at the wreck, measuring only 0.41m. All 3 timbers of the master frame run across and between the keel and the keelson, two of them ending somewhere under the ceiling planking. The middle one continues until it ends under the first stringer for a total length of 7.05m (from the keelson to stringer #1). As the strakes of the ceiling haven't been dismantled we do not know if this middle timber of the master frame is only one piece or if the part that ends in the stringer is a first futtock joined to the master frame under the ceiling. (Fig.86)

FIG.86

Keelson   Ceiling Planking

Master frame (3)

The master frame is located afore the mast step at a distance of 3.02m (almost exactly 2 *rumos*), measured from the centre of the mortise of the mast step to the centre of the middle timber of the master frame.

The tailframes (stern and bow) are also made of 3 timbers each, reinforcing their structure. They have almost the same total width as the master frame. The bow tailframe's width is 0.73m and the stern tailframe's width is 0.74m. The main difference between the measurements of the tailframes and the master frame is the height over the keel, which in the case of the bow tailframe is 0.72m, considerably higher than the one of the master frame. It was impossible to determine the height over the keel in the stern tailframe due to a hard concretion of ballast stones and remains of iron, but it was possible to observe that it is higher than 0.50m.

The stern tailframe is 9.21m (6 *rumos*) abaft the main frame and the bow tailframe is 9.35m (approximately 6 *rumos*) afore it, measured from centre to centre of the middle timber in each case. Therefore we have a distance between both tailframes at the level of the keel of 18.56m or 12.05 *rumos*, with 36 floor timbers in between not counting the 9 that made the master frame (3) and the tailframes (3 each).

The measurement of the width of these 36 floor timbers varies slightly between 0.23m and 0.25m (around 1 *palmo de goa*), taking into account the normal loss of material after almost 400 years of immersion and organic decay. Although the height over the keel increases when moving away from the master frame, it was only possible to measure it in the southern direction, towards the bow tailframe. The highest height over the keel was measured in the bow tailframe, with 0.72m; further north we measured 0.61m in floor timber V-10 and 0.41m in the master frame. In fact, the timbers of the bow tailframe are made with 2 timbers assembled vertically to reach this height. These composed floor timbers were observed from V-1 to V-13. (Fig.87)

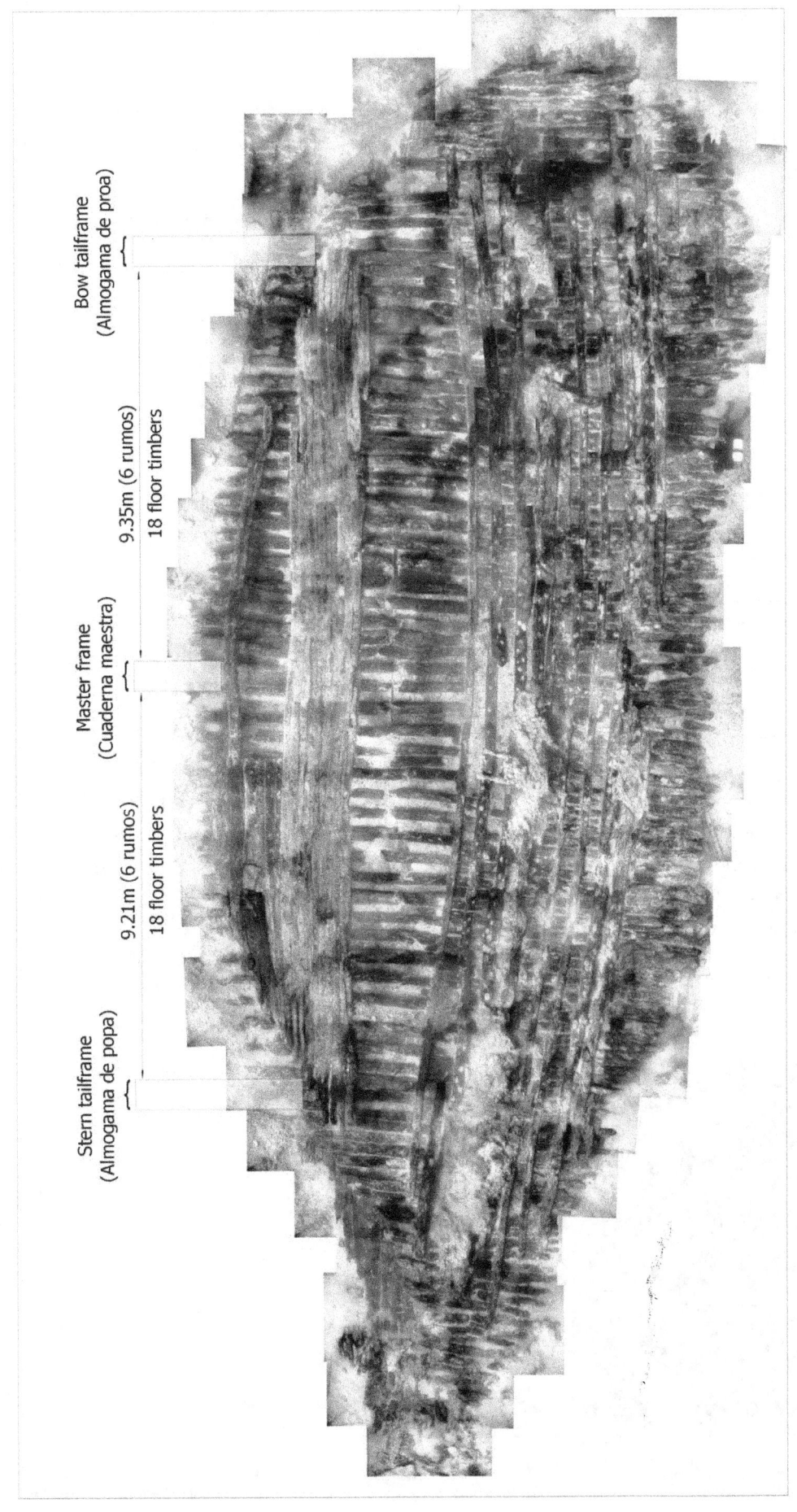

Bow tailframe
(Almogama de proa)

9.35m (6 rumos)
18 floor timbers

Master frame
(Cuaderna maestra)

9.21m (6 rumos)
18 floor timbers

Stern tailframe
(Almogama de popa)

In the fore face of floor timbers V-1 to V-16 (most of the composite ones), we found scarfs in trapezoidal shape, carved in their axis over the keel.

These scarfs have perforations in their lower ends, with countersink holes to allow spikes of a square section of 0.02m to attach the aforementioned floors to the keel. (Fig.88)

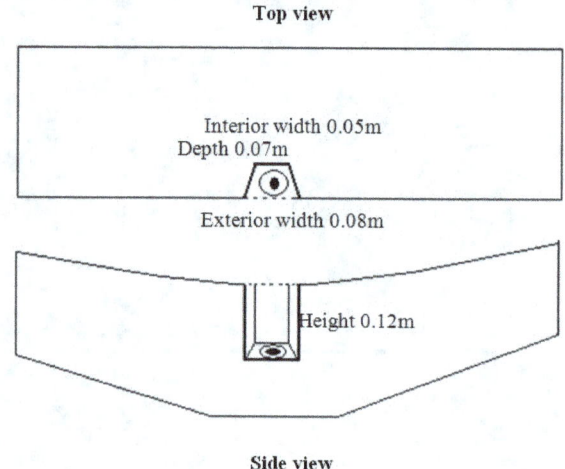

FIG.88
Detail of the scarf on the southern face of some floor timbers. (Drawing: Yuri Romero).

In the upper face of floors V-5, V-8, V-40 and V-42 we observed bolt perforations of 0.03m in diameter. These bolts were 1m or more long and were used to attach the keelson to the keel through the floor timber, leading us to believe that the keelson might have reached that level. Today however, that section is missing. This assumption is reinforced by the fact that these perforations don't have countersink holes for the head of the bolt, suggesting that the bolt continued through the keelson that should have been there.

In the northern face of most of the floor timbers two vertical marks in form of a line are visible, delimiting both edges of the keelson placed on top of the floors.

FIG.89
Mark carved on the northern face of every floor timber under the keelson. This one is part of the starboard side.

No scribe marks were seen in the pre-designed floor timbers although, based on the literature consulted, these are common features. This is probably due to the compact ballast tightly placed between the floors. Its mechanical action on the timbers could have flattened the marks.

The room-and-space, measured between axes of the adjacent floor timbers, including the empty space between them (if any), showed an average value of 0.462m. Individual measurements are shown in Table 3.

It also worth noticing that no limber holes to allow the passage of the bilge water were carved in the floor timbers of this ship.

All surviving floor timbers had lost the portside arm (to the east of the keel) with only approximately 0.50m in length remaining in that direction in most of them, therefore the joining with the first futtocks to the east was lost. To the west, the team was not able to observe the joining scarfs between the floor timbers. The first futtocks and their bolts and spikes also remained unobserved because all are located under the planking of the ceiling. As the heads of the first futtocks and floors were visible under the planking, general measurements of their length and width were taken.

TABLE 3. (MEASUREMENTS FOR ROOM-AND-SPACE)

FLOOR TIMBER	ROOM AND SPACE	REFERENCE AMIDST	COMMENTS
V-1	0.50m	1&2	
V-2	0.50m	2&3	
V-3	0.47m	3&4	
V-4	0.45m	4&5	
V-5	0.52m	5&6	Bolt perforation on top ø = 0.03m, in line with the keelson
V-6	0.49m	6&7	
V-7	0.49m	7&8	Scarf on the south side under keel son axis for bolt.
V-8	0.46m	8&9	Bolt perforation on top ø = 0.03m, in line with the keelson
V-9	0.46m	9&10	Scarf on the south side under keel son axis for bolt.
V-10	0.49m	10&11	Scarf on the south side under keel son axis for bolt.
V-11	0.47m	11&12	Scarf on the south side under keel son axis for bolt.
V-12	0.52m	12&13	Scarf on the south side under keel son axis for bolt.
V-12	0.52m	12&13	Scarf on the south side under keel son axis for bolt.
V-13	0.48m	13&14	Scarf on the south side under keel son axis for bolt.
V-14	0.40m	14&15	Scarf on the south side under keel son axis for bolt.
V-15	0.42m	15&16	Scarf on the south side under keel son axis for bolt.
V-16	0.47m	16&17	Scarf on the south side under keel son axis for bolt.
V-17	0.44m	17&18	
V-18	0.45m	18&19	
V-19	0.49m	19&20	
V-20	0.44m	20&21	
V-21	0.50m	21&22	
V-22	0.28m	22&23	
V-23	0.25m	23&24	
V-24	0.48m	24&25	
V-25	0.47m	25&26	
V-26	0.48m	26&27	
V-27	0.49m	27&28	
V-28	0.45m	28&29	
V-29	0.44m	29&30	
V-30	0.51m	30&31	
V-31	0.23m	31&32	
V-32	0.21m	32&33	
V-33	0.50m	33&34	
V-34	0.51m	34&35	
V-35	0.44m	35&36	
V-36	0.45m	36&37	
V-37	0.57m	37&38	
V-38	0.53m	38&39	
V-37	0.57m	37&38	
V-39	0.52m	39&40	
V-40	0.52m	40&41	Bolt perforation on top ø = 0.03m, in line with the keelson
V-41	0.57m	41&42	
V-42	0.50m	42&43	Bolt perforation on top ø = 0.03m, in line with the keelson
V-43	0.50m	43&44	
V-44	0.53m	44&45	V-45 was the last floor timber observed

FUTTOCKS *(LIGAZONES)*

In the structural remains of the hull it was possible to identify 60 first futtocks. The team was able to take the measurements of 27 of them. In the master section of the ship all first futtocks start almost under the planking of the ceiling, therefore length and width measurements were possible. Jointing was not observed. All studied first futtocks are associated to second and third futtocks, in such a way that their assemblage forms the framing of the ship. All follow quite a regular pattern, more coherent in their structural function than in their measurements.

All are made of a thick timber, which varies in height and width between 0.24m and 0.26m (1 *palmo de goa*). Their length varies according to their joining with the frames (which are not all the same measurements) and their location in the structure. In all cases they tend to end under the first deck clamp or its waterway (Table 4). Thus, we can conclude that all identified first futtocks begin under the planking of the ceiling (where they join the floor timbers) and end between the deck clamp and the waterway of the orlop deck (where they join the second and third futtocks), exception made with Ft1-14, Ft1-20 and Ft1-22 which exceed this level and end on the contiguous stringer.

To reinforce the comment above we have the examples of the first futtocks composed of more than one piece. This is the case with Ft1-2, Ft1-9, Ft1-11, Ft1-13, Ft1-14, Ft1-17, Ft1-36 and Ft1-37, made by two pieces joined in a flat scarf. This phenomenon evidently responds to the need to reach the level of the orlop deck when no timbers of that length were available. The best examples are probably Ft1-11 and Ft1-36 where the second pieces are only 0.80m and 0.70m respectively, a characteristic that could not fulfil any other function, as these pieces don't end in scarfs to allow for the joining of one futtock to the next one. All first futtocks are connected on both sides (aft and fore) with one piece each (second futtocks) that connects the first with the third futtocks. For further explanation we will take the ones connected to the fore face and refer to them using the same number as the floor timber corresponding in axis and with which the assemblage of the frame is formed. (Fig.90)

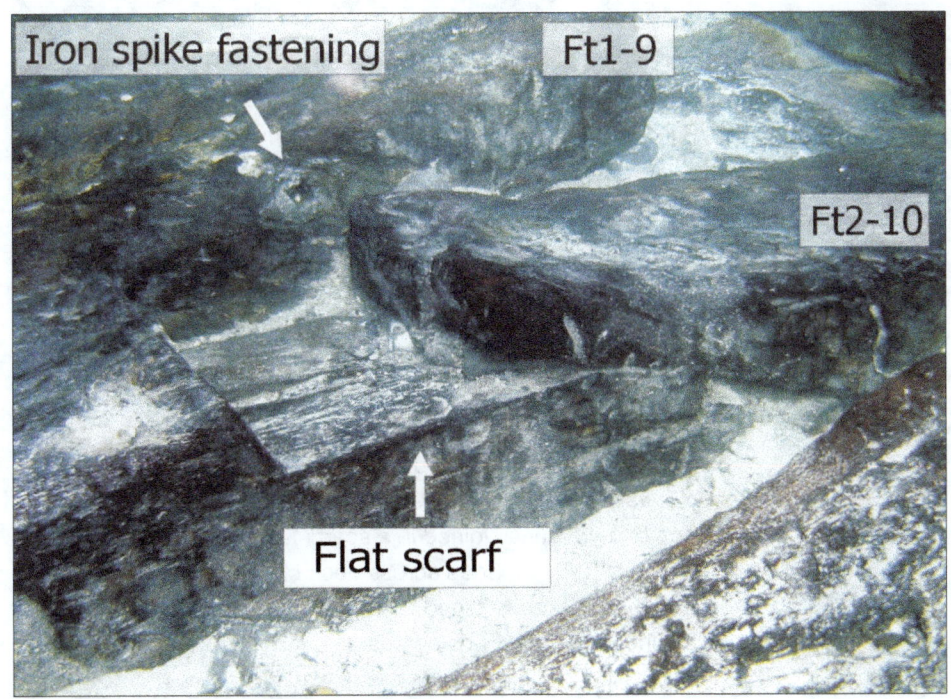

FIG.90
Ft1-9 and Ft2-10 connects laterally at the level of the flat scarf of the latter by a square section iron fastening. No lateral scarfs were observed between futtocks.

TABLE 4. (MEASUREMENTS AND DESCRIPTIONS OF FIRST FUTTOCKS)

ID	REF. AMIDST	LENGTH	COMMENTS
Ft1-1	V 1 & 2	5.30m	No scarping in W limit. Run and ends under deck clamp
Ft1-2	V 2 & 3	5.40m	Made by two pieces joined in a scarp. No scarping in W limit. Run and ends under deck clamp
Ft1-3	V 3 & 4	5.15m	No scarping in W limit. Run under deck clamp
Ft1-4	V 4 & 5	6.08m	No scarping in W limit. Run and ends under deck clamp
Ft1-5	V 5 & 6	5.80m	No scarping in W limit. Run and ends under deck clamp
Ft1-6	V 6 & 7	5.40m	Side scarf in W limit. Ends just in the deck clamp
Ft1-7	V 7 & 8	5.05m	Measured until the scarp-bolt. End not observed
Ft1-8	V 8 & 9	5.05m	No scarping in W limit. Run and ends under deck clamp
Ft1-9	V 9 & 10	5.95m	Made by two pieces joined in a scarf (4.48m and 2.40m) No scarping in W limit. Run and ends under deck clamp
Ft1-10	V 10 & 11	6.05m	Scarp in W limit. Joined under deck clamp
Ft1-11	V 11 & 12	5.50m	Made by two pieces joined in a scarf (5.05 and 0.80m) No scarping in W limit. Run and ends under deck clamp
Ft1-12	V 12 & 13	6.25m	No scarping in W limit. Run and ends under deck clamp
Ft1-13	V 13 & 14		Made by two pieces. End not observed
Ft1-14	V 14 & 15	6.50m	Made by two pieces joined in a scarf (4.30m and 2.45m) No scarping in W limit. Ends under stringer.
Ft1-15	V 15 & 16	5.75m	No scarping in W limit. Run and ends under deck clamp.
Ft1-16	V 16 & 17	6.20m	No scarping in W limit. Across deck clamp and ends under waterway.
Ft1-17	V 17 & 18	6.35m	Made by two pieces joined in a scarf (5.15m and 2.05m) No scarping in W limit. Ends under waterway.
Ft1-18	V 18 & 19	5.75m	No scarping in W limit. Across deck clamp and ends just before waterway.
Ft1-19	V 19 & 20	5.40m	No scarping in W limit. Run and ends under deck clamp.
Ft1-20	V 20 & 21	6.50m	No scarping in W limit. Across deck clamp and waterway. Ends under contiguous stringer.
Ft1-21	V 21 & 22	5.80m	No scarping in W limit. Across deck clamp and ends under waterway.
Ft1-22	V 22 & 24	7.05m	No scarping in W limit. It is the central one from the master frame. Measured from the keelson axis.

From floor timbers V-24 to V-31 it was not possible to determine the length of the first futtocks, because these are under the planking around the mast step and are too heavily concreted at the west limit.

ID	REF. AMIDST	LENGTH	COMMENTS
Ft1-32	V 32 & 33	5.80m	No scarping in W limit. Across deck clamp and ends just before waterway.
Ft1-33	V 33 & 34		Not observed.
Ft1-34	V 34 & 35	5.90m	No scarping in W limit. Ends across waterway.
Ft1-35	V 35 & 36	5.30m	No scarping in W limit. Across deck clamp and ends just before waterway.
Ft1-36	V 36 & 37	5.00m	Made by two pieces joined in a scarf (4.60m and 0.70m) No scarping in W limit. Ends across deck clamp.
Ft1-37	V 37 & 38	5.75m	Made by two pieces joined in a scarf (4.80m and 1.15m) No scarping in W limit. Ends across waterway.
Ft1-38	V 38 & 39	5.50m	No scarping in W limit. Ends under waterway.

MARKS

When measuring the first futtocks, an interesting feature was noticed: the first futtocks afore the stern tailframe, are numbered consecutively in Roman numerals, starting with "0" and ending with "XV", the latter coinciding with the master frame (Table 5). All marks are on the upper face of the futtock and are approximately 0.50m from the first stringer, right under the orlop deck. (Fig.91)

FIG.91
Marks on the first futtocks Ft1-26 and Ft1-25 depicting "XI" and "XII" in Roman numerals respectively. In the lower right corner of the photo the first stringer is visible.

TABLE 5. (MARKS ON THE FIRST FUTTOCKS)

FUTTOCK	ROMAN NUMERAL	COMMENTS
Ft1-22	XV	Very faint. On the central timber of the master frame.
Ft1-23	XIV	Well defined.
Ft1-24	XIII	Very well defined.
Ft1-25	XII	Very well defined.
Ft1-26	XI	Very well defined, apparently framed inside a pentagon.
Ft1-27	X	Well defined, upper part very faint.
Ft1-28	IX	Well defined, apparently framed inside a pentagon.
Ft1-29		Not observed
Ft1-30		Not observed
Ft1-31	VI	Very faint.
Ft1-32	V	Very faint.
Ft1-33	IV	Very faint.
Ft1-34	III	Deep incisions but very irregular marks.
Ft1-35	II	Well defined.
Ft1-36	I	Well defined.
Ft1-37	0	Well defined.

The following is worth mentioning about these marks. Firstly, one must note the use of the zero ("0") among the Roman numerals, which are known to include only seven symbols (I, V, X, L, C, D and M) and no zero. It is not until the adoption of the Arabic numeral notation (developed from the Hindu numeration system during the 7th and 8th centuries) that the numeral zero appears. The main innovation of the Arabic numeration system is the use of the positional notation, in which the individual symbols change their value according to their position in the written number. It is only possible to use the positional notation if a symbol for the zero exists.

Although the first written reference of the use of the Arabic numeration system in Europe dates back to the year 976 and therefore well before the date in which the ship was presumably built, as far as the writer is aware, it was not of common use in Portuguese shipbuilding of the early 17th century.

Another striking coincidence in this matter is the presence of the Arabic number "12" in Ft1-25; which is also marked with the Roman numeral "XII". (Fig.92)

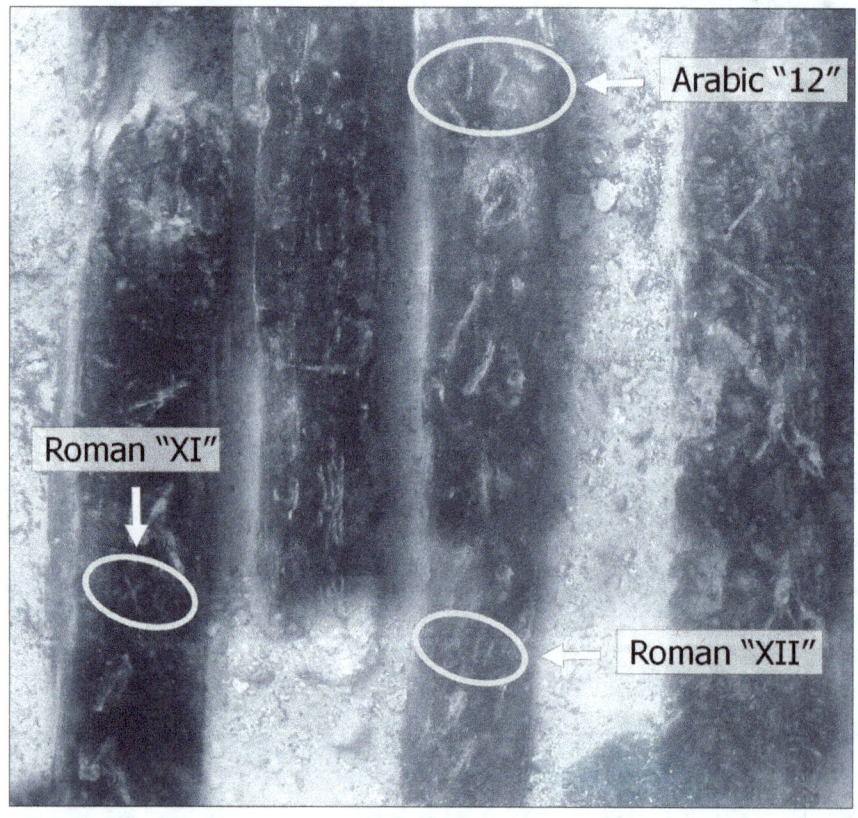

FIG.92
Futtocks Ft1-26 and Ft1-25 with "XI" and "XII" marks in Roman numerals respectively and mark "12" in Arabic characters on Ft1-25.

All comments above regarding the use of Arabic characters are based on the assumption that the observed marks are actually numbers and not random scratches produced either by marine organisms after immersion or by the adzes during the construction process.

Several other marks are visible on the timbers' surfaces with no apparent meaning, but the fact that the two particular marks mentioned above are coincidentally in the right places, lead us to believe that they were intentionally made.

The use of both numeral systems might respond to the cultural level of the shipwright responsible for marking the pre-designed timbers. In this case it would have been a person with above average knowledge compared to other shipwrights of his time. To reinforce this theory we have the correct use of the Roman numerals "IX" (for 9) and "IV" (for 4), instead of the archaic "VIIII" and "IIII" found on floor timbers C3 and C8 of another Portuguese ship, presumably built during the same time period as our case. (*Castro*, F. 2003b.)

Another interesting feature of these marks is that they are upside down and right below the orlop deck when the ship is in upright position; therefore we think that they were made before the assemblage of the pieces into the structure.

As an example of the building techniques of the frames, we will describe two of the better-preserved assemblages as study cases.

Description of futtocks' assemblage of frame # 1

The first futtock, Ft1-1 that is 5.30m long, appears between floor timbers V-1 and V-2; ending only after going across and under the first deck clamp (D1). The third futtock (Ft3-1) follows in the same direction with a thicker timber than the former and a width of 0.30m. This piece, 3.95m long, ends in a flat scarf connected from below to another piece that could not be measured. Apparently both made up the same piece but if this were not the case, it would be connected to the fifth futtock (Ft5-1).

The second futtock starts under the first stringer, connecting laterally on its fore face to Ft1-1 and Ft3-1. It has a total length of 4.84m and is made up of two pieces joined laterally. The first one, 4.35m in length, and a second one, 2.35m long, the latter with a lateral 2m long scarf, acting as a filling arm between the fore face of Ft1-1 and the aft face of Ft3-1 aiming to widen the structure towards the upper part of the side of the ship. This assemblage of two pieces ends just under the waterway of the second deck.

Ft4-1 follows Ft2-1 (not measured because it is incomplete) and ends at the western limit of the surviving structure. There are filling wood pieces in the shape of wedges between Ft1-1 and Ft2-1 and further to the west between Ft3-1 and what could be Ft4-1. The wood fillings between the timbers as well as the filling "arm" of the second piece of Ft2-1 serve the same purpose which is to widen the assemblage towards the upper part of the side. As a confirmation of this, we see that the width in the connection of V1 with Ft1-1 is 0.50m, which is the sum of the width of both timbers, but it is 0.85m in the connection between Ft3-1 and Ft4-1, including one filling piece.

Description of futtocks' assemblage of frame # 2

The first futtock (Ft1-2) of this frame starts between floor timbers V-2 and V-3. It is composed of two pieces connected on a flat scarf for a total length of 5.40m, ending almost at the level of the first waterway. It is followed in the same direction by Ft3-2, made from thicker timber, which reaches 0.32m in width and a length of 3.75m, finishing at the western end of the assemblage where the third deck may have been.

Ft2-2 starts at V-2 (but is not connected to it) and ends under the second waterway. It is made of a group with three pieces: the first one acting as reinforcement in the fore face of Ft1-2 with a length of 2.80m and joined by a flat scarf to the next timber. This next timber is 4.70m long, connected by a lateral scarf, the third piece is 1.80m long, with a lateral scarf as a filling "arm" that ends under the second waterway.

Second futtocks and filling frames

A total of 59 second futtocks have been identified in the remaining wood structure of IDM-003 and all follow the assemblage system described above. Most of them increase in width towards the upper decks by joining thicker timbers (up to 0.30m) before the connection with third and fourth futtocks.

Counting the futtocks or connecting timbers - which form the frames - becomes difficult at the level of the second deck because it is the level where the filling frames start to appear. These filling frames generally appear between the third and fourth futtocks of the same frame, but also between each one, i.e. between the third futtock of one frame and the fourth of the next one.

From the second deck upwards, the number of filling frames starts to increase, becoming higher in the aft and fore sections of the ship, more precisely fore of V-2 and aft of V-40 floors. The master section of the ship only presents filling frames at the level of floors V-11 and V-21, which reinforces the theory that at least at the level of the third deck, the filling frames were placed to achieve the curve of the ship towards the bow and stern. The width of the frames at the level of the third deck varies from 0.15m (one filling frame) to 0.35m (one reinforced frame); most of the frames are 0.22m wide. The height was 0.22m in every frame.

As an example of this gradual increase of pieces we can point out that the number of timbers at the level of the first deck is 119 whilst it is 136 at the level of the third deck (end of the surviving structure to the west).

All frames have squared scarfs at the level of the stringers to home the timbers which these are made of. On several occasions we also observed that these scarfs were wider than the timber they hold. (Fig.93)

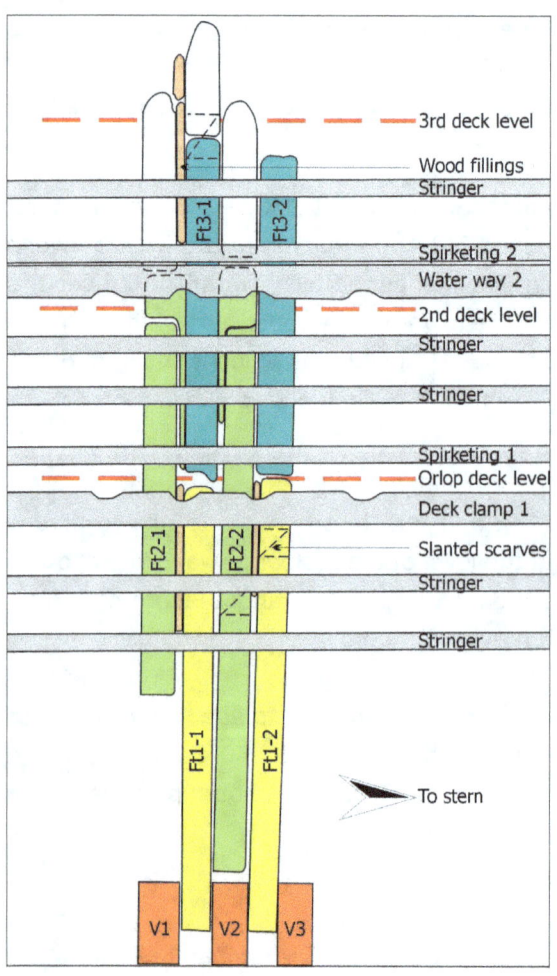

FIG.93
Diagram showing the assemblage between floors and futtocks. Not to scale.

CEILING PLANKING *(PLAN)*

The remaining part of the ceiling planking seems to compose the entire section of the flat amidships of the ship's starboard side, with only both ends (fore and aft) slightly damaged. It runs from the bow tailframe until the stern tailframe, with a width at the level of the main frame of 2.84m, measured from the middle of the keelson to the edge of the ceiling. The assumption that this half of the flat is complete is based on the fact that the external strakes ended in rounded edges at the level of the turn of the bilge. It is this characteristic that would make it very difficult (if not impossible) to attach them to other strakes. Moreover, these external strakes have 9 rectangular holes (0.1m x 0.2m) across them, apparently to support baulks, at relatively regular distances from one another (between 1.8m and 2m). The planking of the ceiling is made up of 65 strakes with a width that varies from 0.15m to 0.3m. The most common value is 0.2m in width along with a thickness of 0.1m. These strakes are nailed to the floors and first futtocks by squared section iron spikes of 0.02m and with countersink holes of a circular section of 0.06m. The connection between the longitudinally contiguous strakes is made by flat scarfs that overlap between one and the next. (Fig.95) (Fig.96)

FIG.95

FIG.95/ 96
Two views of the planking of the ceiling at the level of the mast step. In the lower photo the scarfs used in the strakes to home the baulks are visible.

HULL'S EXTERNAL PLANKING *(TRACAS DEL FORRO)*

Very little of the external planking of the hull was possible to observe as the entire surviving assemblage of timber which makes up the wood structure is resting on it. Due to the decision not to dismantle any part of the structure during this initial phase of the study, the planking of the hull remained mostly inaccessible. Nevertheless, it was possible to take limited measurements between the floor timbers and in the fractured section at the level of the first futtocks.

Judging by the colour and appearance of the hull planks we believe they are made of the same wood as the stringers and planking of the ceiling. They are lighter in colour and softer than the wood used for the floor timbers, deck clamps and other structural parts. No analysis of the wood has been done in this first phase in order to determine the species of trees used. Therefore this conjecture is based on observation only. It is worth noting that various knots in the wood of the planks were observed, but none of them are close to the edges, demonstrating the great care taken when the strakes were selected and laid.

The measured strakes of the hull planking vary in width from 0.17m to 0.27m, with 0.22m being the most common value. They are very close together, with an average separation of 0.001m between them at the level of the master frame, giving the vessel the necessary impermeability. Lead caulking was also observed between strakes and external lead sheathing was visible in the west end of the structure. (Fig.97)

FIG.97
Strakes of the hull's planking visible between the floor timbers. Their thickness was measured in the area of the fracture at the level of the first futtocks.

DECKS *(CUBIERTAS)*

Although the decks had disappeared for obvious reasons, some structural parts of the assemblage of timbers which survived give a good indication of where the decks were placed. The quantity and location of the deck clamps and waterways provide physical evidence that the ship had at least three decks. The orlop deck (first deck going up from the bottom or lower deck) and the first of the twin decks (2nd deck) still conserve their complete set of deck clamps, waterways and spirketings, therefore it was possible to measure the distance between them and the ceiling planking of the hold. The height of the orlop deck over the ceiling was 4.3m, but as this section of the ship had been fractured and flattened by the weight of the ballast and therefore had lost its curvature, we estimated the real height, at approximately 4m. The distance between the orlop deck and the first of the twin decks was 2.4m, exactly the same as the distance between the 2nd deck and what could be the remains of the third deck or upper twin deck. The location of the 3rd deck is suggested by a fragmented deck clamp, still attached to the frames but at the very end of the wood assemblage and unfortunately no part of the waterway nor the deck beams related to it had survived. From the 25 deck beams ends which had survived, none belong to the deck clamp of the 3rd deck, only the scarfs to hold them are visible. The distance between the twin decks was measured from the upper face of the first waterway to the lower face of the second deck clamp.

It is interesting to point out that no port holes nor loop holes are present in the section of the hull between the decks. As we know that the ship was armed with iron cannons this suggests that either the cannons were placed in the weather deck or there was a fourth deck of which no traces have survived. (Fig.94)

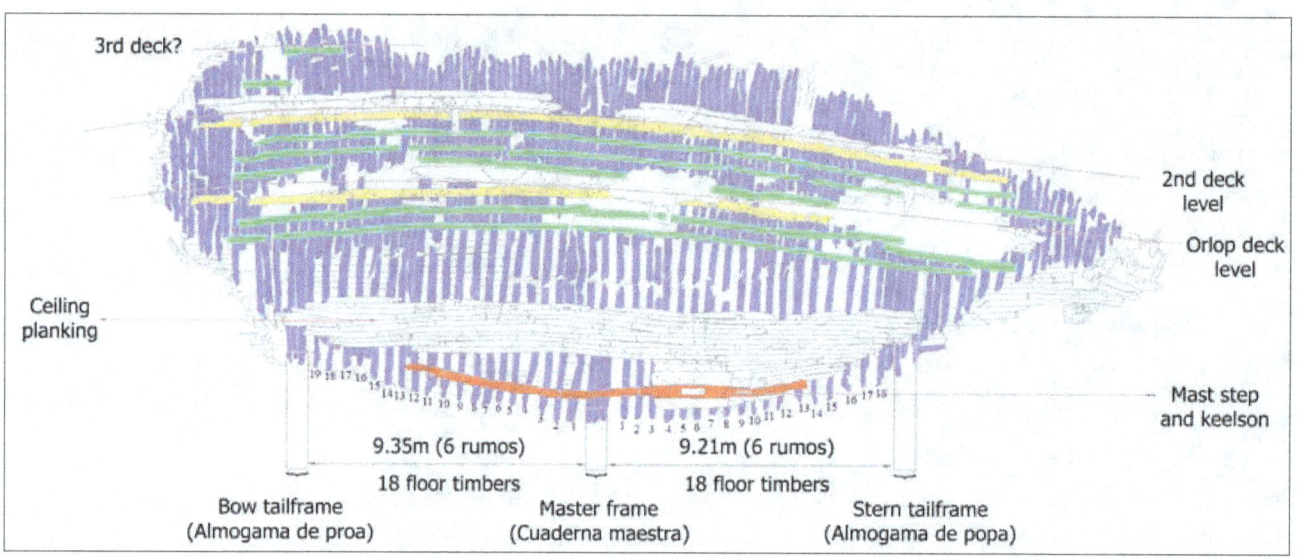

FIG.94
Diagram showing the assemblage of all the main structural parts of IDM-003.

MEASUREMENTS AND RECONSTRUCTION OF THE SHIP

With the recorded measurements of the wood structure pieces and relationship between them, as well as comparative studies, we can venture some very general considerations regarding the size of the IDM-003 ship.

To begin with, it is necessary to identify the measurement units in use in the different Portuguese shipyards during the 16th and 17th centuries that although they were not standardized and varied between shipyards and riverside carpenters, they can give us an idea of the constructive proportions. The table below is taken from Castro, F. 2003. The Pepper Wreck, an early 17th century Portuguese Indiaman at the mouth of the Tagus River, Portugal. *The International Journal of Nautical Archaeology,* Vol. 32. 1, pg. 10.

Units in use in Portuguese shipyards of the 16th and 17th centuries:

UNIT	EQUIVALENT 16TH /17TH CENTURY	METRIC EQUIVALENT
Palmo de vara	1/7 of a *rumo*	220 mm
Palmo de goa	1/6 of a *rumo*	256.7 mm
Vara	5 *palmos de vara*	1.10 m
Goa	3 *palmos de goa*	770 mm
Rumo	2 *goas*, 6 *palmos de goa*	1.54 m
Polegada comum	1/8 of a *palmo de vara*	27.5 mm
Polegada de goa	1 *palmo de goa*	36.7 mm

The structural parts we were able to measure at our wreck and that gave us more information to analyze it in comparison with the above listed units were the following:

Surviving length of the keel	**20.55m** (13.34 *rumos*)
Distance between tailframes	**18.66m** (12.1 *rumos*)
Width of the floor timbers	**0.25m** (1 *Palmo de goa*)
Width of the first futtocks	**0.22m** (1 *Palmo de vara*)
Room-and-space (average)	**0.462m** (1 *Palmo de goa* + 1 *P. de vara*)
No. of timbers of the master frame	**3**
No. of floors between tailframes	**36** (18 each side of the master frame)
Width of the flat amidships (starboard)	**2.84m** (11.09 *Palmos de goa*)

As the planking of the ceiling at the level of the master frame appears to be complete we can safely calculate the total width of the flat amidships in our wreck, therefore:

-Total width of the flat amidships	5.68m (22.18 *Palmos de goa*)

Due to the estimated age of IDM-003 we favoured Fernando Oliveira's *Livro da Fabrica das Naus* dated 1580, to compare the measurements and proportions recorded from the timber assemblage. Due to the surviving length of the keel that we were able to measure (20.55m) the model proposed by Fernando Oliveira which seems to better match our wreck is that of a *nau* of 18 *rumos* of keel (27.72m). For a *nau* of 18 *rumos* Oliveira prescribes three master frames and 18 pre-designed frames, before and after the master frames. IDM-003 presents 18 floor timbers at either side of the master frame until the bow and stern tailframes respectively. In the direction of the bow, a 19th floor timber was observed, but as it was dislodged from the rest of the structure we can't be sure if it belonged there.

The maximum breadth indicated by Oliveira for a *nau* with 18 *rumos* of keel is actually a range between 1/3 and 1/2 of the keel length on the second deck. That is to say, between 6 and 9 *rumos* (9.24m to 13.86m). Oliveira also gives the value of 8 *rumos*, or 48 *palmos de goa* (12.32m) as recommended. He indicates that the flat of the master frames should also be between 1/3 and 1/2 of the maximum breadth, meaning between a minimum of 2 *rumos* (3.08m) and a maximum of 4.5 *rumos* (6.93m). Using his recommended value of 48 *palmos de goa*, we reach the range of 16 to 24 *palmos de goa* (4.11m to 6.16m) for the flat amidships. In our case, it was possible to measure what we think is the complete starboard half of the flat amidships and therefore calculate the total width of the flat amidships at 5.68m (22.18 *palmos de goa*) which perfectly suits the theoretical interval given by Oliveira. Fixing the variable of the width of the flat amidships and following the proportions indicated by Oliveira, we can calculate backwards the maximum breadth of the ship. This gives us a range of between 11.36m (7.38 *rumos*) and 17.04m (11.09 *rumos*). The higher value falls outside the range given by the proportion with the length of the keel, helping us narrow down the theoretical breadth of our *nau* to an interval of between 11.36m (7.38 *rumos*) and 13.86m (9 *rumos*).

The overall length of the ship can be calculated by adding the length of the keel, the spring of the stem post (1/3 of the keel) and the rake of the stern post (1/4 of the spring of the stem post).

With the measurements taken *in situ* and the values obtained following the proportions given in Fernando Oliveira's *Livro da Fabrica das Naus* of 1580, we can list the possible dimensions of our ship as follows:

Keel	27.72m
Overall length	39.27m
Maximum breadth	11.36m to 13.86m
Height of the orlop deck	4m
Height of the twin decks	2.4m each
Depth of the hold	8.8m

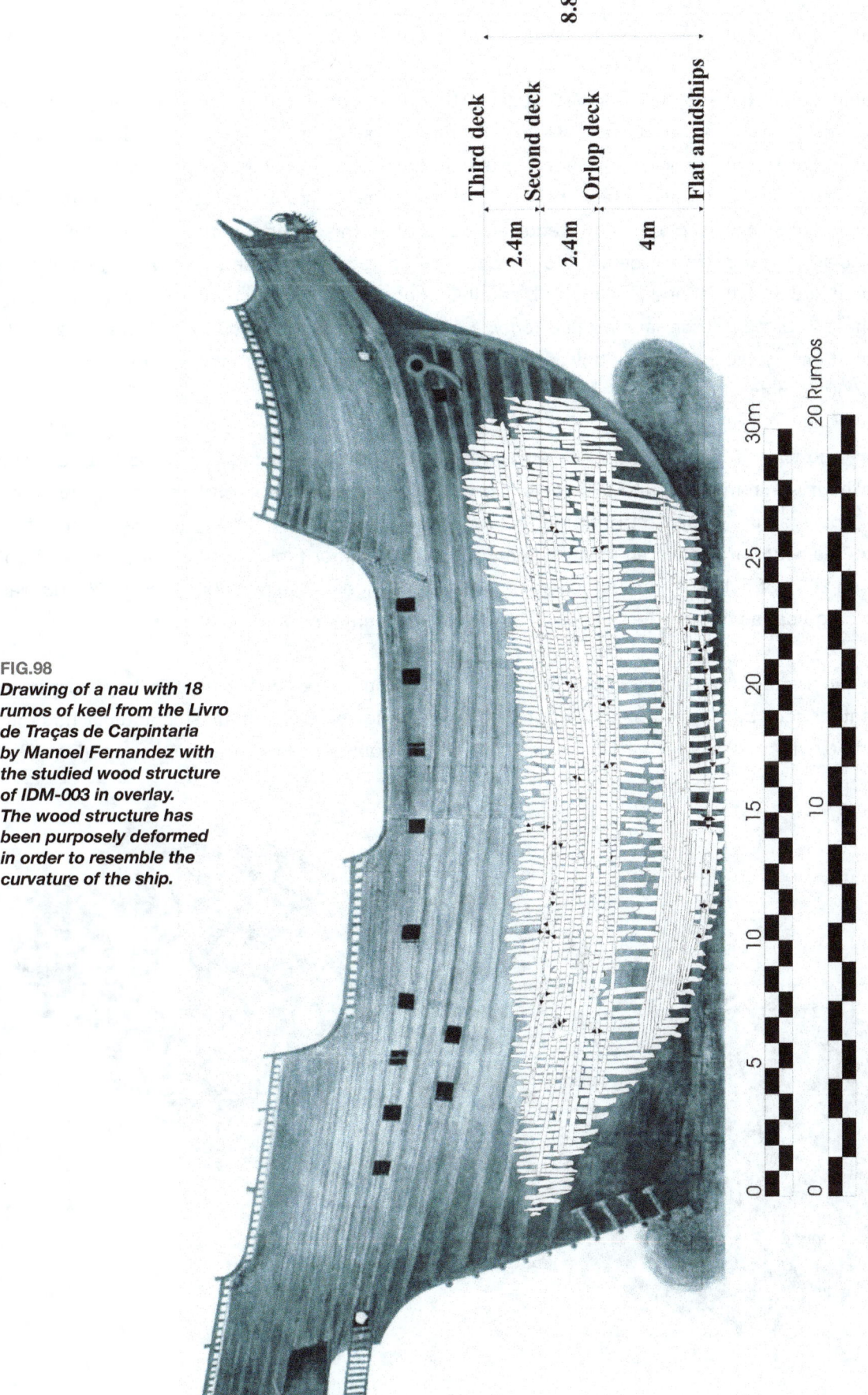

FIG.98
Drawing of a nau with 18 rumos of keel from the Livro de Traças de Carpintaria by Manoel Fernandez with the studied wood structure of IDM-003 in overlay. The wood structure has been purposely deformed in order to resemble the curvature of the ship.

Third deck

Second deck

Orlop deck

Flat amidships

8.8m

2.4m

2.4m

4m

30m

25

20

15

10

5

0

20 Rumos

10

0

Although the measurements and dimensions of IDM-003 perfectly respect the instructions given by Oliveira for the construction of a three-decked *nau* of 600 *tonéis* and 18 *rumos* of keel, they also often coincide with the *"regimentos"* (set of rules) stated by Manoel Fernandez in his Livro de *Traças de Carpintaria*, written in about 1616 for a four-decked *nau* with 17.5 *rumos* of keel. Apparently, the fact that a ship had three or four decks would not have a big impact on its size and displacement. Recurrent debates on this subject took place in 1605, 1619, 1622 and 1627 by especially created committees, without reaching an agreement. There were supporters of both options. A curious example dated 1623 and written by Manuel Gomes Galego, who was in favour of the three-decked *naus*, states that *"se deviam fazer naus de 800 tonéis com três cobertas, pois eram melhores que as de 500 tonéis com quatro"* (*Domingues*, 2004). (It is better to build ships of 800 *tonéis* with three decks, as they are better than the ones of 500 *tonéis* with four)

The fact is that we have no way of knowing with certainty if IDM-003 had three or four decks as both options are feasible based on the measurements found. However, we can't help noting that in almost every case in our wreck, the dimensions observed are closer to the higher ends of the ranges given by Oliveira for the construction of a three-decked *nau*. The width of the flat amidships, the intriguing 19th floor timber to the bow, the height of the decks, the more than 200 t of ballast found in the wreck, all of this suggests the possibility that IDM-003 was built to favour a larger cargo capacity than the building instructions recommended.

Nevertheless, there is one thing we can safely confirm: if IDM-003 had only three decks, the artillery must have been placed on the weather deck due to the absence of port holes on the lower decks. If the ship actually had four decks, the question on how many decks with artillery (one or two) she would have had, remains open. (Fig.99)

FIG.99
A 3D representation of the wood structure studied. Deck beams of the second deck are visible on the left side of the picture.

SECTION 7

Backfilling the Archaeological Station

At the beginning of 2009, 24 months after the fieldwork on IDM-003 had ended, the marine archaeological team in place decided to cover the wreck's exposed hull. Nevertheless, the academic study on the wood structure continued.

The reason for covering the surviving section of the hull of IDM-003 was to stop, or slow down, the natural decay of the wood in a marine context. After the excavation phase, the wood structure was exposed to a new and oxygen-enriched environment, which facilitates the growth of marine organisms with the subsequent impact on the timbers. Furthermore, the mechanical action of human activity, such as fisheries, dragging nets, anchoring and diving, was a threat to the integrity of the wooden hull.

The objectives of backfilling the wreck site were as follows:

1) To create a mechanical barrier in order to avoid currents and/or human activity displacing or damaging the timbers of the hull.

2) To create a "mesh" or "trap" to capture drifting sediment and slowly decrease the oxygen levels in the close vicinity of the wood.

3) To create large areas of shade which rapidly inhibit the growth of marine organisms.

4) To protect the remaining wood structure for peer review and future study.

5) To leave the wreck site as similar as possible to how it was when it was discovered. This objective will have the added benefit that the wreck site can be used in the future for "archaeological tourism".

In order to achieve these objectives, we decided to cover the exposed hull with the same ballast stones that were removed during the archaeological excavation. These ballast stones were located all around the remaining wood structure. From the 250 tons of stones originally removed from the wreck, approximately 100 tons were placed back over the wood structure during the works of the 2009 season.

The divers picked up the ballast stones by hand, one by one and placed them in plastic crates, which were immediately transported to the wood structure and placed on top of it. Then another diver started locating the stones, seeking maximum coverage and gently covering the more fragile sections. The coverage was applied in two layers. The first layer was in direct contact with the wood, filling up all irregularities and cavities formed by the floor timbers and hull planking. After covering the entire wood structure with this layer, a second load of stones was placed over it. This second layer was then spread evenly, taking special care to close every hole between the stones in order to avoid the penetration of sunlight.

At the end of July 2009 the last ballast stones were placed at the IDM-003 wreck site, closing the field phase of the archaeological intervention on this wreck and leaving the site protected *in-situ* from further degradation. (Fig.100)

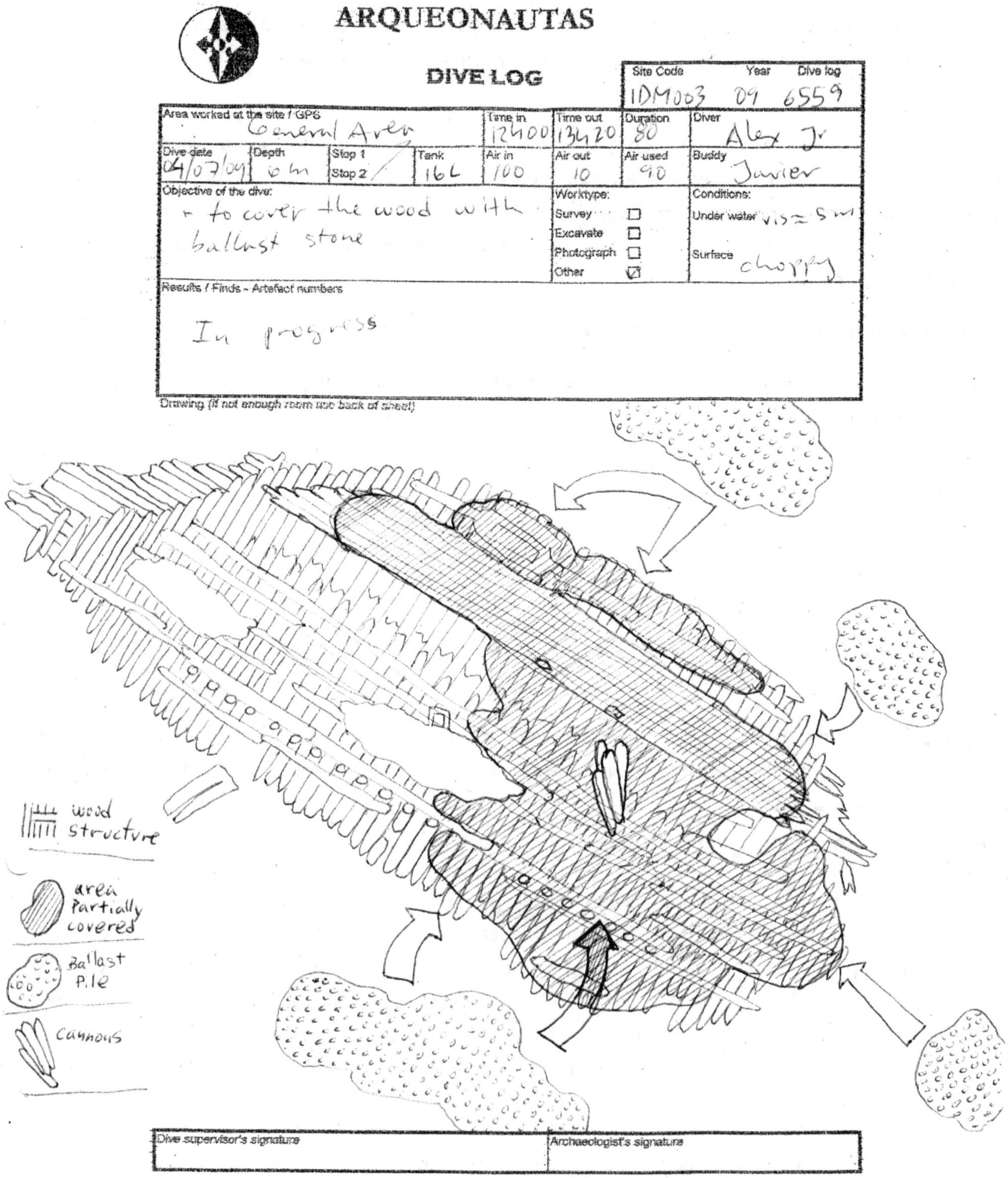

ARQUEONAUTAS

DIVE LOG

Site Code	Year	Dive log
IDM003	09	6559

Area worked at the site / GPS				Time in	Time out	Duration	Diver
General Area				12400	13h20	80	Alex Jr

Dive date	Depth	Stop 1	Tank	Air in	Air out	Air used	Buddy
04/07/09	10 m	Stop 2 /	16 L	100	10	90	Javier

Objective of the dive:	Worktype:		Conditions:	
→ to cover the wood with ballast stone	Survey ☐		Under water vis = 5m	
	Excavate ☐			
	Photograph ☐		Surface choppy	
	Other ☑			

Results / Finds – Artefact numbers

In progress

Drawing (if not enough room use back of sheet)

wood structure

area Partially covered

Ballast P.le

Cannons

Dive supervisor's signature	Archaeologist's signature

FIG.100

Dive Log by the archaeological draftsman Alejandro Raul Mirabal with a working sketch of the backfilling works.

SECTION 8

Conclusion

Based on the information recovered during the archaeological excavation of this site we can start getting a rough idea of the position of the wreck. There is a strong possibility that the ship had run aground on the shoal when sailing from inside the Mozambican bay to the open sea. This is completely in line with the references in the archival documents that the ship was being towed out of the bay by the attacking Dutch fleet. What we have confirmed is that the bow section of the ship is pointing SSW, almost parallel to the navigation channel in that spot and heading outwards, the stern section is pointing in NNE direction towards the inside of the bay.

The horizontal and vertical distribution pattern of artefacts in this wreck is quite typical of a ship sunk in shallow waters but in a relatively calm area. There are no strong currents that need to be taken into account when analyzing the scattering of artefacts. Nevertheless, the action of moderate swell produced by storms coming from the south is of some importance. The fact that this area is of fast sediment deposition, normally carried by the current during ebb and high tide, helped create a "trap". The trap holds the artefacts stored in the interior of the ship, with no sensitive horizontal displacement. Therefore the artefacts found in a specific section of the wreck are likely to belong originally to that section of the ship, at the different levels of decks and hold.

The stratigraphic arrangement of the wreck material at this site is simple, showing a typical pattern of the collapsing of decks and their contents. The objects found shallower in the sediment are the ones which belonged to the upper decks. There is a certain amount of horizontal displacement (to the west) in the case of the upper decks' material due to the natural inclination of a ship stranded in such shallow waters.

The depth of the overburden increases to the west of the debris field where the wreck material is scarcer, from a minimum of 0.30m in the eastern grids to a maximum of 0.90m to the west of S7 where wreck material was found at a depth of 1m.

The depth of the archaeological layer varies from 0.15m to 0.60m mostly modulated by the location of the stone ballast mound at the centre of the ship (where the cultural layer is thinner), increasing to the west like the depth of the overburden. The kind of sediment observed in the area makes it highly likely that the spots towards the west, not containing wreck material at levels deeper than 1m, were part of the rigging and loose elements of the upper decks.

The type of artefacts found include Cargo, Domestic, Personal belongings, Professional instruments and Ordnance categories. This provides rich insight into the trade, navigation and life on board ships, during the early 17th century.

TENTATIVE IDENTIFICATION

Identifying an early shipwreck, based on very often scarce and vague archival documentation and limited and highly degraded physical remains, is a difficult exercise. Sometimes, if we are lucky, we can estimate a certain period of time (few decades) and country of origin of the ship. Less frequently, a particular artefact(s), known to have been transported on the ship or a very accurate description of the location of the loss, can help narrow down the possible identity to a few ships. The IDM-003 wreck was no exception; therefore all conjectures regarding its identity should be understood as no more than an educated guess.

Evidence gathered during excavation and archival research suggests that IDM-003 was a Portuguese Indiaman from the early 17th century and has been tentatively identified as *"Nossa Senhora da Consolação"*, lost at this location in July, 1608, when seized by the Dutch on her trip from Lisbon to Goa and wintering at the Island of Mozambique.

As the *"Nossa Senhora da Consolação"* was lost together with another ship, not named in the archive files but referred to as a *Galeão do trato*, during the research process we kept open the possibility that IDM-003 could be either of the two.

One of the documents studied in our historical research reads as follows:

Aquando da chegada dos holandeses a Moçambique, estavam no porto a nau Nossa Senhora da Consolação, que ali invernara, e um galeão do trato que fazia o comércio entre Goa e Moçambique. Os navios encalharam no lado da Cabeceira após uma tentativa falhada dos holandeses de os rebocar, tendo de noite sido incendiados pelos portugueses. (Botelho, 1948)

[Upon the arrival of the Dutch to Mozambique, there were in the harbour the *nau Nossa Senhora da Consolação*, which had wintered there, and a galleon which made the annual trade voyage between Goa and Mozambique. Both ships were stranded at the side of *Cabeceira* after a failed attempt from the Dutch to take them and were burned during the night by the Portuguese.]

We expected that the archaeological excavation of IDM-003 and the study of its naval construction would help us answer this question, as they were two different kinds of ships, built for different purposes.

The geographical location "at the side of *Cabeceira*" (north side of the entry channel to the bay) matches the location of IDM-003, but other ships have also been reported as lost in that general area. The fact that most of the ends of surviving wood timbres of the hull presented clear signs of having been burnt, added an important clue as to the identity of the ship as we know that *Nossa Senhora da Consolação* was purposely set on fire. The few and much eroded silver coins found in the wreck were minted in Mexico and Potosi and none of them have an inscribed date. Dates only started to be struck on coins in the Mexican mint house from 1607 onwards. One of the Mexican coins shows the assayer mark **"F"**, which corresponds to Francisco de Morales who is known to have worked, between 1589 and 1608, at the Mexican mint house *(Mirabal, 2012)*. Therefore it is fairly safe to say that the coins in the wreck were struck before 1607.

Moreover, in an eye witness account of the Dutch siege of Mozambique Island in 1608, written by Johann Verken in his *"Molukkenreise 1607-1612"* we found the following passages (translation by historian Torsten Arnold):

"…they reached the land and island of Mozambique where they found two "Carracks" *(naus)*, one galleon and a small ship; the small ship lay on land under the fortress (together with the galleon), the two other "Carracks" between the firm land and the island of Mozambique. … As soon as the four hunting ships had lifted their anchors they started to attack the two naus, passing the fortress at full speed. The Portuguese started to shoot at them with massive force but only managed to hit the ship called *Falck* with one shot which ripped off the head of a man. There were only five shots fired by one of the *naus* without causing any hit. Therefore the two hunting ships, the *Falck* and the *Greyff* approached the bigger *nau (Nossa Senhora da Consolação)* and took her into possession. But as they entered the ship they encountered six Portuguese and about sixty moors or slaves on board. The other people, around 200, had fled to land seeking shelter in the fortress abandoning the ship laden with "enlightening" cargo such as precious cloth, "Turkish green spices", elephant tusks, different types of oil, wine and other goods for the Dutch. They cut off the ropes of the anchors in order to float her towards their ships but as soon as they got too close to the ships she got stuck as she was heavily laden and in shallow waters. Therefore they were forced to unload her and take the goods into the hunting ships, taking the best goods from the upper deck and leaving her until the next morning. As they tried to approach her the next morning, they saw the nau on fire... Seeing that the ship was on fire, they approached her and still managed to remove some cloth and "Turkish green spices" as well as some elephant tusks and some two hundred barrels of Lisbon oils. Many of the goods had already been destroyed by the fire causing a great loss as there were at least a hundred and fifty big barrels on board."

After the analysis of the artefacts recovered, the presence of royal seals, a cargo of lead ingots, olive jars of Iberian origin, elephant tusks and the size and characteristics of the ship itself, our opinion is that IDM-003 is most probably the *"nau da India" Nossa Senhora da Consolação* rather than a *"galeão do trato"*.

The surviving part of the wooden hull of *Nossa Senhora da Consolação*, one of the best preserved examples found so far of a 17th century Portuguese Indiaman, has been left protected *in situ* for the benefit of future generations and researchers. There is still a large wealth of knowledge that we can extract from this archaeological site when appropriate infrastructures are available at reasonably close geographical areas.

The entire collection of artefacts recovered from the wreck was donated to the *Museu da Marinha* at *Ilha de Moçambique* in August 2009 and has been on public display ever since.

SECTION 9

Bibliography and Sources.

Alves, F., Castro, F., Rodrigues, P., Garcia, C. & Aleluia, M., 1998, Archaeology of a Shipwreck. In S. L. Afonso, *Nossa Senhora dos Mártires: The Last Voyage.* Lisbon.

Bell, Christopher Richard. *Portugal and the Quest for the Indies.* New York: Harper & Row, 1974, p. 201

Biblioteca Nacional de Lisboa; Fondo General 1871.

Biblioteca Nacional de Lisboa; Reservados; Caixa 26, n° 153.

Botelho de Sousa, A. 1948 *Subsídios para a história militar marítima da Índia*, vol. II, pp. 110-112.

Boxer, Charles Ralph, 1961, *Moçambique Island and the "Carreira da Índia"*, Centro de Estudos Históricos Ultramarinos, sep. STVDIA, Revista Semestral, No. 8, Lisboa,

Boxer, Charles Ralph, Carcanet, (1991) *The Portuguese Seaborne Empire 1415-1825*

Díaz Gamez, Alfredo. (1998) *Naufragio en Inés de Soto: Un hallazgo de cuatro siglos.* Carisub, S.A., Corporación CIMEX, S.A., Ciudad de La Habana, Cuba

Castro, F. 2003, The Pepper Wreck, an early 17th century Portuguese Indiaman at the mouth of the Tagus River, Portugal, *IJNA* **32.1:** 6–23.

Domingues, Francisco C., 2004, *Os navios do mar oceano: teoria e empiria na arquitectura naval portuguesa dos séculos XVI e XVII.* Centro de História da Universidade de Lisboa, Lisboa. pp.249-250

Domínguez, L. *Cerámicas Históricas.* Puerto Rico, Instituto de Cultura Puertorriqueña, 1977.

Durão, António, Prestage, Edgar, Boxer, Charles Ralph *"Cercos de Moçambique defendidos por Dom Estêvão de Ataíde, Capitão General, Governador daquela Praça"*, Tipografia Silvas, Lisboa, 1937.

Escalante de Mendoza, Juan De. *Itinerario de navegación de los mares y tierras occidentales.* 1575. Madrid, Museo Naval, 1985.

Fernandez, M. (1616/1989) *Livro de Traças de Carpintaria.* Facsimile of the manuscript.

García de Palacio, Diego. *Instrucción Náutica para Navegar.* 1587. Madrid, Colección de Incunables Americanos, Siglo XVI, Talleres Graficas Ultra, S.A., 1944

Goggin, J.M. *Spanish Majolica in the New World.* New Haven, Yale University Press. No. 72, 1968.

Hambly, M. 1988 *Drawing Instruments, 1580-1980.* Sotheby's Publications, London, UK.

Hurst, John G. (1995) *Post-Medieval Pottery from Seville Imported into North-West Europe. In Trade and Discovery: The Scientific Study of Artefacts from Post-Medieval Europe and Beyond,* British Museum Occasional Paper 109, edited by Duncan R. Hook and David R.M. Gaimster, pp.45-54. The British Museum, London

Marken, Mitchell W. (1994) *Pottery from Spanish Shipwrecks.* University Press of Florida, Gainesville

Mirabal, A. (1998) *Naufragio en Inés de Soto: Un hallazgo de cuatro siglos.* Carisub, S.A., Corporación CIMEX, S.A., Ciudad de La Habana, Cuba, pp. 69-86

Mirabal, A. (2012) *Spanish Coins in Mozambican Waters. The Numismatic Collection of the São Jose, 1622.* Arqueonautas Worldwide publications, Portugal, p. 26.

Murteira, André Alexandre Martins, (2012) *"A Carreira da Índia e o Corso Neerlandês 1595-1625",* Tipografia Lousanense, Lisboa.

Lavanha, J. B. (1608-1616/1996) *Livro Primeiro de Architectura Naval.* Facsimile, transcription and translation in English of the manuscript of the Real Academia de la Historia of Madrid.

Lopes, Maria de Lurdes, *Ilha e Fortaleza de Moçambique no Século XVII 1620-1668,* Dissertação para a Licenciatura em Ciências Históricas e Filosóficas, Faculdade de Letras da Universidade de Lisboa, 1960.

Nilsson, Jan-Erik, Göteborg 1999, *South East Asian Martaban Jar.*

Oliveira, F., 1580, *O Livro da Fabrica das Naos,* facsimile, transcription and translation into English, 1991, Lisbon.

Pearson, Colin. *Conservation of Marine Archaeology Objects.* London, Buttenworth and Co, 1982.

Pinto de Matos, Maria Antonia. (2006) Ceramic expert, *personal communication.*

Rego, A. De Silva, Baxter, T. W. (cord.) *"Documentos sobre os Portugueses em Moçambique e na África Central: 1497-1840",* Vol. IX, Instituto de Investigação Científica Tropical, Lisboa, 1989.

Turner, Gerard L'E. 1980 *Antique Scientific Instruments.* Blandford Press Ltd., Dorset, UK.

Verken, J., *Molukkenreise 1607–1612, in Reisebeschreibungen von Deutschen Beamten und Kriegsleuten im Dienst der Niederländisch West- und Ost-Indischen Kompanien, 1602–1797,* ed. S. P. l'Honoré Naber, II (The Hague: Martinus Nijhoff, 1930), pp. 22-25.

Vinh, Augustine H, (2005), Ceramic expert, lecturer at Ha Noi National University, Vietnam, *personal communication.*

Waters, D. W. 1958 *The Art of Navigation in England in Elizabethan and Early Stuart Times.* Yale University Press, New Haven, CT.

Complete Catalogue of Artefacts from the
NOSSA SENHORA DA CONSOLAÇÃO

ARTEFACT NO IDM-003- 03- 2005.000

MATERIAL Ceramics

DESCRIPTION Small olive jar, rounded, attached to a small fragment of wood

CATEGORY Cargo

ASSOCIATION Other olive jars and fragments

DATE EXCAVATED 06-Sept-03

DATE CONSERVED 20-Aug-05

LOCATION Marine Conservation Center (CCM), Island of Mozambique

POST CONSERVATION PHOTO

PRE CONSERVATION PHOTO

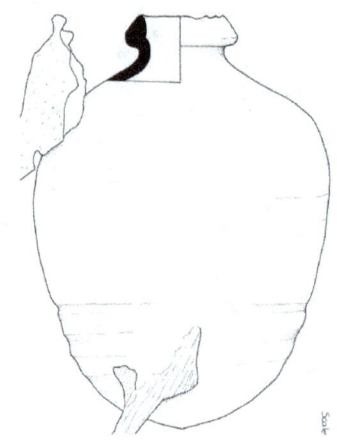

ARTEFACT DRAWING

ARTEFACT NO IDM-003- 03- 2006.000

MATERIAL Ceramics

DESCRIPTION Small olive jar, rounded, with small hole on the side

CATEGORY Cargo

ASSOCIATION Other olive jars and fragments

DATE EXCAVATED 06-Sept-03

DATE CONSERVED 20-Aug-05

LOCATION Marine Conservation Center (CCM), Island of Mozambique

POST CONSERVATION PHOTO

PRE CONSERVATION PHOTO

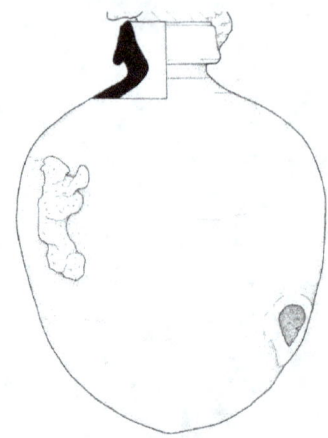

ARTEFACT DRAWING

ARTEFACT NO IDM-003- 03-**2007.000**

MATERIAL Ceramics

DESCRIPTION Fragments (6) of a martaban with remains of tar on the surface. Typically decorated

CATEGORY Cargo

ASSOCIATION Other olive jars and fragments

DATE EXCAVATED 06-Sept-03

DATE CONSERVED 14-Oct-05

LOCATION Marine Conservation Center (CCM), Island of Mozambique

POST CONSERVATION PHOTO

PRE CONSERVATION PHOTO

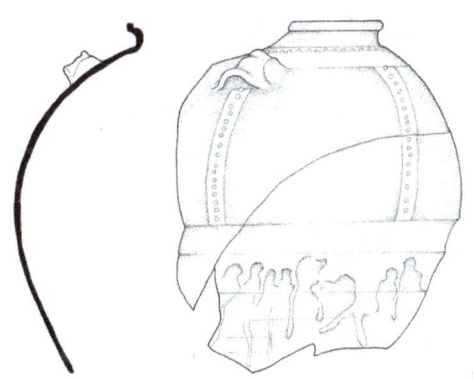

ARTEFACT DRAWING

ARTEFACT NO IDM-003- 03- **2008.000**

MATERIAL Pewter

DESCRIPTION Pewter jar with wide mouth and flat base, the mouth is mishaped and the handle is missing

CATEGORY Domestic

ASSOCIATION Ballast stones

DATE EXCAVATED 06-Sept-03

DATE CONSERVED 14-July-05

LOCATION Marine Conservation Center (CCM), Island of Mozambique

POST CONSERVATION PHOTO

PRE CONSERVATION PHOTO

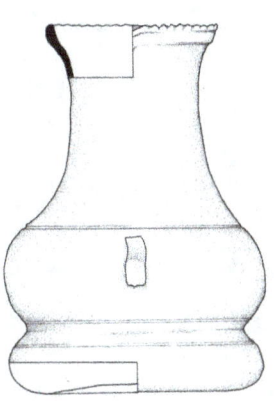

ARTEFACT DRAWING

ARTEFACT NO IDM-003- 03- **2009.000**

MATERIAL Ceramics

DESCRIPTION Small delicated ceramic flask (crude pottery) with some decoration. Appears to be of Indian manufacture

CATEGORY Cargo

ASSOCIATION Olive jars and timbers

DATE EXCAVATED 06-Sept-03

DATE CONSERVED 01-June-05

LOCATION Marine Museum (MUSIM), Island of Mozambique

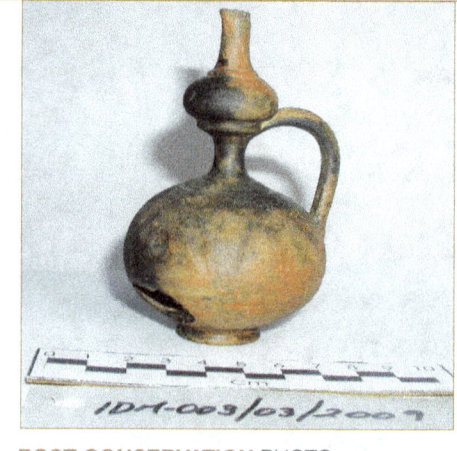

POST CONSERVATION PHOTO

PRE CONSERVATION PHOTO

ARTEFACT DRAWING

ARTEFACT NO IDM-003- 03- **2010.000**

MATERIAL Ceramics

DESCRIPTION Fragments (6) of a delicate ceramic flask. Handle concreted in a stone

CATEGORY Cargo

ASSOCIATION Olive jars and timbers

DATE EXCAVATED 06-Sept-03

DATE CONSERVED 06-June-05

LOCATION Marine Conservation Center (CCM), Island of Mozambique

POST CONSERVATION PHOTO

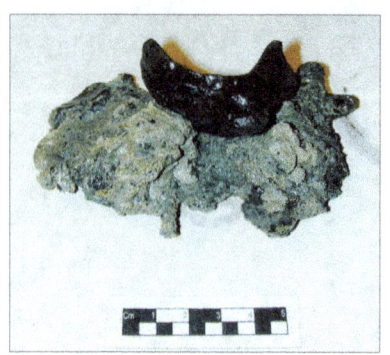

PRE CONSERVATION PHOTO

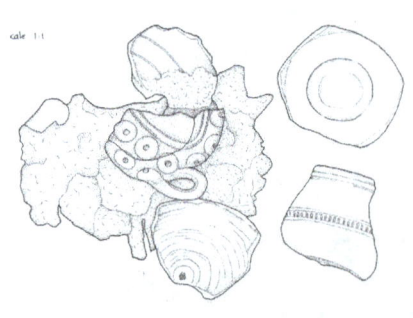

ARTEFACT DRAWING

ARTEFACT NO IDM-003- 03- **2011.000**

MATERIAL Ceramics

DESCRIPTION Small cup of ceramic (like a bell upside down). Some decoration on the rim and the body

CATEGORY Domestic

ASSOCIATION Fragments of ceramics

DATE EXCAVATED 06-Sept-03

DATE CONSERVED 01-June-05

LOCATION Marine Conservation Center (CCM), Island of Mozambique

POST CONSERVATION PHOTO

PRE CONSERVATION PHOTO

ARTEFACT DRAWING

ARTEFACT NO IDM-003- 03- **2012.000**

MATERIAL Stone

DESCRIPTION Medium size pendant representing a hand with half closed fist (Mano Fico) or "fig-hand". Depression in the back, possibly for a stone

CATEGORY Personal belongings

ASSOCIATION Fragments of ceramics and timbers

DATE EXCAVATED 06-Sept-03

DATE CONSERVED 26-May-05

LOCATION Marine Conservation Center (CCM), Island of Mozambique

POST CONSERVATION PHOTO

PRE CONSERVATION PHOTO   **ARTEFACT DRAWING**

ARTEFACT NO IDM-003- 03- **2013.000**

MATERIAL Stone

DESCRIPTION Small pendant representing a hand closed as a fist (Mano Fico) or "fig-hand". Rectangular base

CATEGORY Personal belongings

ASSOCIATION Fragments of ceramics and timbers

DATE EXCAVATED 06-Sept-03

DATE CONSERVED 26-May-05

LOCATION Marine Conservation Center (CCM), Island of Mozambique

POST CONSERVATION PHOTO

PRE CONSERVATION PHOTO

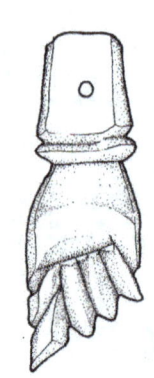

ARTEFACT DRAWING

ARTEFACT NO IDM-003- 03- **2014.000**

MATERIAL Ceramics

DESCRIPTION Delicate ceramic flask with narrow mouth. Small holes on the side and at the bottom

CATEGORY Domestic

ASSOCIATION Ceramic fragments and timbers

DATE EXCAVATED 06-Sept-03

DATE CONSERVED 01-June-05

LOCATION Marine Conservation Center (CCM), Island of Mozambique

POST CONSERVATION PHOTO

PRE CONSERVATION PHOTO

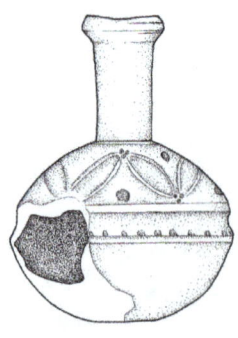

ARTEFACT DRAWING

ARTEFACT NO IDM-003- 03- **2015.000**

MATERIAL Ceramics

DESCRIPTION Delicate ceramic flask with wide mouth. Handle missing and rim chipped

CATEGORY Domestic

ASSOCIATION Fragments of ceramics and timbers

DATE EXCAVATED 06-Sept-03

DATE CONSERVED 01-June-05

LOCATION Marine Conservation Center (CCM), Island of Mozambique

POST CONSERVATION PHOTO

PRE CONSERVATION PHOTO

ARTEFACT DRAWING

ARTEFACT NO IDM-003- 03- **2016.000**

MATERIAL Ceramics

DESCRIPTION Ceramic flask with neck missing. Flat base

CATEGORY Domestic

ASSOCIATION Fragments of ceramics and timbers

DATE EXCAVATED 06-Sept-03

DATE CONSERVED 01-June-05

LOCATION Marine Conservation Center (CCM), Island of Mozambique

POST CONSERVATION PHOTO

PRE CONSERVATION PHOTO

ARTEFACT DRAWING

ARTEFACT NO IDM-003- 03- **2017.000**

MATERIAL Ceramics

DESCRIPTION Ceramic dispenser (for salt or pepper) with 4 reinforcing rings on the body

CATEGORY Domestic

ASSOCIATION Fragments of ceramics and timbers

DATE EXCAVATED 06-Sept-03

DATE CONSERVED 06-June-05

LOCATION Marine Museum (MUSIM), Island of Mozambique

POST CONSERVATION PHOTO

PRE CONSERVATION PHOTO

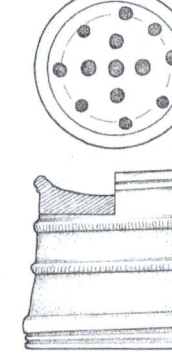

ARTEFACT DRAWING

ARTEFACT NO IDM-003- 03- **2018.000**

MATERIAL Ceramics

DESCRIPTION Ceramic stopper with thread

CATEGORY Domestic

ASSOCIATION Fragments of ceramics and timbers

DATE EXCAVATED 06-Sept-03

DATE CONSERVED 01-June-05

LOCATION Marine Conservation Center (CCM), Island of Mozambique

POST CONSERVATION PHOTO

PRE CONSERVATION PHOTO

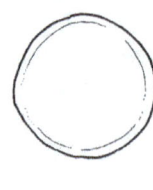

ARTEFACT DRAWING

ARTEFACT NO IDM-003- 03- **2019.000**

MATERIAL Ceramics

DESCRIPTION 4 bowls of ceramic, different sizes.
Found as a stack, the larger ones containing the smaller ones

CATEGORY Cargo

ASSOCIATION Fragments of ceramics and timbers

DATE EXCAVATED 06-Sept-03

DATE CONSERVED 06-June-05

LOCATION Marine Conservation Center (CCM), Island of Mozambique

POST CONSERVATION PHOTO

PRE CONSERVATION PHOTO

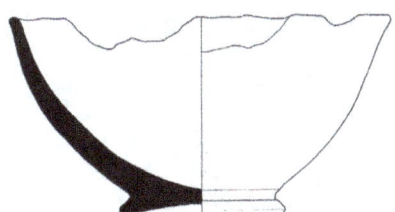

ARTEFACT DRAWING

ARTEFACT NO IDM-003- 03- **2020.000**

MATERIAL Ceramics

DESCRIPTION Small olive jar. Tap *in situ*, rounded

CATEGORY Cargo

ASSOCIATION Fragments of ceramics and timbers

DATE EXCAVATED 06-Sept-03

DATE CONSERVED 20-Aug-05

LOCATION Marine Conservation Center (CCM), Island of Mozambique

POST CONSERVATION PHOTO

PRE CONSERVATION PHOTO

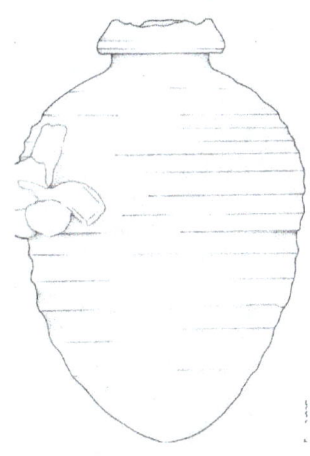

ARTEFACT DRAWING

ARTEFACT NO IDM-003- 03- **2021.000**

MATERIAL Ceramics

DESCRIPTION Ceramic flask, neck missing, flat base

CATEGORY Domestic

ASSOCIATION Fragments of ceramics and timbers

DATE EXCAVATED 06-Sept-03

DATE CONSERVED 01-June-05

LOCATION Marine Conservation Center (CCM), Island of Mozambique

POST CONSERVATION PHOTO

PRE CONSERVATION PHOTO

ARTEFACT DRAWING

ARTEFACT NO IDM-003- 03- **2023.000**

MATERIAL Ceramics

DESCRIPTION Olive jar, small, rounded

CATEGORY Cargo

ASSOCIATION Timbers and fragments of ceramics

DATE EXCAVATED 08-Sept-03

DATE CONSERVED 02-Sept-05

LOCATION Marine Conservation Center (CCM), Island of Mozambique

POST CONSERVATION PHOTO

PRE CONSERVATION PHOTO

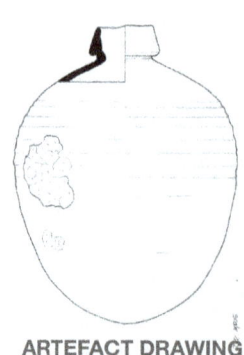

ARTEFACT DRAWING

ARTEFACT NO IDM-003- 03- **2024.000**

MATERIAL Ceramics

DESCRIPTION Olive jar, small, rounded

CATEGORY Cargo

ASSOCIATION Timbers and fragments of ceramics

DATE EXCAVATED 08-Sept-03

DATE CONSERVED 02-Sept-05

LOCATION Marine Conservation Center (CCM), Island of Mozambique

POST CONSERVATION PHOTO

PRE CONSERVATION PHOTO

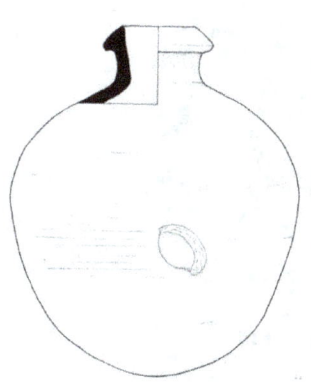

ARTEFACT DRAWING

ARTEFACT NO IDM-003- 03- **2025.000**

MATERIAL Ceramics

DESCRIPTION Olive jar, small, rounded

CATEGORY Cargo

ASSOCIATION Timbers and fragments of ceramics

DATE EXCAVATED 08-Sept-03

DATE CONSERVED 20-Aug-05

LOCATION Marine Conservation Center (CCM), Island of Mozambique

POST CONSERVATION PHOTO

PRE CONSERVATION PHOTO

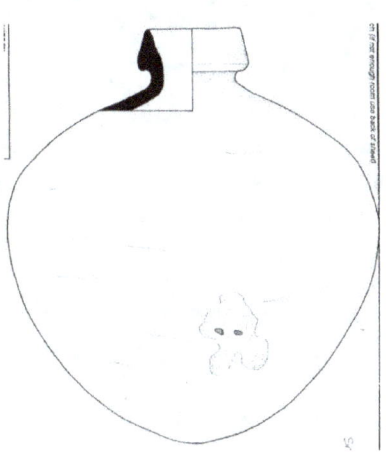

ARTEFACT DRAWING

ARTEFACT NO IDM-003- 03- **2026.000**

MATERIAL Silver

DESCRIPTION 8 silver coins in two clumps
(one of 5 coins and the other with 3)

CATEGORY Personal belongings

ASSOCIATION Olive jars, fragments of ceramics and timbers

DATE EXCAVATED 08-Sept-03

DATE CONSERVED 31-May-05

POST CONSERVATION PHOTO

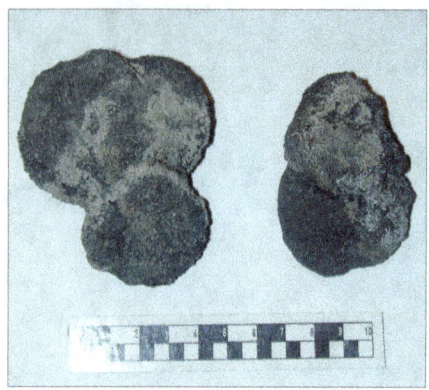

PRE CONSERVATION PHOTO

ARTEFACT DRAWING

ARTEFACT NO IDM-003 - 05 - **15000.000**

MATERIAL Ivory

DESCRIPTION One elephant tusk and two hippopotamus fangs

CATEGORY Cargo

ASSOCIATION Ballast stones, wood, olive jars

DATE EXCAVATED 06-July-05

DATE CONSERVED 24-Aug-05

LOCATION Marine Conservation Center (CCM), Island of Mozambique

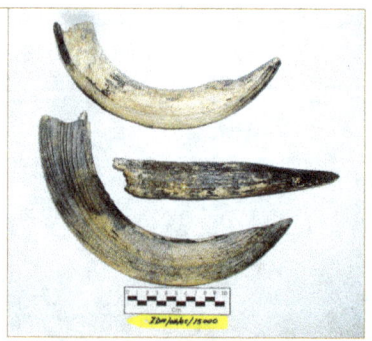

POST CONSERVATION PHOTO

PRE CONSERVATION PHOTO

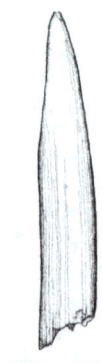

ARTEFACT DRAWING

ARTEFACT NO IDM-003 - 05 - **15001.000**

MATERIAL Ceramics

DESCRIPTION Olive jar.

CATEGORY Cargo

ASSOCIATION Ballast stones, wood, fragments of olive jars

DATE EXCAVATED 06-July-05

DATE CONSERVED 20-Aug-05

LOCATION Marine Conservation Center (CCM), Island of Mozambique

POST CONSERVATION PHOTO

PRE CONSERVATION PHOTO

ARTEFACT DRAWING

ARTEFACT NO IDM-003 - 05 - **15002.000**

MATERIAL Glass

DESCRIPTION 2 fragmented necks of glass bottles.
Fine glass decorated with strips

CATEGORY Domestic

ASSOCIATION Ballast stones, wood, olive jars

DATE EXCAVATED 06-July-05

DATE CONSERVED 09-Aug-05

LOCATION Marine Conservation Center (CCM), Island of Mozambique

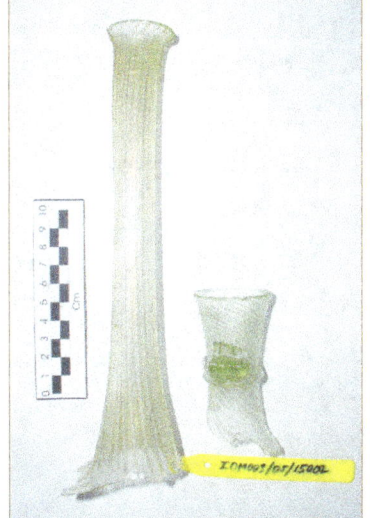

POST CONSERVATION PHOTO

PRE CONSERVATION PHOTO

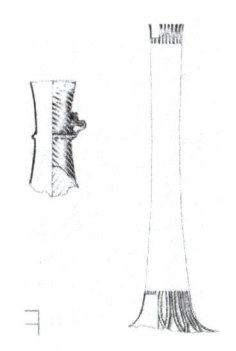

ARTEFACT DRAWING

ARTEFACT NO IDM-003 - 05 - **15003.000**

MATERIAL Ceramics

DESCRIPTION Pitcher jar, wide mouth, flat base and handle

CATEGORY Domestic

ASSOCIATION Ballast stones, wood, fragments of olive jars

DATE EXCAVATED 06-July-05

DATE CONSERVED 18-Aug-05

LOCATION Marine Museum (MUSIM), Island of Mozambique

POST CONSERVATION PHOTO

PRE CONSERVATION PHOTO

ARTEFACT DRAWING

ARTEFACT NO IDM-003 - 05 - **15004.000**

MATERIAL Ceramics

DESCRIPTION Olive jar

CATEGORY Cargo

ASSOCIATION Ballast stones, wood, other olive jars

DATE EXCAVATED 06-July-05

DATE CONSERVED 02-Sept-05

LOCATION Marine Conservation Center (CCM), Island of Mozambique

POST CONSERVATION PHOTO

PRE CONSERVATION PHOTO

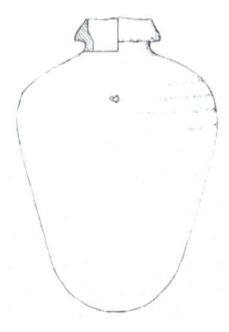

ARTEFACT DRAWING

ARTEFACT NO IDM-003 - 05 - **15005.000**

MATERIAL Ceramics

DESCRIPTION Olive jar

CATEGORY Cargo

ASSOCIATION Ballast stones, wood, other olive jars

DATE EXCAVATED 06-July-05

DATE CONSERVED 20-Aug-05

LOCATION Marine Conservation Center (CCM), Island of Mozambique

POST CONSERVATION PHOTO

PRE CONSERVATION PHOTO

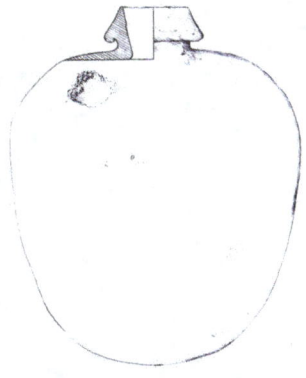

ARTEFACT DRAWING

ARTEFACT NO IDM-003 - 05 - **15005.001**

MATERIAL Ivory

DESCRIPTION Elephant tusk, small

CATEGORY Cargo

ASSOCIATION Ballast stones, wood, other olive jars

DATE EXCAVATED 06-July-05

DATE CONSERVED 24-Aug-05

LOCATION Marine Conservation Center (CCM), Island of Mozambique

POST CONSERVATION PHOTO

ARTEFACT DRAWING

ARTEFACT NO IDM-003 - 05 - **15006.000**

MATERIAL Ceramics

DESCRIPTION Olive jar

CATEGORY Cargo

ASSOCIATION Ballast stones, wood, other olive jars

DATE EXCAVATED 06-July-05

DATE CONSERVED 20-July-05

LOCATION Marine Conservation Center (CCM), Island of Mozambique

POST CONSERVATION PHOTO

PRE CONSERVATION PHOTO

ARTEFACT DRAWING

ARTEFACT NO IDM-003 - 05 - **15007.000**

MATERIAL Glass

DESCRIPTION Fragment of glass bottle, transparent ornamented glass

CATEGORY Domestic

ASSOCIATION Ballast stones, wood, other olive jars

DATE EXCAVATED 06-July-05

DATE CONSERVED 09-Aug-05

LOCATION Marine Conservation Center (CCM), Island of Mozambique

POST CONSERVATION PHOTO

PRE CONSERVATION PHOTO

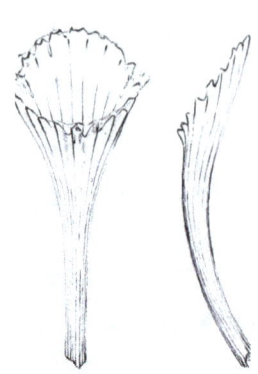

ARTEFACT DRAWING

ARTEFACT NO IDM-003 - 05 - **15009.000**

MATERIAL Ivory

DESCRIPTION Elephant tusk

CATEGORY Cargo

ASSOCIATION Wood, ballast stones

DATE EXCAVATED 07-July-05

DATE CONSERVED 29-Aug-05

LOCATION Marine Conservation Center (CCM), Island of Mozambique

POST CONSERVATION PHOTO

PRE CONSERVATION PHOTO

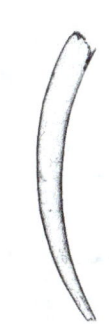

ARTEFACT DRAWING

ARTEFACT NO IDM-003 - 05 - **15010.000**

MATERIAL Ivory

DESCRIPTION Elephant tusk

CATEGORY Cargo

ASSOCIATION Wood, ballast stones

DATE EXCAVATED 07-July-05

DATE CONSERVED 29-Aug-05

LOCATION Marine Conservation Center (CCM), Island of Mozambique

POST CONSERVATION PHOTO

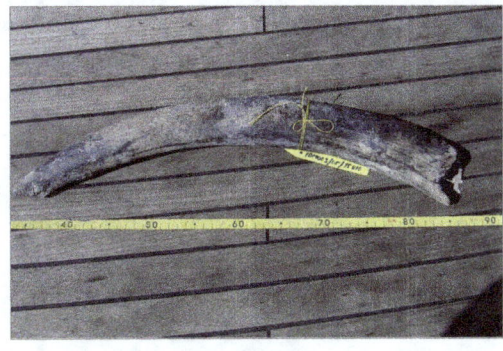

PRE CONSERVATION PHOTO

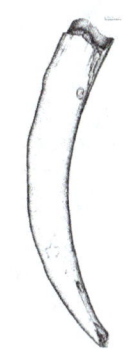

ARTEFACT DRAWING

ARTEFACT NO IDM-003 - 05 - **15011.000**

MATERIAL Pewter

DESCRIPTION Pewter lid in a concretion.
After cleaning seems to be part of Art. No 2008

CATEGORY Domestic

ASSOCIATION Iron concretion, wood

DATE EXCAVATED 07-July-05

DATE CONSERVED 21-Sept-05

LOCATION Marine Conservation Center (CCM), Island of Mozambique

POST CONSERVATION PHOTO

PRE CONSERVATION PHOTO

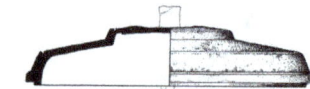

ARTEFACT DRAWING

ARTEFACT NO IDM-003 - 05 - **150012.000**

MATERIAL Copper / copper alloy

DESCRIPTION Metallic object, with handle in an iron concretion

CATEGORY Domestic

ASSOCIATION Iron concretion, wood, ballast stones

DATE EXCAVATED 07-July-05

DATE CONSERVED 11-Nov-05

LOCATION Marine Conservation Center (CCM), Island of Mozambique

POST CONSERVATION PHOTO

PRE CONSERVATION PHOTO

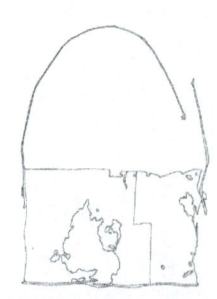

ARTEFACT DRAWING

ARTEFACT NO IDM-003 - 05 - **15013.000**

MATERIAL Copper / copper alloy

DESCRIPTION Metallic solid flattened cone

CATEGORY Unknown

ASSOCIATION Wood, ballast stones

DATE EXCAVATED 07-July-05

DATE CONSERVED 10-Aug-05

LOCATION Marine Conservation Center (CCM), Island of Mozambique

POST CONSERVATION PHOTO

PRE CONSERVATION PHOTO

ARTEFACT DRAWING

ARTEFACT NO IDM-003 - 05 - **150014.000**

MATERIAL Ceramics

DESCRIPTION Intact ceramic lid depressed in the centre

CATEGORY Domestic

ASSOCIATION Wood, ballast stones and broken ceramic

DATE EXCAVATED 09-July-05

DATE CONSERVED 17-July-05

LOCATION Marine Conservation Center (CCM), Island of Mozambique

POST CONSERVATION PHOTO

PRE CONSERVATION PHOTO

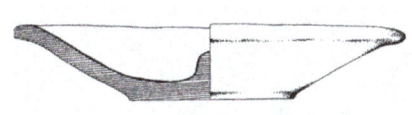

ARTEFACT DRAWING

ARTEFACT NO IDM-003 - 05 - **15015.000**

MATERIAL Ceramics

DESCRIPTION Broken side of an olive jar with handle

CATEGORY Domestic

ASSOCIATION Wood, ballast stones

DATE EXCAVATED 09-July-05

DATE CONSERVED 04-Oct-05

LOCATION Marine Conservation Center (CCM), Island of Mozambique

POST CONSERVATION PHOTO

PRE CONSERVATION PHOTO

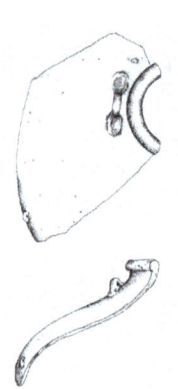

ARTEFACT DRAWING

ARTEFACT NO IDM-003 - 05 - **150016.000**

MATERIAL Copper / copper alloy

DESCRIPTION Broken copper handle

CATEGORY Domestic

ASSOCIATION Wood, ballast stones

DATE EXCAVATED 09-July-05

DATE CONSERVED 10-Nov-05

LOCATION Marine Conservation Center (CCM), Island of Mozambique

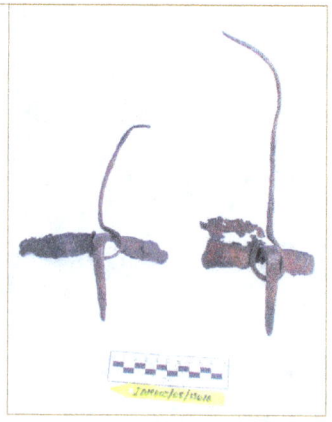

POST CONSERVATION PHOTO

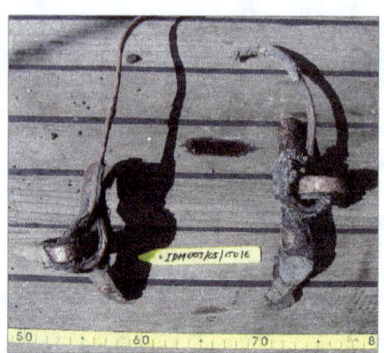

PRE CONSERVATION PHOTO

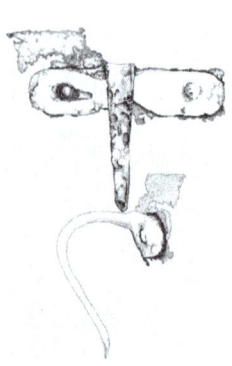

ARTEFACT DRAWING

ARTEFACT NO IDM-003 - 05 - **15017.000**

MATERIAL Ceramics

DESCRIPTION Neck of broken martaban with handle

CATEGORY Cargo

ASSOCIATION Wood, ballast stones

DATE EXCAVATED 09-July-05

DATE CONSERVED 10-Oct-05

LOCATION Marine Conservation Center (CCM), Island of Mozambique

POST CONSERVATION PHOTO

PRE CONSERVATION PHOTO

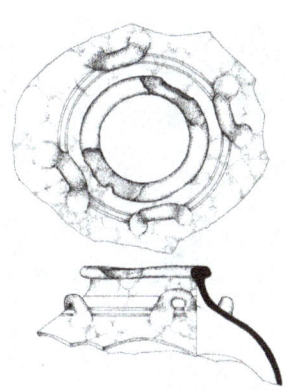

ARTEFACT DRAWING

ARTEFACT NO IDM-003 - 05 - **150018.000**

MATERIAL Silver

DESCRIPTION Clump of approx. 4 silver coins.
After treatment in the lab there were 5 eroded coins

CATEGORY Personal belongings

ASSOCIATION Seabed sediments

DATE EXCAVATED 11-July-05

DATE CONSERVED 26-July-05

LOCATION Marine Conservation Center (CCM), Island of Mozambique

POST CONSERVATION PHOTO

PRE CONSERVATION PHOTO

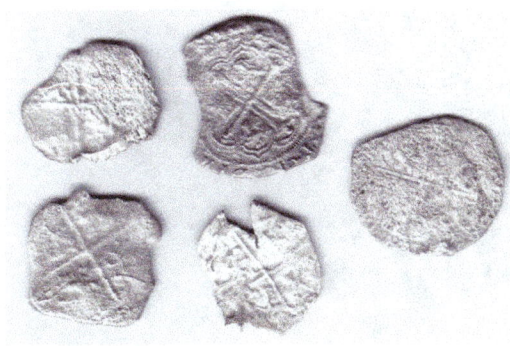

ARTEFACT DRAWING

ARTEFACT NO IDM-003 - 05 - **15019.000**

MATERIAL Copper / copper alloy

DESCRIPTION Copper jar handle

CATEGORY Domestic

ASSOCIATION Timber and sediments

DATE EXCAVATED 12-July-05

DATE CONSERVED 10-Nov-05

LOCATION Marine Conservation Center (CCM), Island of Mozambique

POST CONSERVATION PHOTO

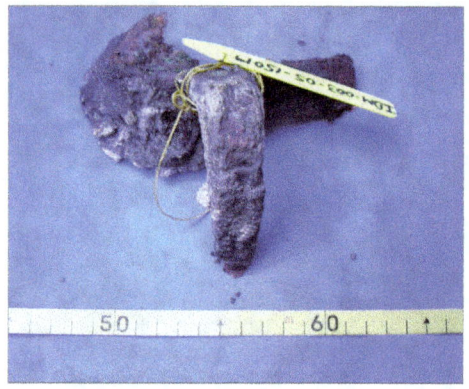

PRE CONSERVATION PHOTO

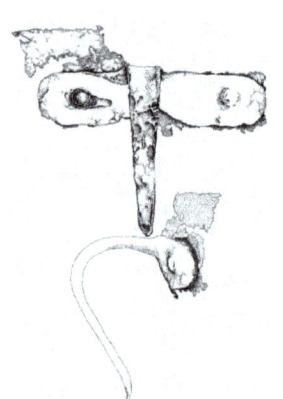

ARTEFACT DRAWING

ARTEFACT NO IDM-003 - 05 - **150020.000**

MATERIAL Silver

DESCRIPTION Clump of silver coins. After treatment there were only 10 eroded coins. Some of them minted in Mexico, the others had no recognisable mint

CATEGORY Personal belongings

ASSOCIATION Timbers and sediments

DATE EXCAVATED 13-July-05

DATE CONSERVED 27-July-05

LOCATION Marine Conservation Center (CCM), Island of Mozambique

POST CONSERVATION PHOTO

PRE CONSERVATION PHOTO

ARTEFACT DRAWING

ARTEFACT NO IDM-003 - 05 - **15021.000**

MATERIAL Copper / copper alloy

DESCRIPTION Copper jar handle

CATEGORY Domestic

ASSOCIATION Sendiments and wood

DATE EXCAVATED 13-July-05

DATE CONSERVED 10-Nov-05

LOCATION Marine Conservation Center (CCM), Island of Mozambique

POST CONSERVATION PHOTO

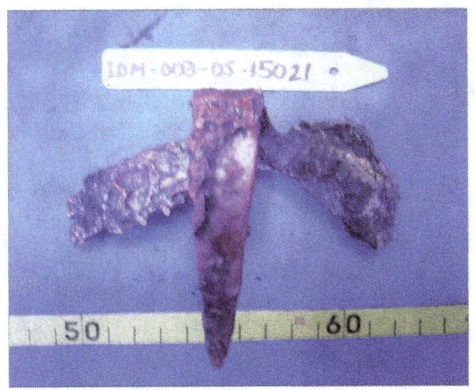

PRE CONSERVATION PHOTO

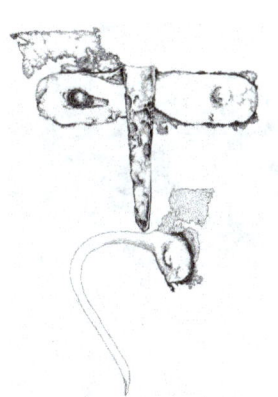

ARTEFACT DRAWING

ARTEFACT NO IDM-003 - 05 - **15022.000**

MATERIAL Ceramics

DESCRIPTION Neck and handle of a small flask

CATEGORY Domestic

ASSOCIATION Timbers and sediments

DATE EXCAVATED 13-July-05

DATE CONSERVED 03-Nov-05

LOCATION Marine Conservation Center (CCM), Island of Mozambique

POST CONSERVATION PHOTO

PRE CONSERVATION PHOTO

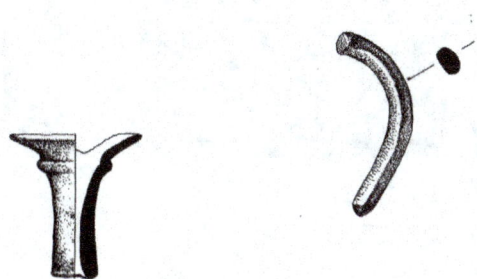

ARTEFACT DRAWING

ARTEFACT NO IDM-003 - 05 - **15024.000**

MATERIAL Other

DESCRIPTION Black bead, ornamented with floral motifs
and diagonal lines forming a rectangular frame

CATEGORY Personal belongings

ASSOCIATION Wood

DATE EXCAVATED 13-July-05

DATE CONSERVED 15-Aug-05

LOCATION Marine Conservation Center (CCM), Island of Mozambique

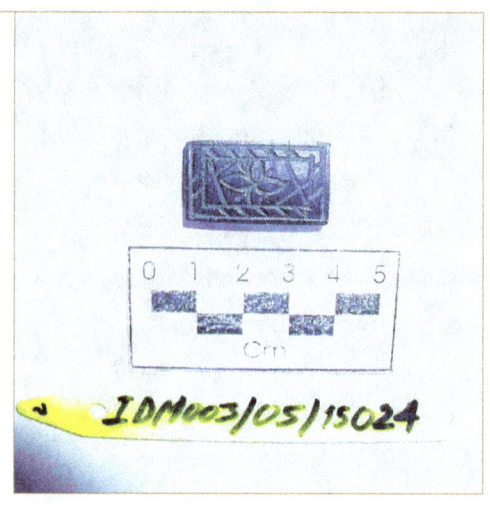

POST CONSERVATION PHOTO

PRE CONSERVATION PHOTO

ARTEFACT DRAWING

ARTEFACT NO IDM-003 - 05 - **15025.000**

MATERIAL Other

DESCRIPTION Black bead, ornamented with floral motifs
and diagonal lines forming a rectangular frame

CATEGORY Personal belongings

ASSOCIATION Wood

DATE EXCAVATED 14-July-05

DATE CONSERVED 15-Aug-05

LOCATION Marine Conservation Center (CCM), Island of Mozambique

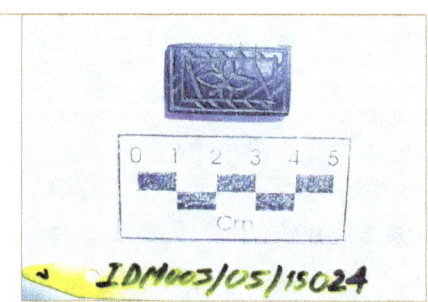

POST CONSERVATION PHOTO

PRE CONSERVATION PHOTO

ARTEFACT DRAWING

ARTEFACT NO IDM-003 - 05 - **15027.000**

MATERIAL Ceramics

DESCRIPTION Broken glazed ceramic lid. Reconstructed in the laboratory

CATEGORY Domestic

ASSOCIATION Coral and wood

DATE EXCAVATED 14-July-05

DATE CONSERVED 30-Aug-05

LOCATION Marine Museum (MUSIM), Island of Mozambique

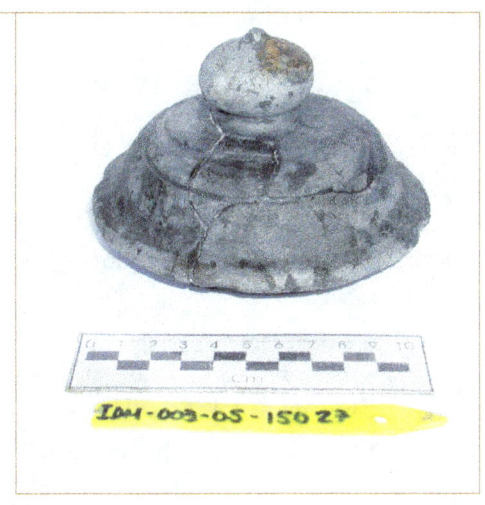

POST CONSERVATION PHOTO

PRE CONSERVATION PHOTO

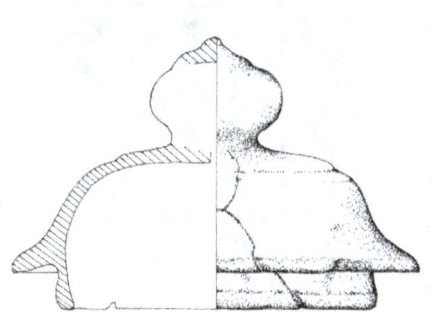

ARTEFACT DRAWING

ARTEFACT NO IDM-003 - 05 - **15028.000**

MATERIAL Copper / copper alloy

DESCRIPTION Copper alloy block

CATEGORY Ships fittings

ASSOCIATION Sediment

DATE EXCAVATED 14-July-05

DATE CONSERVED 08-Nov-05

LOCATION Marine Conservation Center (CCM), Island of Mozambique

POST CONSERVATION PHOTO

PRE CONSERVATION PHOTO

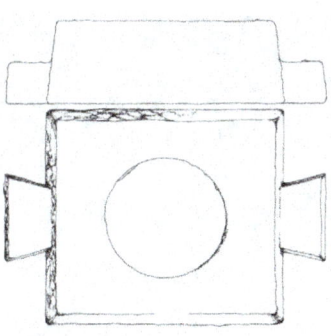

ARTEFACT DRAWING

ARTEFACT NO IDM-003 - 05 - **15030.000**

MATERIAL Silver

DESCRIPTION 1 little clump of silver coins. After treatment in the lab there was 1 coin and 2g of fragments

CATEGORY Personal belongings

ASSOCIATION Wood

DATE EXCAVATED 14-July-05

DATE CONSERVED 18-Aug-05

LOCATION Marine Conservation Center (CCM), Island of Mozambique

POST CONSERVATION PHOTO

PRE CONSERVATION PHOTO

ARTEFACT DRAWING

ARTEFACT NO IDM-003 - 05 - **15033.000**

MATERIAL Ceramics

DESCRIPTION Ceramic jar with handle

CATEGORY Domestic

ASSOCIATION Iron concretion

DATE EXCAVATED 15-July-05

DATE CONSERVED 20-July-05

LOCATION Marine Conservation Center (CCM), Island of Mozambique

POST CONSERVATION PHOTO

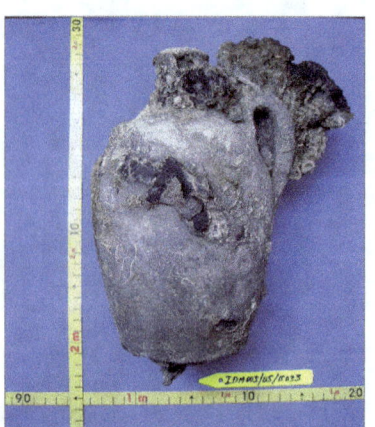

PRE CONSERVATION PHOTO

ARTEFACT DRAWING

ARTEFACT NO IDM-003 - 05 - **15035.000**

MATERIAL Ceramics

DESCRIPTION Olive jar

CATEGORY Cargo

ASSOCIATION Wood and sediments

DATE EXCAVATED 16-July-05

DATE CONSERVED 27-July-05

LOCATION Marine Conservation Center (CCM), Island of Mozambique

POST CONSERVATION PHOTO

PRE CONSERVATION PHOTO

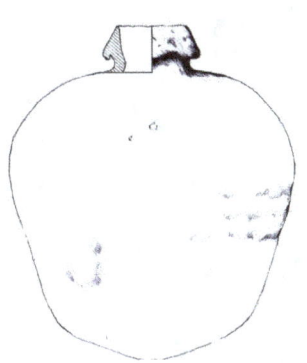

ARTEFACT DRAWING

ARTEFACT NO IDM-003 - 05 - **15036.000**

MATERIAL Ceramics

DESCRIPTION Olive jar

CATEGORY Cargo

ASSOCIATION Wood and sediments

DATE EXCAVATED 16-July-05

DATE CONSERVED 29-July-05

LOCATION Marine Conservation Center (CCM), Island of Mozambique

POST CONSERVATION PHOTO

PRE CONSERVATION PHOTO

ARTEFACT DRAWING

ARTEFACT NO IDM-003 - 05 - **15037.000**

MATERIAL Ceramics

DESCRIPTION Olive jar

CATEGORY Cargo

ASSOCIATION Wood and sediments

DATE EXCAVATED 16-July-05

DATE CONSERVED 24-July-05

LOCATION Marine Conservation Center (CCM), Island of Mozambique

POST CONSERVATION PHOTO

PRE CONSERVATION PHOTO

ARTEFACT DRAWING

ARTEFACT NO IDM-003 - 05 - **15038.000**

MATERIAL Ceramics

DESCRIPTION Olive jar

CATEGORY Cargo

ASSOCIATION Wood and sediments

DATE EXCAVATED 16-July-05

DATE CONSERVED 20-Aug-05

LOCATION Marine Conservation Center (CCM), Island of Mozambique

POST CONSERVATION PHOTO

PRE CONSERVATION PHOTO

ARTEFACT DRAWING

ARTEFACT NO IDM-003 - 05 - **15039.000**

MATERIAL Ceramics

DESCRIPTION Olive jar

CATEGORY Cargo

ASSOCIATION Wood and sediments

DATE EXCAVATED 16-July-05

DATE CONSERVED 24-July-05

LOCATION Marine Conservation Center (CCM), Island of Mozambique

POST CONSERVATION PHOTO

PRE CONSERVATION PHOTO

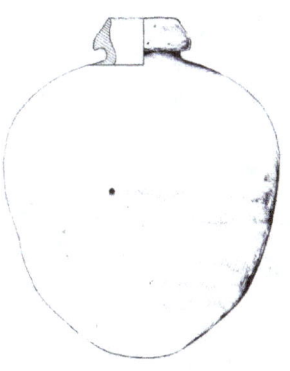

ARTEFACT DRAWING

ARTEFACT NO IDM-003 - 05 - **15040.000**

MATERIAL Ceramics

DESCRIPTION Olive jar

CATEGORY Cargo

ASSOCIATION Wood and sediments

DATE EXCAVATED 16-July-05

DATE CONSERVED 02-Sept-05

LOCATION Marine Conservation Center (CCM), Island of Mozambique

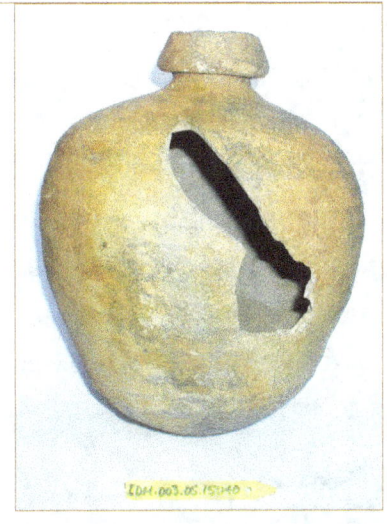

POST CONSERVATION PHOTO

PRE CONSERVATION PHOTO

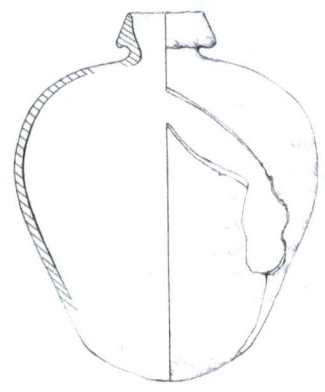

ARTEFACT DRAWING

ARTEFACT NO IDM-003 - 05 - **15041.000**

MATERIAL Ceramics

DESCRIPTION Olive jar

CATEGORY Cargo

ASSOCIATION Wood and sediments

DATE EXCAVATED 16-July-05

DATE CONSERVED 29-July-05

LOCATION Marine Conservation Center (CCM), Island of Mozambique

POST CONSERVATION PHOTO

PRE CONSERVATION PHOTO

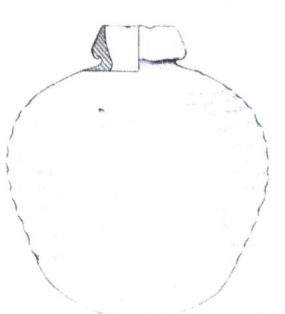

ARTEFACT DRAWING

ARTEFACT NO IDM-003 - 05 - **15042.000**

MATERIAL Ceramics

DESCRIPTION Olive jar

CATEGORY Cargo

ASSOCIATION Wood and sediments

DATE EXCAVATED 16-July-05

DATE CONSERVED 27-July-05

LOCATION Marine Conservation Center (CCM), Island of Mozambique

POST CONSERVATION PHOTO

PRE CONSERVATION PHOTO

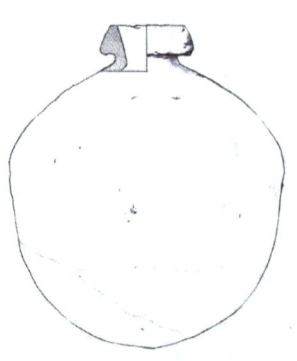

ARTEFACT DRAWING

ARTEFACT NO IDM-003 - 05 - **15043.000**

MATERIAL Ceramics

DESCRIPTION Olive jar

CATEGORY Cargo

ASSOCIATION Wood and sediments

DATE EXCAVATED 16-July-05

DATE CONSERVED 24-July-05

LOCATION Marine Conservation Center (CCM), Island of Mozambique

POST CONSERVATION PHOTO

PRE CONSERVATION PHOTO

ARTEFACT DRAWING

ARTEFACT NO IDM-003 - 05 - **15044.000**

MATERIAL Ceramics

DESCRIPTION Olive jar

CATEGORY Cargo

ASSOCIATION Wood and sediments

DATE EXCAVATED 16-July-05

DATE CONSERVED 24-July-05

LOCATION Marine Conservation Center (CCM), Island of Mozambique

POST CONSERVATION PHOTO

PRE CONSERVATION PHOTO

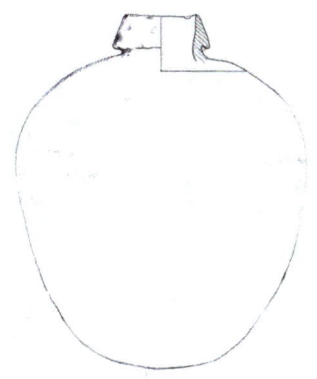

ARTEFACT DRAWING

ARTEFACT NO IDM-003 - 05 - **15045.000**

MATERIAL Ceramics

DESCRIPTION Olive jar

CATEGORY Cargo

ASSOCIATION Wood and sediments

DATE EXCAVATED 16-July-05

DATE CONSERVED 27-July-05

LOCATION Marine Conservation Center (CCM), Island of Mozambique

POST CONSERVATION PHOTO

PRE CONSERVATION PHOTO

ARTEFACT DRAWING

ARTEFACT NO IDM-003 - 05 - **15046.000**

MATERIAL Ceramics

DESCRIPTION Olive jar

CATEGORY Cargo

ASSOCIATION Wood and sediments

DATE EXCAVATED 16-July-05

DATE CONSERVED 27-July-05

LOCATION Marine Conservation Center (CCM), Island of Mozambique

POST CONSERVATION PHOTO

PRE CONSERVATION PHOTO

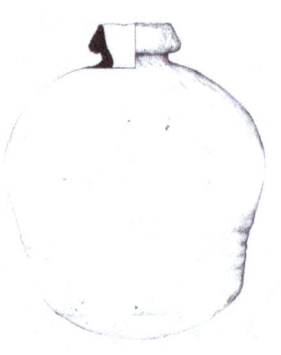

ARTEFACT DRAWING

ARTEFACT NO IDM-003 - 05 - **15047.000**

MATERIAL Ceramics

DESCRIPTION Olive jar

CATEGORY Cargo

ASSOCIATION Wood and sediments

DATE EXCAVATED 16-July-05

DATE CONSERVED 24-July-05

LOCATION Marine Conservation Center (CCM), Island of Mozambique

POST CONSERVATION PHOTO

PRE CONSERVATION PHOTO

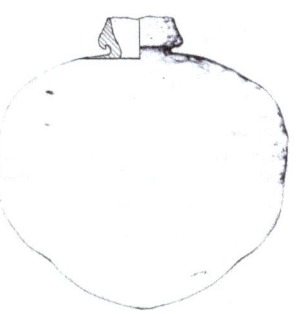

ARTEFACT DRAWING

ARTEFACT NO IDM-003 - 05 - **15048.000**

MATERIAL Ceramics

DESCRIPTION Olive jar

CATEGORY Cargo

ASSOCIATION Wood and sediments

DATE EXCAVATED 16-July-05

DATE CONSERVED 02-Sept-05

LOCATION Marine Conservation Center (CCM), Island of Mozambique

POST CONSERVATION PHOTO

PRE CONSERVATION PHOTO

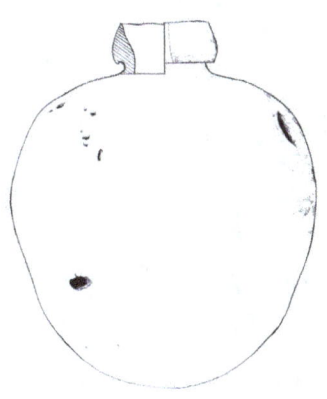

ARTEFACT DRAWING

ARTEFACT NO IDM-003 - 05 - **15049.000**

MATERIAL Ceramics

DESCRIPTION Olive jar (deformed body)

CATEGORY Cargo

ASSOCIATION Wood and sediments

DATE EXCAVATED 16-July-05

DATE CONSERVED 27-July-05

LOCATION Marine Conservation Center (CCM), Island of Mozambique

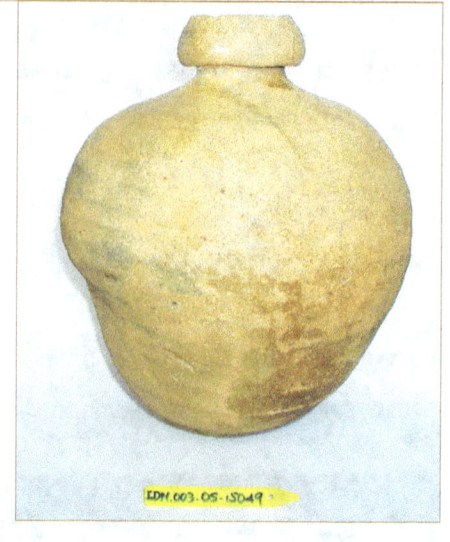

POST CONSERVATION PHOTO

PRE CONSERVATION PHOTO

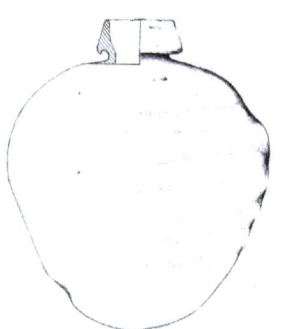

ARTEFACT DRAWING

ARTEFACT NO IDM-003 - 05 - **15050.000**

MATERIAL Ceramics

DESCRIPTION Olive jar (neck broken, reconstructed in the laboratory)

CATEGORY Cargo

ASSOCIATION Wood and sediments

DATE EXCAVATED 16-July-05

DATE CONSERVED 20-Aug-05

LOCATION Marine Conservation Center (CCM), Island of Mozambique

POST CONSERVATION PHOTO

PRE CONSERVATION PHOTO

ARTEFACT DRAWING

ARTEFACT NO IDM-003 - 05 - **15051.000**

MATERIAL Ceramics

DESCRIPTION Olive jar

CATEGORY Cargo

ASSOCIATION Wood and sediments

DATE EXCAVATED 16-July-05

DATE CONSERVED 24-July-05

LOCATION Marine Conservation Center (CCM), Island of Mozambique

POST CONSERVATION PHOTO

PRE CONSERVATION PHOTO

ARTEFACT DRAWING

ARTEFACT NO IDM-003 - 05 - **15052.000**

MATERIAL Ceramics

DESCRIPTION Olive jar

CATEGORY Cargo

ASSOCIATION Wood and sediments

DATE EXCAVATED 16-July-05

DATE CONSERVED 02-Sept-05

LOCATION Marine Conservation Center (CCM), Island of Mozambique

POST CONSERVATION PHOTO

PRE CONSERVATION PHOTO

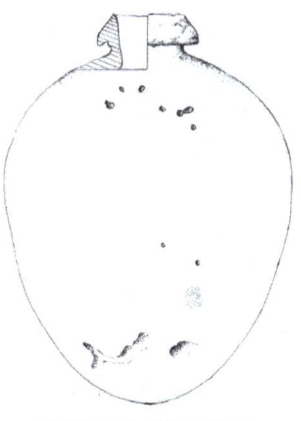

ARTEFACT DRAWING

ARTEFACT NO IDM-003 - 05 - **15053.000**

MATERIAL Ceramics

DESCRIPTION Olive jar

CATEGORY Cargo

ASSOCIATION Wood and sediments

DATE EXCAVATED 16-July-05

DATE CONSERVED 24-July-05

LOCATION Marine Conservation Center (CCM), Island of Mozambique

POST CONSERVATION PHOTO

PRE CONSERVATION PHOTO

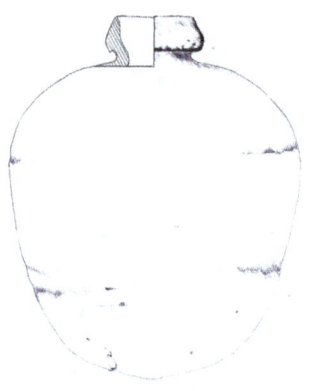

ARTEFACT DRAWING

ARTEFACT NO IDM-003 - 05 - **15054.000**

MATERIAL Ceramics

DESCRIPTION Olive jar, completely mishaped from the origin

CATEGORY Cargo

ASSOCIATION Wood and sediments

DATE EXCAVATED 16-July-05

DATE CONSERVED 20-Aug-05

LOCATION Marine Museum (MUSIM), Island of Mozambique

POST CONSERVATION PHOTO

PRE CONSERVATION PHOTO

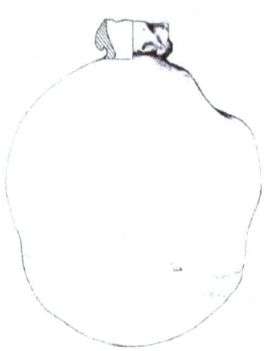

ARTEFACT DRAWING

ARTEFACT NO IDM-003 - 05 - **15055.000**

MATERIAL Lead

DESCRIPTION Lead seal depicting the Portuguese "Esfera Armilar"

CATEGORY Personal belongings

ASSOCIATION Wood, olive jars

DATE EXCAVATED 16-July-05

DATE CONSERVED 09-Aug-05

LOCATION Marine Conservation Center (CCM), Island of Mozambique

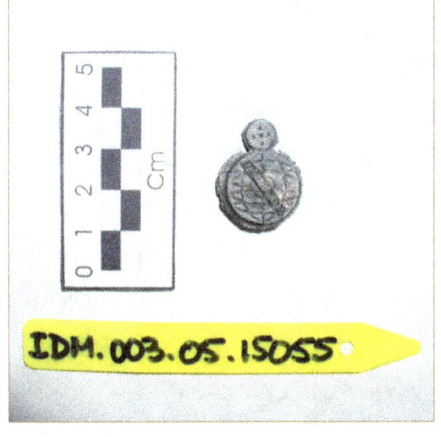

POST CONSERVATION PHOTO

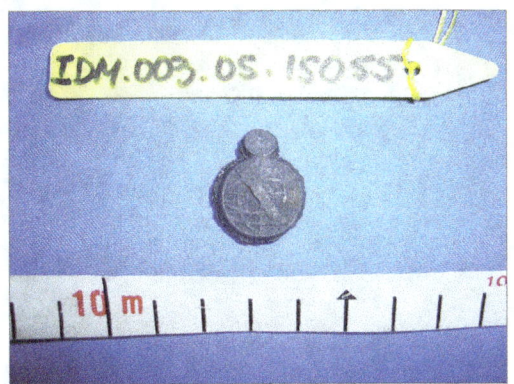

PRE CONSERVATION PHOTO

ARTEFACT DRAWING

ARTEFACT NO IDM-003 - 05 - **15056.000**

MATERIAL Lead

DESCRIPTION Lead seal with a coat of arms.

CATEGORY Personal belongings

ASSOCIATION Wood, olive jars

DATE EXCAVATED 16-July-05

DATE CONSERVED 09-Aug-05

LOCATION Marine Conservation Center (CCM), Island of Mozambique

POST CONSERVATION PHOTO

PRE CONSERVATION PHOTO

ARTEFACT DRAWING

ARTEFACT NO IDM-003 - 05 - **15057.000**

MATERIAL Ceramics

DESCRIPTION Olive jar

CATEGORY Cargo

ASSOCIATION Wood and sediments

DATE EXCAVATED 16-July-05

DATE CONSERVED 02-Sept-05

LOCATION Marine Conservation Center (CCM), Island of Mozambique

POST CONSERVATION PHOTO

PRE CONSERVATION PHOTO

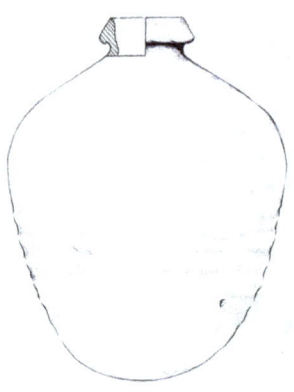

ARTEFACT DRAWING

ARTEFACT NO IDM-003 - 05 - **15059.000**

MATERIAL Copper / copper alloy

DESCRIPTION Sailmaker's palm

CATEGORY Professional instruments

ASSOCIATION Wood timbers and sediments

DATE EXCAVATED 30-July-05

DATE CONSERVED 02-Nov-05

LOCATION Marine Conservation Center (CCM), Island of Mozambique

POST CONSERVATION PHOTO

PRE CONSERVATION PHOTO

ARTEFACT DRAWING

ARTEFACT NO IDM-003 - 05 - **15060.000**

MATERIAL Lead

DESCRIPTION 1 lead roll. Probably modern contamination

CATEGORY Other

ASSOCIATION Wood timbers and sediments

DATE EXCAVATED 30-July-05

DATE CONSERVED 29-Aug-05

LOCATION Marine Conservation Center (CCM), Island of Mozambique

POST CONSERVATION PHOTO

PRE CONSERVATION PHOTO

ARTEFACT DRAWING

ARTEFACT NO IDM-003 - 05 - **15061.000**

MATERIAL Ceramics

DESCRIPTION Olive jar

CATEGORY Cargo

ASSOCIATION Wood and sediments

DATE EXCAVATED 01-Aug-05

DATE CONSERVED 02-Sept-05

LOCATION Marine Conservation Center (CCM), Island of Mozambique

POST CONSERVATION PHOTO

PRE CONSERVATION PHOTO

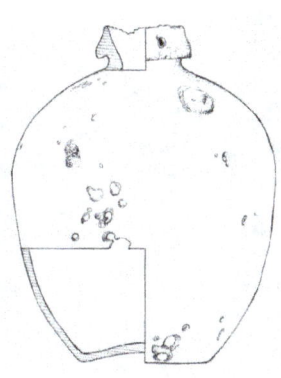

ARTEFACT DRAWING

ARTEFACT NO IDM-003 - 05 - **15064.000**

MATERIAL Other

DESCRIPTION One black bead, ornamented with floral motifs and diagonal lines forming a rectangular frame

CATEGORY Personal belongings

ASSOCIATION Ceramics pieces, wood and coral.

DATE EXCAVATED 03-Aug-05

DATE CONSERVED 30-Nov-05

LOCATION Marine Conservation Center (CCM), Island of Mozambique

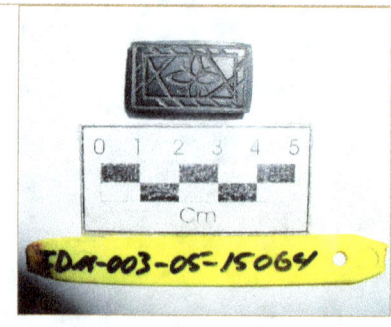

POST CONSERVATION PHOTO

PRE CONSERVATION PHOTO

ARTEFACT DRAWING

ARTEFACT NO IDM-003 - 05 - **15065.000**

MATERIAL Wood

DESCRIPTION 1 wooden handle

CATEGORY Unknown

ASSOCIATION Wood and sendiments

DATE EXCAVATED 05-Aug-05

DATE CONSERVED 05-July-06

LOCATION Marine Conservation Center (CCM), Island of Mozambique

POST CONSERVATION PHOTO

PRE CONSERVATION PHOTO

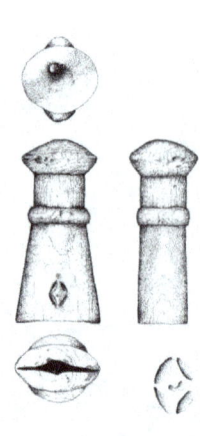

ARTEFACT DRAWING

ARTEFACT NO IDM-003 - 05 - **15066.000**

MATERIAL Copper / copper alloy

DESCRIPTION One metallic object (part of an ornament)

CATEGORY Unknown

ASSOCIATION Coral and wood

DATE EXCAVATED 05-Aug-05

DATE CONSERVED 02-Nov-05

LOCATION Marine Conservation Center (CCM), Island of Mozambique

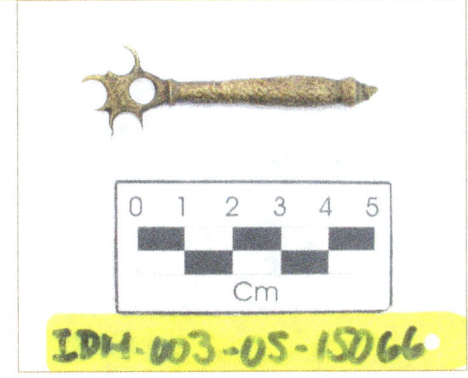

POST CONSERVATION PHOTO

PRE CONSERVATION PHOTO

ARTEFACT DRAWING

ARTEFACT NO IDM-003 - 05 - **15068.000**

MATERIAL Ceramics

DESCRIPTION Ceramic jar, neck missing

CATEGORY Domestic

ASSOCIATION Wood and sediments

DATE EXCAVATED 06-Aug-05

DATE CONSERVED 05-Oct-05

LOCATION Marine Conservation Center (CCM), Island of Mozambique

POST CONSERVATION PHOTO

PRE CONSERVATION PHOTO

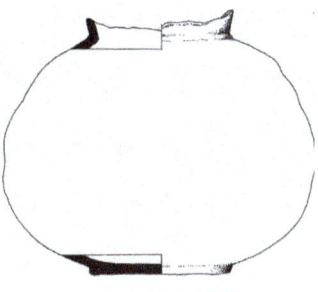

ARTEFACT DRAWING

143

ARTEFACT NO IDM-003 - 05 - **15069.000**

MATERIAL Ceramics

DESCRIPTION Olive jar

CATEGORY Cargo

ASSOCIATION Sand and sediments

DATE EXCAVATED 08-Aug-05

DATE CONSERVED 02-Sept-05

LOCATION Marine Conservation Center (CCM), Island of Mozambique

POST CONSERVATION PHOTO

PRE CONSERVATION PHOTO

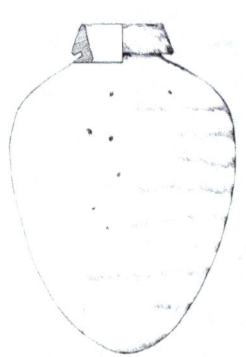

ARTEFACT DRAWING

ARTEFACT NO IDM-003 - 05 - **15070.000**

MATERIAL Copper / copper alloy

DESCRIPTION Sailmaker's palm

CATEGORY Professional instruments

ASSOCIATION Wood and sediments

DATE EXCAVATED 11-Aug-05

DATE CONSERVED 02-Nov-05

LOCATION Marine Conservation Center (CCM), Island of Mozambique

POST CONSERVATION PHOTO

PRE CONSERVATION PHOTO

ARTEFACT DRAWING

ARTEFACT NO IDM-003 - 05 - **15071.000**

MATERIAL Ceramics

DESCRIPTION Olive jar

CATEGORY Cargo

ASSOCIATION Wood and sediments

DATE EXCAVATED 15-Aug-05

DATE CONSERVED 02-Sept-05

LOCATION Marine Conservation Center (CCM), Island of Mozambique

POST CONSERVATION PHOTO

PRE CONSERVATION PHOTO

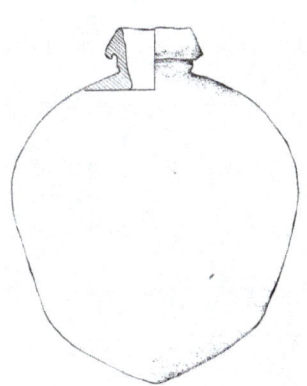

ARTEFACT DRAWING

ARTEFACT NO IDM-003 - 05 - **15072.000**

MATERIAL Ceramics

DESCRIPTION Olive jar

CATEGORY Cargo

ASSOCIATION Wood and sediments

DATE EXCAVATED 17-Aug-05

DATE CONSERVED 02-Sept-05

LOCATION Marine Conservation Center (CCM), Island of Mozambique

POST CONSERVATION PHOTO

PRE CONSERVATION PHOTO

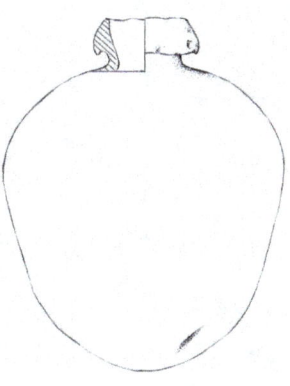

ARTEFACT DRAWING

ARTEFACT NO IDM-003 - 05 - **15073.000**

MATERIAL Ceramics

DESCRIPTION Olive jar

CATEGORY Cargo

ASSOCIATION Wood and sediments

DATE EXCAVATED 18-Aug-05

DATE CONSERVED 02-Sept-05

LOCATION Marine Conservation Center (CCM), Island of Mozambique

POST CONSERVATION PHOTO

PRE CONSERVATION PHOTO

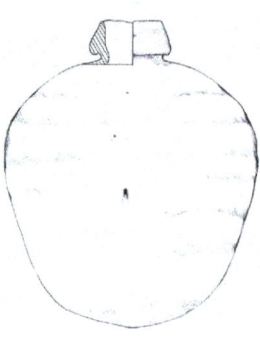

ARTEFACT DRAWING

ARTEFACT NO IDM-003 - 05 - **15074.000**

MATERIAL Ceramics

DESCRIPTION Olive jar

CATEGORY Cargo

ASSOCIATION Wood and sediments

DATE EXCAVATED 18-Aug-05

DATE CONSERVED 02-Sept-05

LOCATION Marine Conservation Center (CCM), Island of Mozambique

POST CONSERVATION PHOTO

PRE CONSERVATION PHOTO

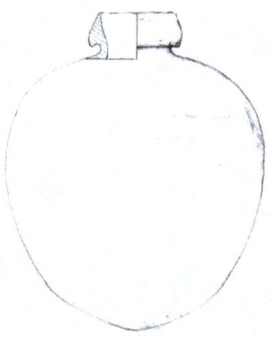

ARTEFACT DRAWING

ARTEFACT NO IDM-003 - 05 - **15075.000**

MATERIAL Ceramics

DESCRIPTION Round ornamented flask, stem missing

CATEGORY Domestic

ASSOCIATION Timbers and coarse ceramics pieces

DATE EXCAVATED 18-Aug-05

DATE CONSERVED 29-Aug-05

LOCATION Marine Conservation Center (CCM), Island of Mozambique

POST CONSERVATION PHOTO

PRE CONSERVATION PHOTO

ARTEFACT DRAWING

ARTEFACT NO IDM-003 - 05 - **15076.000**

MATERIAL Ceramics

DESCRIPTION Ceramic lid, apparently from an olive jar

CATEGORY Cargo

ASSOCIATION Sediments

DATE EXCAVATED 19-Aug-05

DATE CONSERVED 29-Aug-05

LOCATION Marine Conservation Center (CCM), Island of Mozambique

POST CONSERVATION PHOTO

PRE CONSERVATION PHOTO

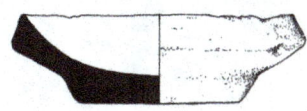

ARTEFACT DRAWING

ARTEFACT NO IDM-003 - 05 - **15077.000**

MATERIAL Ceramics

DESCRIPTION Decorated ceramic flask with handles

CATEGORY Cargo

ASSOCIATION Wood, ballast stones, coarse ceramics pieces

DATE EXCAVATED 19-Aug-05

DATE CONSERVED 29-Aug-05

LOCATION Marine Museum (MUSIM), Island of Mozambique

POST CONSERVATION PHOTO

PRE CONSERVATION PHOTO

ARTEFACT DRAWING

ARTEFACT NO IDM-003 - 05 - **15078.000**

MATERIAL Copper / copper alloy

DESCRIPTION Sailmaker's palm

CATEGORY Professional instruments

ASSOCIATION Wood, ballast stones, coarse ceramics pieces

DATE EXCAVATED 19-Aug-05

DATE CONSERVED 02-Nov-05

LOCATION Marine Conservation Center (CCM), Island of Mozambique

POST CONSERVATION PHOTO

PRE CONSERVATION PHOTO

ARTEFACT DRAWING

ARTEFACT NO IDM-003 - 05 - **15079.000**

MATERIAL Ceramics

DESCRIPTION Olive jar

CATEGORY Cargo

ASSOCIATION Wood, ballast stones, coarse ceramics pieces

DATE EXCAVATED 19-Aug-05

DATE CONSERVED 02-Sept-05

LOCATION Marine Conservation Center (CCM), Island of Mozambique

POST CONSERVATION PHOTO

PRE CONSERVATION PHOTO

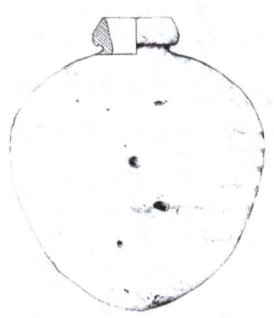

ARTEFACT DRAWING

ARTEFACT NO IDM-003 - 05 - **15080.000**

MATERIAL Ceramics

DESCRIPTION Decorated ceramic pot in the concretion. Apparently of African manufacture

CATEGORY Domestic

ASSOCIATION Wood, ballast stones, coarse ceramic pieces

DATE EXCAVATED 19-Aug-05

DATE CONSERVED 10-Sept-05

LOCATION Marine Conservation Center (CCM), Island of Mozambique

POST CONSERVATION PHOTO

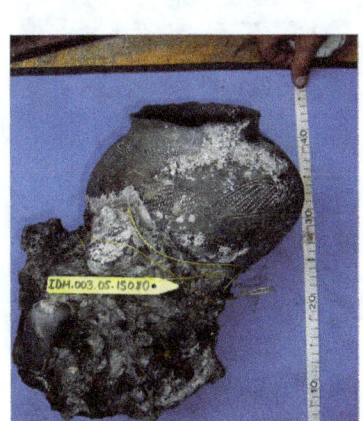

PRE CONSERVATION PHOTO

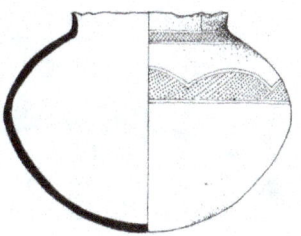

ARTEFACT DRAWING

ARTEFACT NO IDM-003 - 05 - **15081.000**

MATERIAL Ceramics

DESCRIPTION Decorated ceramic jar with one handle

CATEGORY Domestic

ASSOCIATION Wood, ballast stones, coarse ceramic pieces

DATE EXCAVATED 19-Aug-05

DATE CONSERVED 02-Sept-05

LOCATION Marine Conservation Center (CCM), Island of Mozambique

POST CONSERVATION PHOTO

PRE CONSERVATION PHOTO

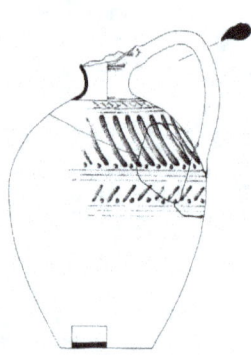

ARTEFACT DRAWING

ARTEFACT NO IDM-003 - 05 - **15082.000**

MATERIAL Ceramics

DESCRIPTION Ceramic lid in the iron concretion with fragments of coarse ceramic

CATEGORY Domestic

ASSOCIATION Wood, ballast stones, coarse ceramic pieces

DATE EXCAVATED 19-Aug-05

DATE CONSERVED 02-Sept-05

LOCATION Marine Conservation Center (CCM), Island of Mozambique

POST CONSERVATION PHOTO

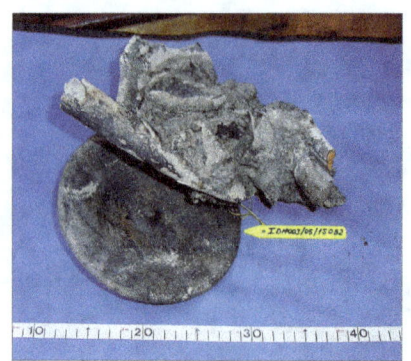

PRE CONSERVATION PHOTO

ARTEFACT DRAWING

ARTEFACT NO IDM-003 - 05 - **15082.001**

MATERIAL Ivory

DESCRIPTION Elephant tusk, small

CATEGORY Cargo

ASSOCIATION Wood, ballast stones, coarse ceramic pieces

DATE EXCAVATED 19-Aug-05

DATE CONSERVED 03-Sept-05

LOCATION Marine Conservation Center (CCM), Island of Mozambique

POST CONSERVATION PHOTO

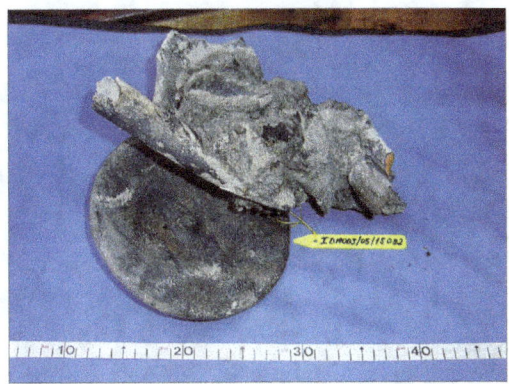

PRE CONSERVATION PHOTO

ARTEFACT DRAWING

ARTEFACT NO IDM-003 - 05 - **15083.000**

MATERIAL Ceramics

DESCRIPTION Ceramic lid, apparently from an olive jar

CATEGORY Cargo

ASSOCIATION Sediments

DATE EXCAVATED 20-Aug-05

DATE CONSERVED 29-Aug-05

LOCATION Marine Conservation Center (CCM), Island of Mozambique

POST CONSERVATION PHOTO

PRE CONSERVATION PHOTO

ARTEFACT DRAWING

ARTEFACT NO IDM-003 - 05 - **15084.000**

MATERIAL Ceramics

DESCRIPTION Ceramic lid, apparently from an olive jar

CATEGORY Cargo

ASSOCIATION Sediments

DATE EXCAVATED 20-Aug-05

DATE CONSERVED 29-Aug-05

LOCATION Marine Conservation Center (CCM), Island of Mozambique

POST CONSERVATION PHOTO

PRE CONSERVATION PHOTO

ARTEFACT DRAWING

ARTEFACT NO IDM-003 - 05 - **15085.000**

MATERIAL Ceramics

DESCRIPTION Porcelain ewer. Kendi made of white porcelain with blue cobalt decoration under the glaze, showing a circular bulge, long straight stem and very prominent spout. It is decorated with a scroll of stylized lotus around the bulge as well as curled and straight leaves around the stem. The base shows a mark of a white hare in front of a blue rock

CATEGORY Domestic

ASSOCIATION Sediment, wood and iron concretion

DATE EXCAVATED 22-Aug-05

DATE CONSERVED 30-Aug-05

LOCATION Marine Museum (MUSIM), Island of Mozambique

POST CONSERVATION PHOTO

PRE CONSERVATION PHOTO

ARTEFACT DRAWING

ARTEFACT NO IDM-003 - 05 - **15086.000**

MATERIAL Ceramics

DESCRIPTION Olive jar

CATEGORY Cargo

ASSOCIATION Sediment and wood

DATE EXCAVATED 22-Aug-05

DATE CONSERVED 02-Sept-05

LOCATION Marine Conservation Center (CCM), Island of Mozambique

POST CONSERVATION PHOTO

PRE CONSERVATION PHOTO

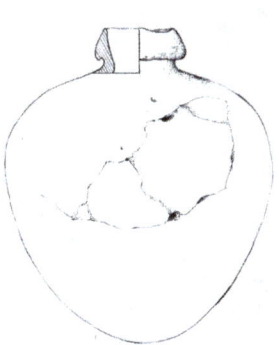

ARTEFACT DRAWING

ARTEFACT NO IDM-003 - 05 - **15087.000**

MATERIAL Ceramics

DESCRIPTION Ceramic lid, apparently from an olive jar

CATEGORY Cargo

ASSOCIATION Sand and sediment

DATE EXCAVATED 22-Aug-05

DATE CONSERVED 29-Aug-05

LOCATION Marine Conservation Center (CCM), Island of Mozambique

POST CONSERVATION PHOTO

PRE CONSERVATION PHOTO

ARTEFACT DRAWING

ARTEFACT NO IDM-003 - 05 - **15088.000**

MATERIAL Ceramics

DESCRIPTION Neck of martaban

CATEGORY Cargo

ASSOCIATION Wood structure, ballast stones, ceramic fragments

DATE EXCAVATED 22-Aug-05

DATE CONSERVED 08-Oct-05

LOCATION Marine Conservation Center (CCM), Island of Mozambique

POST CONSERVATION PHOTO

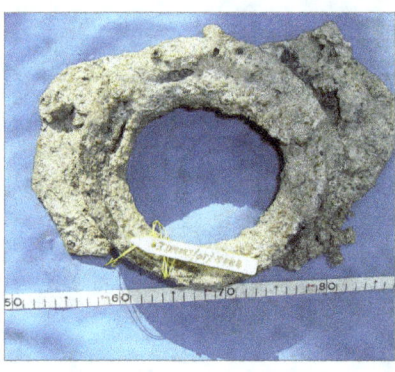

PRE CONSERVATION PHOTO

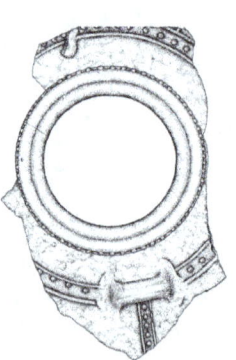

ARTEFACT DRAWING

ARTEFACT NO IDM-003 - 05 - **15089.000**

MATERIAL Ceramics

DESCRIPTION Neck of martaban

CATEGORY Cargo

ASSOCIATION Wood structure, ballast stones

DATE EXCAVATED 22-Aug-05

DATE CONSERVED 05-Oct-05

LOCATION Marine Conservation Center (CCM), Island of Mozambique

POST CONSERVATION PHOTO

PRE CONSERVATION PHOTO

ARTEFACT DRAWING

ARTEFACT NO IDM-003 - 05 - **15090.000**

MATERIAL Glass

DESCRIPTION 4 fragments of glass bottle

CATEGORY Domestic

ASSOCIATION Ceramic fragments, wood stucture, ballast stones

DATE EXCAVATED 22-Aug-05

DATE CONSERVED 30-Aug-05

LOCATION Marine Museum (MUSIM), Island of Mozambique

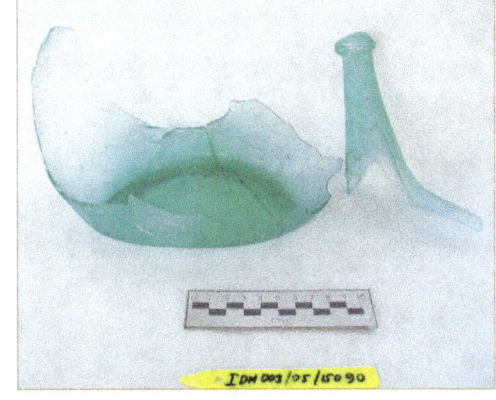

POST CONSERVATION PHOTO

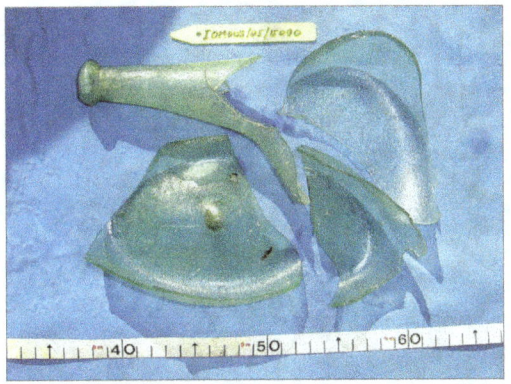

PRE CONSERVATION PHOTO

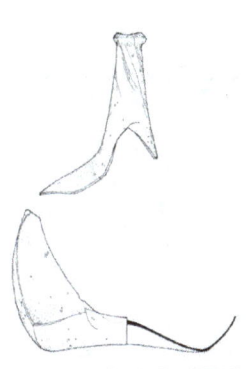

ARTEFACT DRAWING

ARTEFACT NO IDM-003 - 05 - **15091.000**

MATERIAL Glass

DESCRIPTION Intact green drinking glass

CATEGORY Domestic

ASSOCIATION Sediments

DATE EXCAVATED 29-Aug-05

DATE CONSERVED 10-Sept-05

LOCATION Marine Conservation Center (CCM), Island of Mozambique

POST CONSERVATION PHOTO

PRE CONSERVATION PHOTO

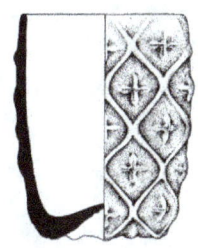

ARTEFACT DRAWING

ARTEFACT NO IDM-003 - 05 - **15092.000**

MATERIAL Ceramics

DESCRIPTION Martaban jar

CATEGORY Cargo

ASSOCIATION Sediments

DATE EXCAVATED 29-Aug-05

DATE CONSERVED 09-Sept-05

LOCATION Marine Conservation Center (CCM), Island of Mozambique

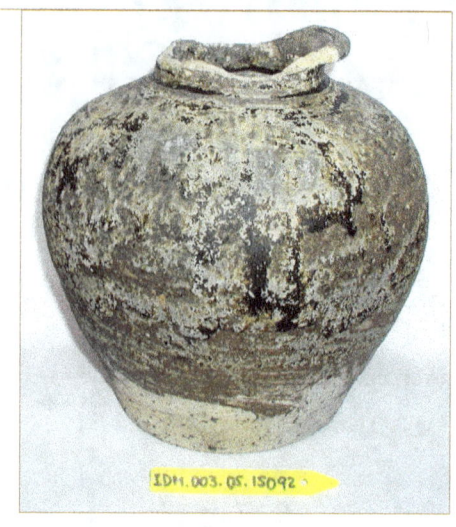

POST CONSERVATION PHOTO

PRE CONSERVATION PHOTO

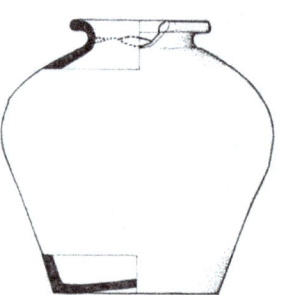

ARTEFACT DRAWING

ARTEFACT NO IDM-003 - 05 - **15093.000**

MATERIAL Ceramics

DESCRIPTION Olive jar

CATEGORY Cargo

ASSOCIATION Wood and sediments

DATE EXCAVATED 29-Aug-05

DATE CONSERVED 09-Sept-05

LOCATION Marine Conservation Center (CCM), Island of Mozambique

POST CONSERVATION PHOTO

PRE CONSERVATION PHOTO

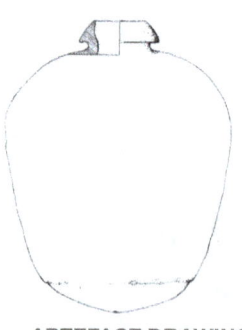

ARTEFACT DRAWING

ARTEFACT NO IDM-003 - 05 - **15094.000**

MATERIAL Pewter

DESCRIPTION Metallic statue of Jesus Christ

CATEGORY Personal belongings

ASSOCIATION Wood and sediment

DATE EXCAVATED 29-Aug-05

DATE CONSERVED 10-Sept-05

LOCATION Marine Conservation Center (CCM), Island of Mozambique

POST CONSERVATION PHOTO

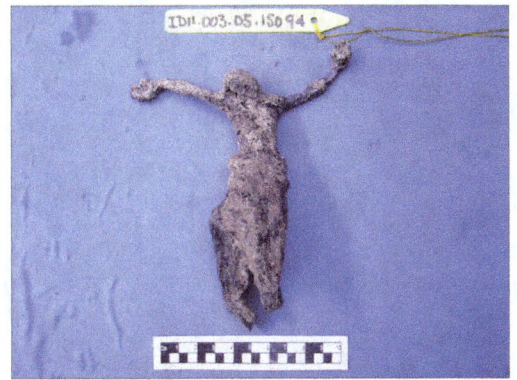

PRE CONSERVATION PHOTO

ARTEFACT DRAWING

ARTEFACT NO IDM-003 - 05 - **15095.000**

MATERIAL Ceramics

DESCRIPTION Olive jar

CATEGORY Cargo

ASSOCIATION Sediment and wood

DATE EXCAVATED 30-Aug-05

DATE CONSERVED 09-Sept-05

LOCATION Marine Conservation Center (CCM), Island of Mozambique

POST CONSERVATION PHOTO

PRE CONSERVATION PHOTO

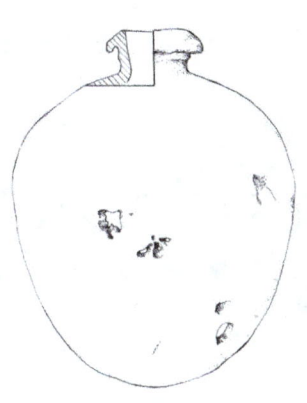

ARTEFACT DRAWING

ARTEFACT NO IDM-003 - 05 - **15096.000**

MATERIAL Ceramics

DESCRIPTION Olive jar

CATEGORY Cargo

ASSOCIATION Sediment and wood

DATE EXCAVATED 30-Aug-05

DATE CONSERVED 09-Sept-05

LOCATION Marine Conservation Center (CCM), Island of Mozambique

POST CONSERVATION PHOTO

PRE CONSERVATION PHOTO

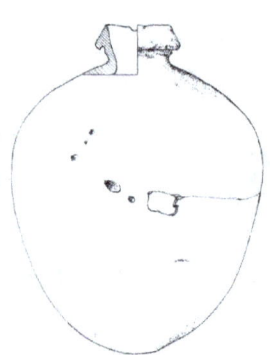

ARTEFACT DRAWING

ARTEFACT NO IDM-003 - 05 - **15097.000**

MATERIAL Pewter

DESCRIPTION Metallic stopper

CATEGORY Personal belongings

ASSOCIATION Wood

DATE EXCAVATED 30-Aug-05

DATE CONSERVED 09-Sept-05

LOCATION Marine Conservation Center (CCM), Island of Mozambique

POST CONSERVATION PHOTO

PRE CONSERVATION PHOTO

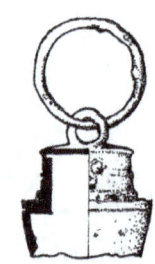

ARTEFACT DRAWING

ARTEFACT NO IDM-003 - 05 - **15098.000**

MATERIAL Ceramics

DESCRIPTION Olive jar

CATEGORY Cargo

ASSOCIATION Wood

DATE EXCAVATED 30-Aug-05

DATE CONSERVED 09-Sept-05

LOCATION Marine Conservation Center (CCM), Island of Mozambique

POST CONSERVATION PHOTO

PRE CONSERVATION PHOTO

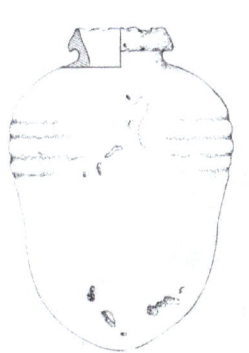

ARTEFACT DRAWING

ARTEFACT NO IDM-003 - 05 - **15099.000**

MATERIAL Copper / copper alloy

DESCRIPTION Copper alloy handle (as for a bucket)

CATEGORY Domestic

ASSOCIATION Sediments

DATE EXCAVATED 31-Aug-05

DATE CONSERVED 10-Nov-05

LOCATION Marine Conservation Center (CCM), Island of Mozambique

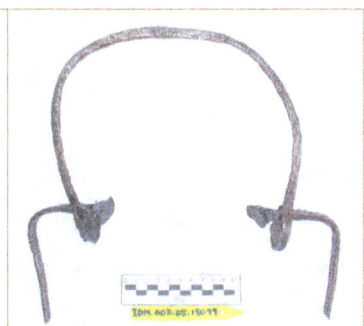

POST CONSERVATION PHOTO

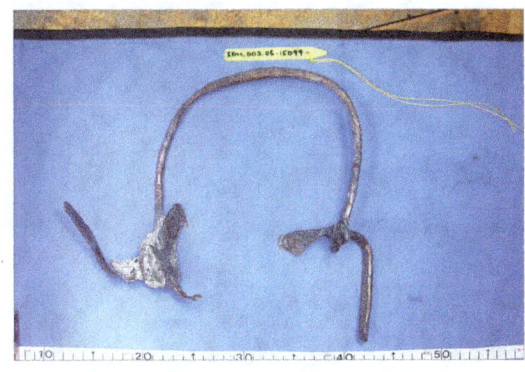

PRE CONSERVATION PHOTO

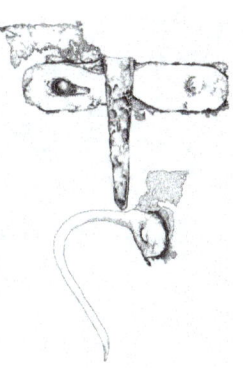

ARTEFACT DRAWING

ARTEFACT NO IDM-003 - 05 - **15100.000**

MATERIAL Copper / copper alloy

DESCRIPTION Sailmaker's palm

CATEGORY Professional instruments

ASSOCIATION Wood and sediments

DATE EXCAVATED 01-Sept-05

DATE CONSERVED 02-Nov-05

LOCATION Marine Conservation Center (CCM), Island of Mozambique

POST CONSERVATION PHOTO

PRE CONSERVATION PHOTO

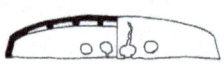
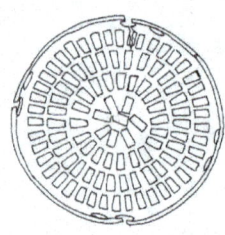

ARTEFACT DRAWING

ARTEFACT NO IDM-003 - 05 - **15101.000**

MATERIAL Pewter

DESCRIPTION Intact plate

CATEGORY Domestic

ASSOCIATION Sediments

DATE EXCAVATED 01-Sept-05

DATE CONSERVED 09-Sept-05

LOCATION Marine Museum (MUSIM), Island of Mozambique

POST CONSERVATION PHOTO

PRE CONSERVATION PHOTO

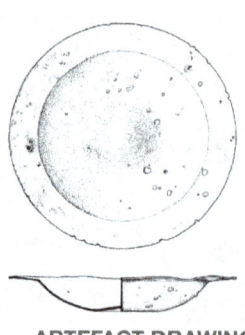

ARTEFACT DRAWING

ARTEFACT NO IDM-003 - 05 - **15102.000**

MATERIAL Ceramics

DESCRIPTION Earthenware pot, apparently of African manufacture

CATEGORY Domestic

ASSOCIATION Wood and sediments

DATE EXCAVATED 02-Sept-05

DATE CONSERVED 10-Sept-05

LOCATION Marine Conservation Center (CCM), Island of Mozambique

POST CONSERVATION PHOTO

PRE CONSERVATION PHOTO

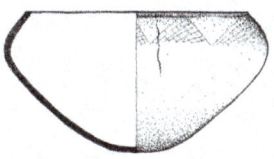

ARTEFACT DRAWING

ARTEFACT NO IDM-003 - 05 - **15103.000**

MATERIAL Pewter

DESCRIPTION A pewter plate, partially cracked and concreted

CATEGORY Domestic

ASSOCIATION Coral, wood and concretion

DATE EXCAVATED 02-Sept-05

DATE CONSERVED 09-Sept-05

LOCATION Marine Conservation Center (CCM), Island of Mozambique

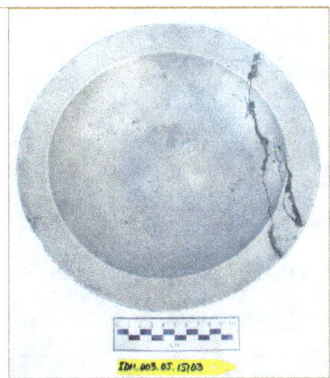

POST CONSERVATION PHOTO

PRE CONSERVATION PHOTO

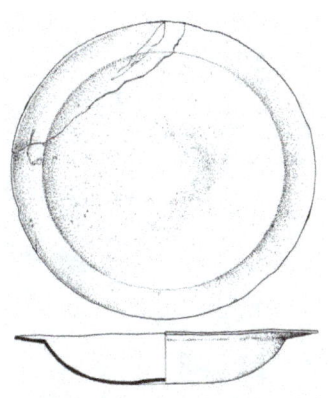

ARTEFACT DRAWING

ARTEFACT NO IDM-003 - 05 - **15103.001**

MATERIAL Ceramics

DESCRIPTION Ceramic lid.

CATEGORY Cargo

ASSOCIATION In concretion with a pewter plate

DATE EXCAVATED 02-Sept-05

DATE CONSERVED 04-Oct-05

LOCATION Marine Conservation Center (CCM), Island of Mozambique

POST CONSERVATION PHOTO

PRE CONSERVATION PHOTO

ARTEFACT DRAWING

ARTEFACT NO IDM-003 - 05 - **15104.000**

MATERIAL Ceramics

DESCRIPTION Olive jar

CATEGORY Cargo

ASSOCIATION Sediments

DATE EXCAVATED 02-Sept-05

DATE CONSERVED 09-Sept-05

LOCATION Marine Conservation Center (CCM), Island of Mozambique

POST CONSERVATION PHOTO

PRE CONSERVATION PHOTO

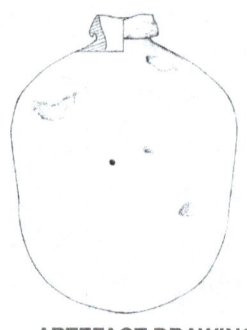

ARTEFACT DRAWING

ARTEFACT NO IDM-003 - 05 - **15105.000**

MATERIAL Ceramics

DESCRIPTION Olive jar

CATEGORY Cargo

ASSOCIATION Sediments

DATE EXCAVATED 02-Sept-05

DATE CONSERVED 09-Sept-05

LOCATION Marine Conservation Center (CCM), Island of Mozambique

POST CONSERVATION PHOTO

PRE CONSERVATION PHOTO

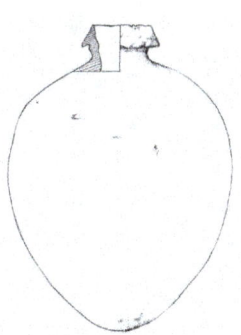

ARTEFACT DRAWING

ARTEFACT NO IDM-003 - 05 - **15106.000**

MATERIAL Copper / copper alloy

DESCRIPTION Plate, or possibly a frying pan

CATEGORY Domestic

ASSOCIATION Sand and sediments.

DATE EXCAVATED 07-Sept-05

DATE CONSERVED 07-Nov-05

LOCATION Marine Conservation Center (CCM), Island of Mozambique

POST CONSERVATION PHOTO

PRE CONSERVATION PHOTO

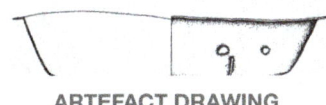

ARTEFACT DRAWING

ARTEFACT NO IDM-003 - 05 - **15107.000**

MATERIAL Ceramics

DESCRIPTION Porcelain plate (fragmented but reconstructed in the laboratory)

CATEGORY Domestic

ASSOCIATION Sediments

DATE EXCAVATED 07-Sept-05

DATE CONSERVED 12-Oct-05

LOCATION Marine Museum (MUSIM), Island of Mozambique

POST CONSERVATION PHOTO

PRE CONSERVATION PHOTO   ARTEFACT DRAWING

ARTEFACT NO IDM-003 - 05 - **15108.000**

MATERIAL Copper / copper alloy

DESCRIPTION A set of dividers, badly corroded

CATEGORY Professional instruments

ASSOCIATION Sediments

DATE EXCAVATED 07-Sept-05

DATE CONSERVED 07-Nov-05

LOCATION Marine Conservation Center (CCM), Island of Mozambique

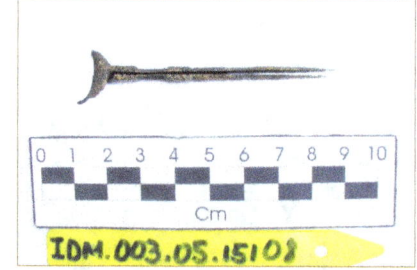

POST CONSERVATION PHOTO

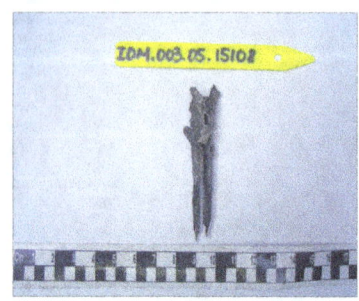

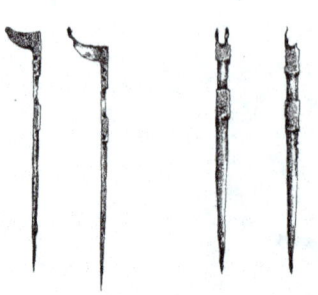

PRE CONSERVATION PHOTO   ARTEFACT DRAWING

ARTEFACT NO IDM-003 - 05 - **15109.000**

MATERIAL Copper / copper alloy

DESCRIPTION A copper alloy object in a concretion

CATEGORY Unknown

ASSOCIATION Concretion of wood and iron

DATE EXCAVATED 09-Sept-05

DATE CONSERVED 05-Nov-05

LOCATION Marine Conservation Center (CCM), Island of Mozambique

POST CONSERVATION PHOTO

PRE CONSERVATION PHOTO

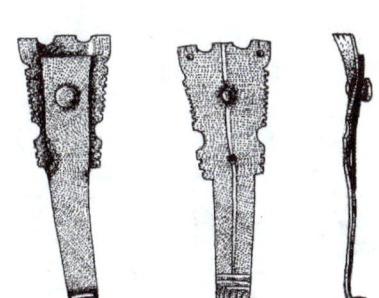

ARTEFACT DRAWING

ARTEFACT NO IDM-003 - 05 - **15110.000**

MATERIAL Copper / copper alloy

DESCRIPTION One hand navigation divider. Perfect condition

CATEGORY Professional instruments

ASSOCIATION Sediments

DATE EXCAVATED 09-Sept-05

DATE CONSERVED 05-Nov-05

LOCATION Marine Conservation Center (CCM), Island of Mozambique

POST CONSERVATION PHOTO

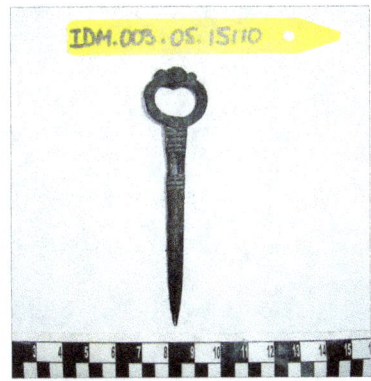

PRE CONSERVATION PHOTO

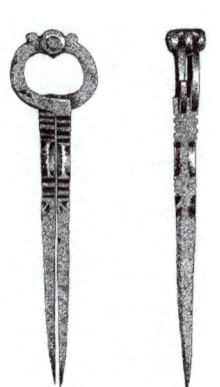

ARTEFACT DRAWING

ARTEFACT NO IDM-003 - 05 - **15111.000**

MATERIAL Ceramics

DESCRIPTION A ceramic lid.

CATEGORY Cargo

ASSOCIATION Sediments

DATE EXCAVATED 09-Sept-05

DATE CONSERVED 04-Oct-05

LOCATION Marine Conservation Center (CCM), Island of Mozambique

POST CONSERVATION PHOTO

PRE CONSERVATION PHOTO

ARTEFACT DRAWING

ARTEFACT NO IDM-003 - 05 - **15113.000**

MATERIAL Ceramics

DESCRIPTION A ceramic lid.

CATEGORY Cargo

ASSOCIATION Sediment

DATE EXCAVATED 10-Sept-05

DATE CONSERVED 04-Oct-05

LOCATION Marine Conservation Center (CCM), Island of Mozambique

POST CONSERVATION PHOTO

PRE CONSERVATION PHOTO

ARTEFACT DRAWING

ARTEFACT NO IDM-003 - 05 - **15115.000**

MATERIAL Ceramics

DESCRIPTION Olive jar

CATEGORY Cargo

ASSOCIATION Wood and sediments

DATE EXCAVATED 12-Sept-05

DATE CONSERVED 26-Sept-05

LOCATION Marine Conservation Center (CCM), Island of Mozambique

POST CONSERVATION PHOTO

PRE CONSERVATION PHOTO

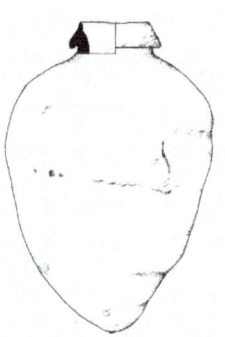

ARTEFACT DRAWING

ARTEFACT NO IDM-003 - 05 - **15116.000**

MATERIAL Ceramics

DESCRIPTION A little ceramic cup, rim broken

CATEGORY Domestic

ASSOCIATION Wood and sediment

DATE EXCAVATED 12-Sept-05

DATE CONSERVED 20-Sept-05

LOCATION Marine Conservation Center (CCM), Island of Mozambique

POST CONSERVATION PHOTO

PRE CONSERVATION PHOTO

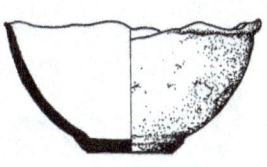

ARTEFACT DRAWING

ARTEFACT NO IDM-003 - 05 - **15117.000**

MATERIAL Ceramics

DESCRIPTION Olive jar

CATEGORY Cargo

ASSOCIATION Sediment and wood

DATE EXCAVATED 12-Sept-05

DATE CONSERVED 26-Sept-05

LOCATION Marine Conservation Center (CCM), Island of Mozambique

POST CONSERVATION PHOTO

PRE CONSERVATION PHOTO

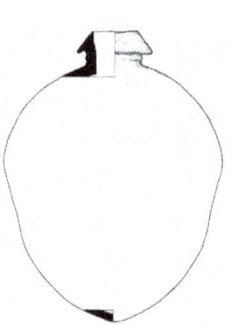

ARTEFACT DRAWING

ARTEFACT NO IDM-003 - 05 - **15118.000**

MATERIAL Ceramics

DESCRIPTION Olive jar

CATEGORY Cargo

ASSOCIATION Sediments and wood

DATE EXCAVATED 12-Sept-05

DATE CONSERVED 26-Sept-05

LOCATION Marine Conservation Center (CCM), Island of Mozambique

POST CONSERVATION PHOTO

PRE CONSERVATION PHOTO

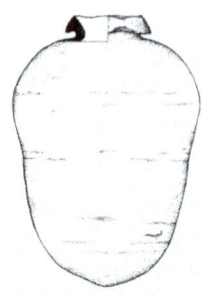

ARTEFACT DRAWING

ARTEFACT NO IDM-003 - 05 - **15119.000**

MATERIAL Ceramics

DESCRIPTION Olive jar

CATEGORY Cargo

ASSOCIATION Sediment

DATE EXCAVATED 13-Sept-05

DATE CONSERVED 26-Sept-05

LOCATION Marine Conservation Center (CCM), Island of Mozambique

POST CONSERVATION PHOTO

PRE CONSERVATION PHOTO

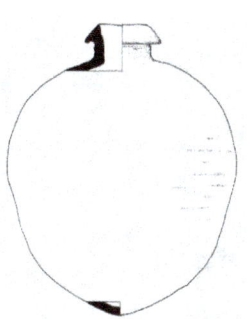

ARTEFACT DRAWING

ARTEFACT NO IDM-003 - 05 - **15120.000**

MATERIAL Pewter

DESCRIPTION A pewter bottle tap

CATEGORY Personal belongings

ASSOCIATION Sediment

DATE EXCAVATED 13-Sept-05

DATE CONSERVED 20-Sept-05

LOCATION Marine Conservation Center (CCM), Island of Mozambique

POST CONSERVATION PHOTO

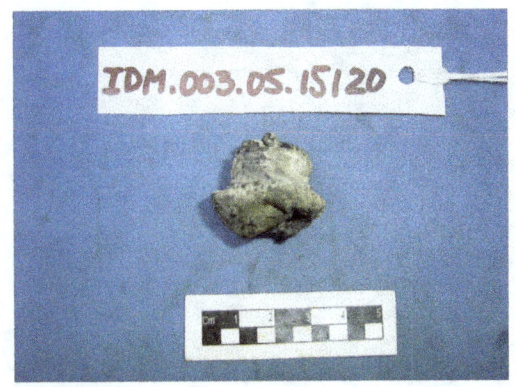

PRE CONSERVATION PHOTO

ARTEFACT DRAWING

169

ARTEFACT NO IDM-003 - 05 - **15121.000**

MATERIAL Pewter

DESCRIPTION A pewter bottle tap in a concretion

CATEGORY Personal belongings

ASSOCIATION Sediment and wood

DATE EXCAVATED 14-Sept-05

DATE CONSERVED 10-Oct-05

LOCATION Marine Conservation Center (CCM), Island of Mozambique

POST CONSERVATION PHOTO

PRE CONSERVATION PHOTO

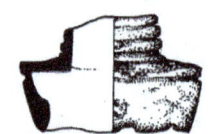

ARTEFACT DRAWING

ARTEFACT NO IDM-003 - 05 - **15122.000**

MATERIAL Ceramics

DESCRIPTION Olive jar

CATEGORY Cargo

ASSOCIATION Sediment and wood

DATE EXCAVATED 14-Sept-05

DATE CONSERVED 26-Sept-05

LOCATION Marine Conservation Center (CCM), Island of Mozambique

POST CONSERVATION PHOTO

PRE CONSERVATION PHOTO

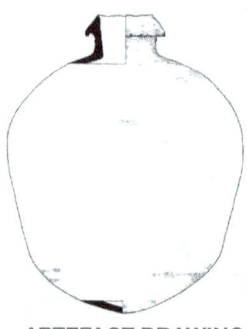

ARTEFACT DRAWING

ARTEFACT NO IDM-003 - 05 - **15124.000**

MATERIAL Pewter

DESCRIPTION A pewter bottle tap

CATEGORY Personal belongings

ASSOCIATION A concretion and sediment

DATE EXCAVATED 14-Sept-05

DATE CONSERVED 10-Oct-05

LOCATION Marine Conservation Center (CCM), Island of Mozambique

POST CONSERVATION PHOTO

PRE CONSERVATION PHOTO

ARTEFACT DRAWING

ARTEFACT NO IDM-003 - 05 - **15125.000**

MATERIAL Pewter

DESCRIPTION A pewter bottle tap

CATEGORY Personal belongings

ASSOCIATION Wood and sediments

DATE EXCAVATED 15-Sept-05

DATE CONSERVED 20-Sept-05

LOCATION Marine Conservation Center (CCM), Island of Mozambique

POST CONSERVATION PHOTO

PRE CONSERVATION PHOTO

ARTEFACT DRAWING

ARTEFACT NO IDM-003 - 05 - **15126.000**

MATERIAL Ceramics

DESCRIPTION A piece of decorated ceramic.
Floral motifs and Swastika in relief

CATEGORY Cargo

ASSOCIATION Sediment and wood

DATE EXCAVATED 16-Sept-05

DATE CONSERVED 10-Oct-05

LOCATION Marine Museum (MUSIM), Island of Mozambique

POST CONSERVATION PHOTO

PRE CONSERVATION PHOTO

ARTEFACT DRAWING

ARTEFACT NO IDM-003 - 05 - **15127.000**

MATERIAL Copper / copper alloy

DESCRIPTION Metal stick with wooden ball on top

CATEGORY Unknown

ASSOCIATION Sediments, wood and broken ceramic

DATE EXCAVATED 19-Sept-05

DATE CONSERVED 12-July-06

LOCATION Marine Conservation Center (CCM), Island of Mozambique

POST CONSERVATION PHOTO

PRE CONSERVATION PHOTO

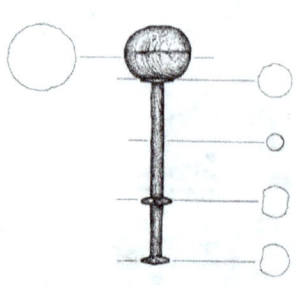

ARTEFACT DRAWING

ARTEFACT NO IDM-003 - 05 - **15128.000**

MATERIAL Copper / copper alloy

DESCRIPTION Sailmaker's palm

CATEGORY Professional instruments

ASSOCIATION Sediments, wood and broken ceramic

DATE EXCAVATED 19-Sept-05

DATE CONSERVED 02-Nov-05

LOCATION Marine Conservation Center (CCM), Island of Mozambique

POST CONSERVATION PHOTO

PRE CONSERVATION PHOTO

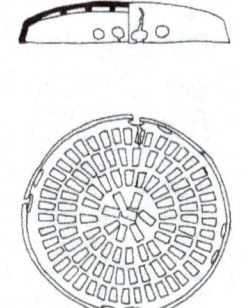

ARTEFACT DRAWING

ARTEFACT NO IDM-003 - 05 - **15129.000**

MATERIAL Copper / copper alloy

DESCRIPTION Measurement instrument with scales on both sides, apparently to measure angular distances or arcs

CATEGORY Professional instruments

ASSOCIATION Sediments

DATE EXCAVATED 30-Sept-05

DATE CONSERVED 02-Nov-05

LOCATION Marine Conservation Center (CCM), Island of Mozambique

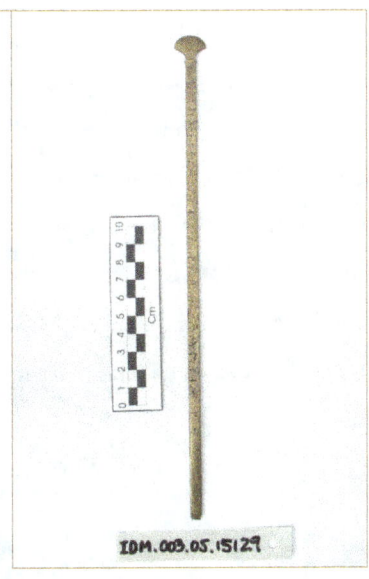

POST CONSERVATION PHOTO

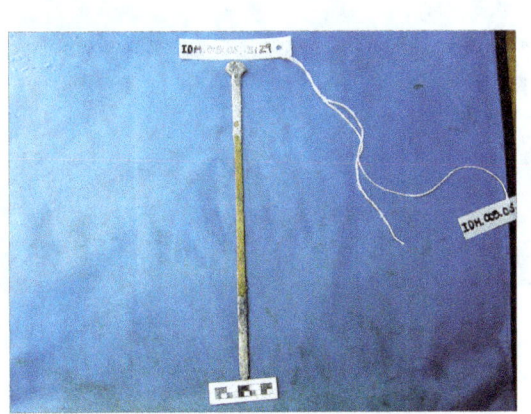

PRE CONSERVATION PHOTO

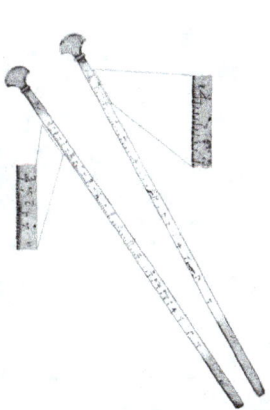

ARTEFACT DRAWING

ARTEFACT NO IDM-003 - 05 - **15130.000**

MATERIAL Copper / copper alloy

DESCRIPTION Straight pattern navigation divider in perfect condition

CATEGORY Professional instruments

ASSOCIATION Sediments

DATE EXCAVATED 30-Sept-05

DATE CONSERVED 02-Nov-05

LOCATION Marine Conservation Center (CCM), Island of Mozambique

POST CONSERVATION PHOTO

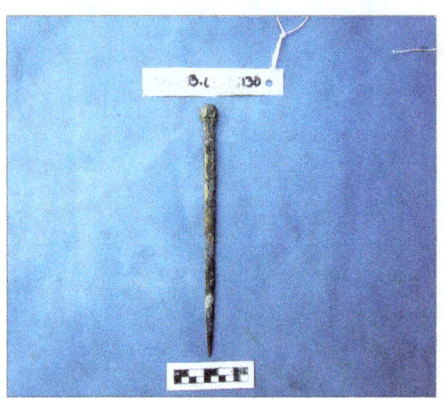

PRE CONSERVATION PHOTO

ARTEFACT DRAWING

ARTEFACT NO IDM-003 - 05 - **15131.000**

MATERIAL Ceramics

DESCRIPTION Ceramic lid with a handle on top, rim chipped

CATEGORY Cargo

ASSOCIATION Sediment and wood

DATE EXCAVATED 05-Oct-05

DATE CONSERVED 03-Nov-05

LOCATION Marine Conservation Center (CCM), Island of Mozambique

POST CONSERVATION PHOTO

PRE CONSERVATION PHOTO

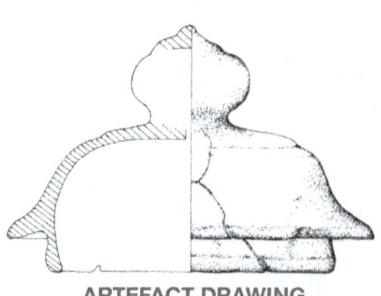

ARTEFACT DRAWING

ARTEFACT NO IDM-003 - 05 - **15132.000**

MATERIAL Ceramics

DESCRIPTION Olive jar

CATEGORY Cargo

ASSOCIATION Sediment and wood

DATE EXCAVATED 05-Oct-05

DATE CONSERVED 03-Nov-05

LOCATION Marine Conservation Center (CCM), Island of Mozambique

POST CONSERVATION PHOTO

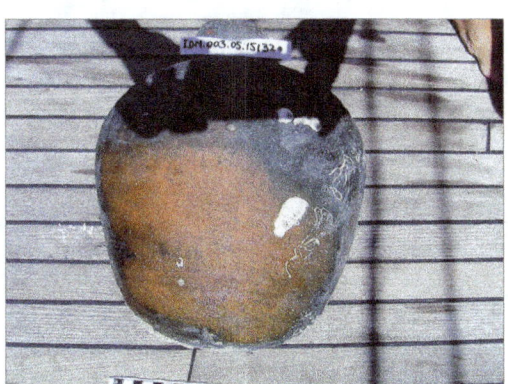

PRE CONSERVATION PHOTO

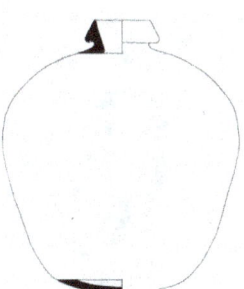

ARTEFACT DRAWING

ARTEFACT NO IDM-003 - 05 - **15133.000**

MATERIAL Ivory

DESCRIPTION Piece of board game, possibly checkers

CATEGORY Personal belongings

ASSOCIATION Timbers of wood

DATE EXCAVATED 06-Oct-05

DATE CONSERVED 03-Nov-05

LOCATION Marine Conservation Center (CCM), Island of Mozambique

POST CONSERVATION PHOTO

PRE CONSERVATION PHOTO

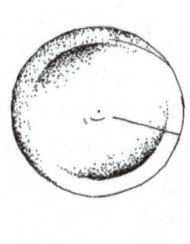

ARTEFACT DRAWING

ARTEFACT NO IDM-003 - 05 - **15134.000**

MATERIAL Pewter

DESCRIPTION A pewter hinge e.g. for a buckle

CATEGORY Personal belongings

ASSOCIATION Timbers and sediment

DATE EXCAVATED 06-Oct-05

DATE CONSERVED 14-Oct-05

LOCATION Marine Conservation Center (CCM), Island of Mozambique

POST CONSERVATION PHOTO

PRE CONSERVATION PHOTO

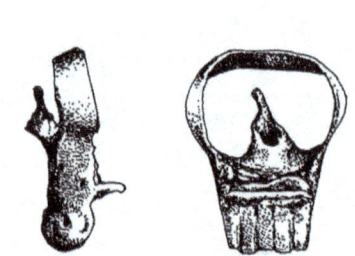

ARTEFACT DRAWING

ARTEFACT NO IDM-003 - 05 - **15135.000**

MATERIAL Lead

DESCRIPTION A lead seal

CATEGORY Personal belongings

ASSOCIATION Sediments and wood

DATE EXCAVATED 07-Oct-05

DATE CONSERVED 14-Oct-05

LOCATION Marine Conservation Center (CCM), Island of Mozambique

POST CONSERVATION PHOTO

PRE CONSERVATION PHOTO

ARTEFACT DRAWING

ARTEFACT NO IDM-003 - 05 - **15136.000**

MATERIAL Ceramics

DESCRIPTION Ceramic lid.

CATEGORY Cargo

ASSOCIATION Sediments and wood

DATE EXCAVATED 07-Oct-05

DATE CONSERVED 03-Nov-05

LOCATION Marine Conservation Center (CCM), Island of Mozambique

POST CONSERVATION PHOTO

PRE CONSERVATION PHOTO   **ARTEFACT DRAWING**

ARTEFACT NO IDM-003 - 05 - **15138.000**

MATERIAL Copper / copper alloy

DESCRIPTION One hand navigation divider. Perfect condition

CATEGORY Professional instruments

ASSOCIATION Wood and iron concretion

DATE EXCAVATED 19-Oct-05

DATE CONSERVED 02-Nov-05

LOCATION Marine Conservation Center (CCM), Island of Mozambique

POST CONSERVATION PHOTO

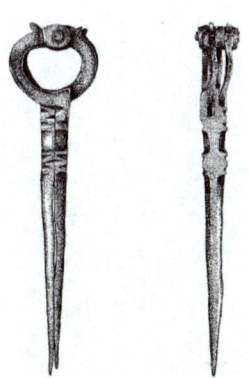

PRE CONSERVATION PHOTO   **ARTEFACT DRAWING**

ARTEFACT NO IDM-003 - 05 - **15140.000**

MATERIAL Copper / copper alloy

DESCRIPTION One hand navigation divider. Perfect condition

CATEGORY Professional instruments

ASSOCIATION Wood and iron concretion

DATE EXCAVATED 20-Oct-05

DATE CONSERVED 05-Nov-05

LOCATION Marine Conservation Center (CCM), Island of Mozambique

POST CONSERVATION PHOTO

PRE CONSERVATION PHOTO

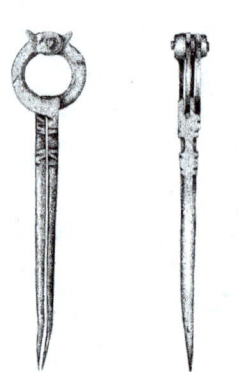

ARTEFACT DRAWING

ARTEFACT NO IDM-003 - 05 - **15141.000**

MATERIAL Ceramics

DESCRIPTION Ceramic bowl

CATEGORY Domestic

ASSOCIATION Sediment and wood

DATE EXCAVATED 22-Oct-05

DATE CONSERVED 03-Nov-05

LOCATION Marine Conservation Center (CCM), Island of Mozambique

POST CONSERVATION PHOTO

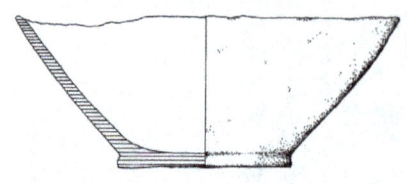

ARTEFACT DRAWING

178

ARTEFACT NO IDM-003 - 05 - **15142.000**

MATERIAL Ceramics

DESCRIPTION Lower section of a glazed ceramic bowl

CATEGORY Domestic

ASSOCIATION Wood and sediment

DATE EXCAVATED 24-Oct-05

DATE CONSERVED 03-Nov-05

LOCATION Marine Conservation Center (CCM), Island of Mozambique

POST CONSERVATION PHOTO

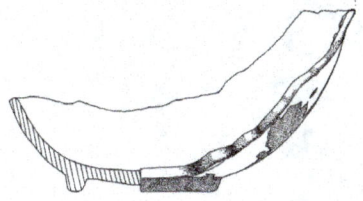

ARTEFACT DRAWING

ARTEFACT NO IDM-003 - 06 - **15143.000**

MATERIAL Ceramics

DESCRIPTION Little ceramic flask with two handles

CATEGORY Domestic

ASSOCIATION Sediment and wood

DATE EXCAVATED 13-Apr-06

DATE CONSERVED 30-May-06

LOCATION Marine Conservation Center (CCM), Island of Mozambique

POST CONSERVATION PHOTO

PRE CONSERVATION PHOTO

ARTEFACT NO IDM-003 - 06 - **15145.000**

MATERIAL Glass

DESCRIPTION Small oil dispenser of blue glass

CATEGORY Domestic

ASSOCIATION Sediments and wood.

DATE EXCAVATED 30-May-06

DATE CONSERVED 07-June-06

LOCATION Marine Museum (MUSIM), Island of Mozambique

POST CONSERVATION PHOTO

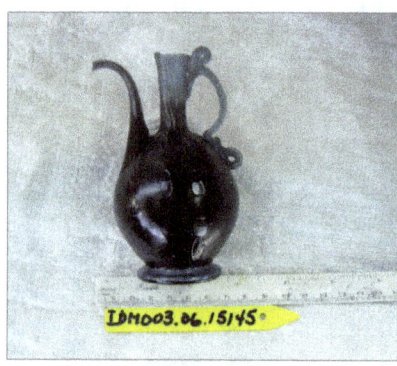

PRE CONSERVATION PHOTO

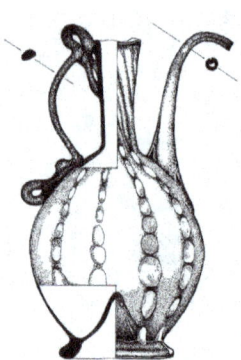

ARTEFACT DRAWING

ARTEFACT NO IDM-003 - 06 - **15146.000**

MATERIAL Lead

DESCRIPTION A little lead seal

CATEGORY Personal belongings

ASSOCIATION Sediments and wood

DATE EXCAVATED 31-May-06

DATE CONSERVED 07-June-06

LOCATION Marine Conservation Center (CCM), Island of Mozambique

POST CONSERVATION PHOTO

PRE CONSERVATION PHOTO

ARTEFACT DRAWING

ARTEFACT NO IDM-003 - 05 - **15152.000**

MATERIAL Ceramics

DESCRIPTION Olive jar

CATEGORY Cargo

ASSOCIATION Sediment, ballast stones and concretions of iron and wood

DATE EXCAVATED 24-July-06

DATE CONSERVED 07-Oct-06

LOCATION Marine Conservation Center (CCM), Island of Mozambique

POST CONSERVATION PHOTO

PRE CONSERVATION PHOTO

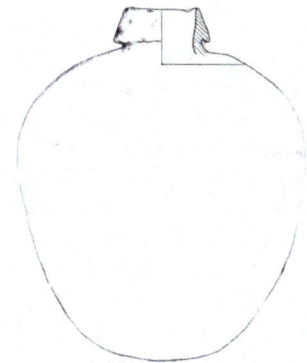

ARTEFACT DRAWING

ARTEFACT NO IDM-003 - 06 - **15153.000**

MATERIAL Copper / copper alloy

DESCRIPTION A little piece of copper alloy, apparently part of an instrument

CATEGORY Professional instruments

ASSOCIATION Ballast stones, sediment and wood

DATE EXCAVATED 25-July-06

DATE CONSERVED 02-Sept-06

LOCATION Marine Conservation Center (CCM), Island of Mozambique

POST CONSERVATION PHOTO

PRE CONSERVATION PHOTO

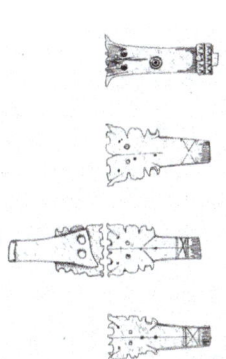

ARTEFACT DRAWING

ARTEFACT NO IDM-003 - 06 - **15154.000**

MATERIAL Copper / copper alloy

DESCRIPTION 5 copper alloy pieces, apparently part of an instrument

CATEGORY Professional instruments

ASSOCIATION Concretion of iron, wood and ballast stones

DATE EXCAVATED 26-July-06

DATE CONSERVED 02-Sept-06

LOCATION Marine Conservation Center (CCM), Island of Mozambique

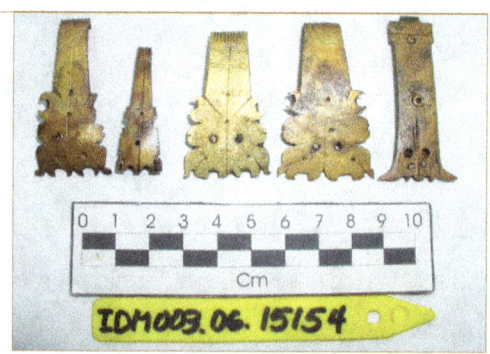

POST CONSERVATION PHOTO

PRE CONSERVATION PHOTO

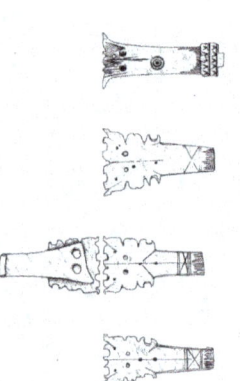

ARTEFACT DRAWING

ARTEFACT NO IDM-003 - 06 - **15155.000**

MATERIAL Ceramics

DESCRIPTION Ceramic lid

CATEGORY Domestic

ASSOCIATION Ballast stones, sediments and wood

DATE EXCAVATED 27-July-06

DATE CONSERVED 31-Aug-06

LOCATION Marine Conservation Center (CCM), Island of Mozambique

POST CONSERVATION PHOTO

PRE CONSERVATION PHOTO

ARTEFACT DRAWING

ARTEFACT NO IDM-003 - 05 - **15156.000**

MATERIAL Copper / copper alloy

DESCRIPTION 12 copper alloy pieces

CATEGORY Professional instruments

ASSOCIATION Concretion of iron, wood and ballast stones

DATE EXCAVATED 31-July-06

DATE CONSERVED 02-Sept-06

LOCATION Marine Conservation Center (CCM), Island of Mozambique

POST CONSERVATION PHOTO

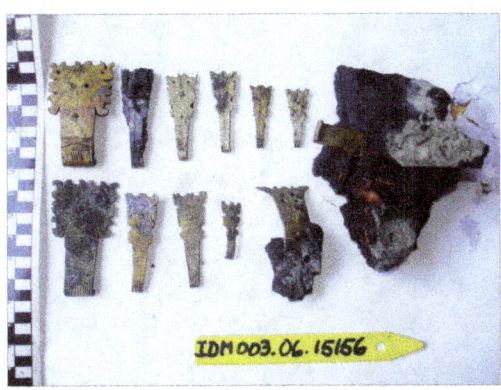

PRE CONSERVATION PHOTO

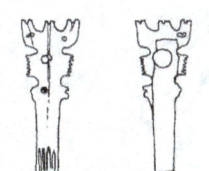

ARTEFACT DRAWING

ARTEFACT NO IDM-003 - 06 - **15157.000**

MATERIAL Lead

DESCRIPTION Lead seal

CATEGORY Personal belongings

ASSOCIATION Concretion of iron, wood and ballast stones

DATE EXCAVATED 31-July-06

DATE CONSERVED 30-Aug-06

LOCATION Marine Conservation Center (CCM), Island of Mozambique

POST CONSERVATION PHOTO

PRE CONSERVATION PHOTO

ARTEFACT DRAWING

ARTEFACT NO IDM-003 - 06 - **15158.000**

MATERIAL Lead

DESCRIPTION Lead seal

CATEGORY Personal belongings

ASSOCIATION Concretion of iron, wood and ballast stones

DATE EXCAVATED 31-July-06

DATE CONSERVED 30-Aug-06

LOCATION Marine Conservation Center (CCM), Island of Mozambique

POST CONSERVATION PHOTO

PRE CONSERVATION PHOTO

ARTEFACT DRAWING

ARTEFACT NO IDM-003 - 06 - **15159.000**

MATERIAL Lead

DESCRIPTION Lead seal

CATEGORY Personal belongings

ASSOCIATION Concretion of iron, wood and ballast stones

DATE EXCAVATED 31-July-06

DATE CONSERVED 30-Aug-06

LOCATION Marine Conservation Center (CCM), Island of Mozambique

POST CONSERVATION PHOTO

PRE CONSERVATION PHOTO

ARTEFACT DRAWING

184

ARTEFACT NO IDM-003 - 05 - **15161.000**

MATERIAL Copper / copper alloy

DESCRIPTION Copper alloy piece

CATEGORY Unknown

ASSOCIATION Concretion of iron, wood and ballast stones

DATE EXCAVATED 31-July-06

DATE CONSERVED 02-Sept-06

LOCATION Marine Conservation Center (CCM), Island of Mozambique

POST CONSERVATION PHOTO

PRE CONSERVATION PHOTO

ARTEFACT DRAWING

ARTEFACT NO IDM-003 - 06 - **15163.000**

MATERIAL Lead

DESCRIPTION A group of 6 lead seals

CATEGORY Personal belongings

ASSOCIATION Concretion of wood, iron and ballast stones

DATE EXCAVATED 01-Aug-06

DATE CONSERVED 30-Aug-06

LOCATION Marine Conservation Center (CCM), Island of Mozambique

POST CONSERVATION PHOTO

PRE CONSERVATION PHOTO

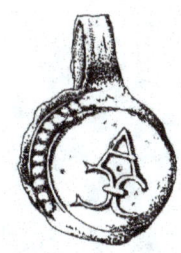

ARTEFACT DRAWING

ARTEFACT NO IDM-003 - 06 - **15164.000**

MATERIAL Lead

DESCRIPTION Lead seal

CATEGORY Personal belongings

ASSOCIATION Concretion of wood, iron and ballast stones

DATE EXCAVATED 01-Aug-06

DATE CONSERVED 30-Aug-06

LOCATION Marine Conservation Center (CCM), Island of Mozambique

POST CONSERVATION PHOTO

PRE CONSERVATION PHOTO

ARTEFACT DRAWING

ARTEFACT NO IDM-003 - 06 - **15165.000**

MATERIAL Lead

DESCRIPTION 4 lead seals

CATEGORY Personal belongings

ASSOCIATION Wood, iron and ballast stones concretion

DATE EXCAVATED 02-Aug-06

DATE CONSERVED 30-Aug-06

LOCATION Marine Conservation Center (CCM), Island of Mozambique

POST CONSERVATION PHOTO

PRE CONSERVATION PHOTO

ARTEFACT DRAWING

ARTEFACT NO IDM-003 - 05 - **15166.000**

MATERIAL Copper / copper alloy

DESCRIPTION Copper alloy wing nut

CATEGORY Professional instruments

ASSOCIATION Wood, iron and ballast stones concretion

DATE EXCAVATED 02-Aug-06

DATE CONSERVED 02-Sept-06

LOCATION Marine Conservation Center (CCM), Island of Mozambique

POST CONSERVATION PHOTO

PRE CONSERVATION PHOTO   **ARTEFACT DRAWING**

ARTEFACT NO IDM-003 - 06 - **15167.000**

MATERIAL Lead

DESCRIPTION Lead seal

CATEGORY Personal belongings

ASSOCIATION Wood, iron and ballast stones concretion

DATE EXCAVATED 03-Aug-06

DATE CONSERVED 30-Aug-06

LOCATION Marine Conservation Center (CCM), Island of Mozambique

POST CONSERVATION PHOTO

PRE CONSERVATION PHOTO   **ARTEFACT DRAWING**

ARTEFACT NO IDM-003 - 06 - **15168.000**

MATERIAL Lead

DESCRIPTION 10 lead seals

CATEGORY Personal belongings

ASSOCIATION Wood, iron and ballast stones concretion

DATE EXCAVATED 07-Aug-06

DATE CONSERVED 30-Aug-06

LOCATION Marine Conservation Center (CCM), Island of Mozambique

POST CONSERVATION PHOTO

PRE CONSERVATION PHOTO

ARTEFACT DRAWING

ARTEFACT NO IDM-003 - 06 - **15169.000**

MATERIAL Ceramics

DESCRIPTION 1 ceramic lid

CATEGORY Domestic

ASSOCIATION Iron, wood and sediment concretion

DATE EXCAVATED 08-Aug-06

DATE CONSERVED 31-Aug-06

LOCATION Marine Conservation Center (CCM), Island of Mozambique

POST CONSERVATION PHOTO

PRE CONSERVATION PHOTO

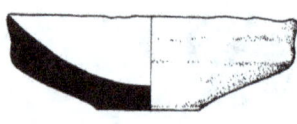

ARTEFACT DRAWING

ARTEFACT NO IDM-003 - 05 - **15170.000**

MATERIAL Lead

DESCRIPTION A group of 6 lead seals

CATEGORY Personal belongings

ASSOCIATION Wood, iron and sediment concretion

DATE EXCAVATED 08-Aug-06

DATE CONSERVED 30-Aug-06

LOCATION Marine Conservation Center (CCM), Island of Mozambique

POST CONSERVATION PHOTO

PRE CONSERVATION PHOTO

ARTEFACT DRAWING

ARTEFACT NO IDM-003 - 06 - **15173.000**

MATERIAL Lead

DESCRIPTION A group of 8 lead seals

CATEGORY Personal belongings

ASSOCIATION Concretion of iron, wood and sediments

DATE EXCAVATED 15-Aug-06

DATE CONSERVED 30-Aug-06

LOCATION Marine Conservation Center (CCM), Island of Mozambique

POST CONSERVATION PHOTO

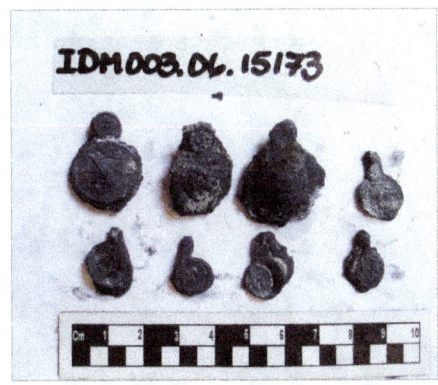

PRE CONSERVATION PHOTO

ARTEFACT DRAWING

ARTEFACT NO IDM-003 - 06 - **15174.000**

MATERIAL Copper / copper alloy

DESCRIPTION 6 copper alloy pieces

CATEGORY Professional instruments

ASSOCIATION Concretion of iron, wood and sediments

DATE EXCAVATED 16-Aug-06

DATE CONSERVED 02-Sept-06

LOCATION Marine Conservation Center (CCM), Island of Mozambique

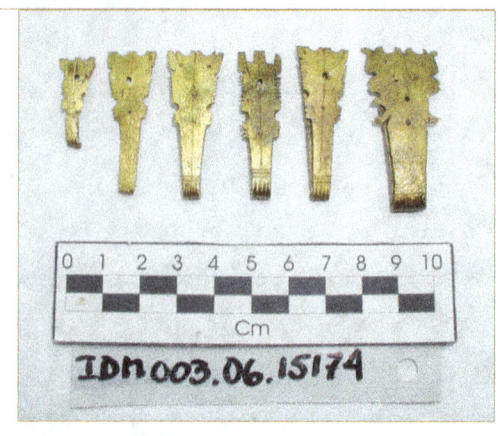

POST CONSERVATION PHOTO

PRE CONSERVATION PHOTO

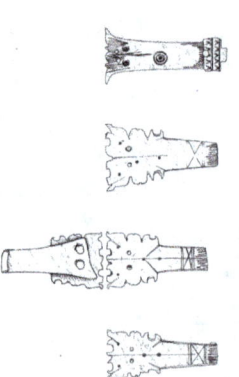

ARTEFACT DRAWING

ARTEFACT NO IDM-003 - 06 - **15175.000**

MATERIAL Ceramics

DESCRIPTION Ceramic flask with stem missing and flat base

CATEGORY Domestic

ASSOCIATION Sand, sediments and wood

DATE EXCAVATED 16-Aug-06

DATE CONSERVED 31-Aug-06

LOCATION Marine Conservation Center (CCM), Island of Mozambique

POST CONSERVATION PHOTO

PRE CONSERVATION PHOTO

ARTEFACT DRAWING

ARTEFACT NO IDM-003 - 05 - **15176.000**

MATERIAL Lead

DESCRIPTION A lead seal

CATEGORY Personal belongings

ASSOCIATION Concretion of sediment, wood and iron

DATE EXCAVATED 16-Aug-06

DATE CONSERVED 30-Aug-06

LOCATION Marine Conservation Center (CCM), Island of Mozambique

POST CONSERVATION PHOTO

PRE CONSERVATION PHOTO

ARTEFACT DRAWING

ARTEFACT NO IDM-003 - 06 - **15180.000**

MATERIAL Lead

DESCRIPTION A group of 4 lead seals

CATEGORY Personal belongings

ASSOCIATION Wood

DATE EXCAVATED 29-Sept-06

DATE CONSERVED 03-Oct-06

LOCATION Marine Conservation Center (CCM), Island of Mozambique

POST CONSERVATION PHOTO

PRE CONSERVATION PHOTO

ARTEFACT DRAWING

ARTEFACT NO IDM-003 - 06 - **15181.000**

MATERIAL Pewter

DESCRIPTION A metal piece (such as an ornament)

CATEGORY Personal belongings

ASSOCIATION Wood and sediment

DATE EXCAVATED 29-Sept-06

DATE CONSERVED 04-Oct-06

LOCATION Marine Conservation Center (CCM), Island of Mozambique

POST CONSERVATION PHOTO

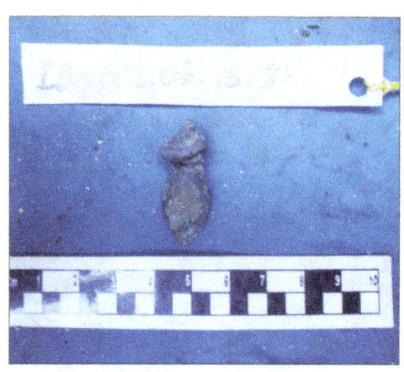

PRE CONSERVATION PHOTO

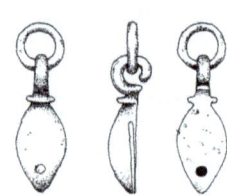

ARTEFACT DRAWING

ARTEFACT NO IDM-003 - 06 - **151482.000**

MATERIAL Pewter

DESCRIPTION A metal piece (such as an ornament)

CATEGORY Personal belongings

ASSOCIATION Wood and sediment

DATE EXCAVATED 29-Sept-06

DATE CONSERVED 04-Oct-06

LOCATION Marine Conservation Center (CCM), Island of Mozambique

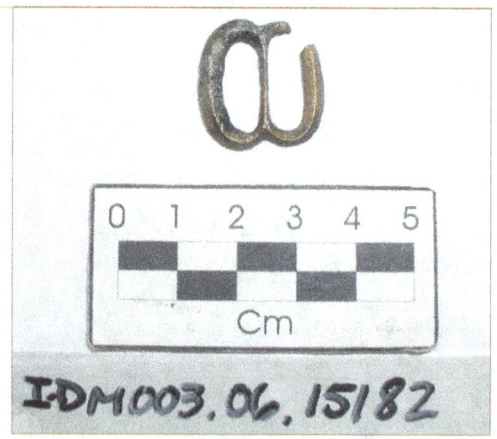

POST CONSERVATION PHOTO

PRE CONSERVATION PHOTO

ARTEFACT DRAWING

ARTEFACT NO IDM-003 - 05 - **15183.000**

MATERIAL Lead

DESCRIPTION Lead seal

CATEGORY Personal belongings

ASSOCIATION Wood and concretions

DATE EXCAVATED 06-Oct-06

DATE CONSERVED 19-Oct-06

LOCATION Marine Conservation Center (CCM), Island of Mozambique

POST CONSERVATION PHOTO

PRE CONSERVATION PHOTO

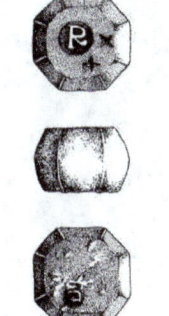

ARTEFACT DRAWING

ANNEX 2

Equipment and Staff

Equipment

The following equipment and peripherals were used in this excavation:

I *Zanj* Explorer Recovery vessel (20m length, accommodation for 14).
I RIB *Humber* (5.5 m length).
I Zodiac *Mark VI* (6 m length).
I 2 x Honda 20 HP four strokes outboard engines.
I 1 x Mercury 25 HP outboard engine.
I 1 x Yamaha 30 HP outboard engine.
I 2 x GPS GARMIN map 168 (with echo sounder) and NMEA interface.
I 2 x GPS GARMIN 128 with NMEA interface.
I GPS Eagle view with NMEA interface.
I Handheld GPS Magellan 3000.
I Echo sounder MAP2000/SAM MODULE.
I Echo sounder GARMIN 160.
I 2 x ELSEC 2000 Metal detectors.
I Aquascan AQUAPULSE Metal detector.
I U/W Digital photo camera Ricoh with housing.
I U/W Digital video camera Sony with housing.
I U/W Digital video camera Panasonic with housing.
I Surface digital camera Ricoh Caplio 3,2 Megapixel.
I 2 x towing sledges for visual survey.
I 16 x full diving gear sets.
I 2 x full diving gear as spare.
I 15 x 16 Lts steel diving bottles.
I 10 x 15 Lts steel diving bottles.
I 1 x 12 Lts aluminium diving bottle.
I Diving compressor BAUER (Electric engine).
I Diving compressor EXPLORER (Diesel engine).
I U/W Scooter Apollo.
I U/W Scooter Submerge.
I 1 x Grundfos Submersible water pump and water dredge system.
I 2 x Honda water pumps, 4,5 bar, 1400 Lts/min.
I Laptop Compaq Presario, Pentium IV.
I Laptop Toshiba Satellite, Pentium IV.
I Laptop Acer Travel Mate, Pentium IV.
I Laptop Gericom, Pentium IV.
I Desktop Acer + scanner HP.
I CMAPecs Navigation software.
I AxLogger editor software.
I AQLogedit software.
I Surfer 8 software.
I Corel Draw 10 software.
I Adobe Photoshop 7.0 software.
I Microsoft Office suite 2004 software.
I Iridium Satellite phone for data transfer.

Staff

For this excavation operation the following team was mobilized:

▮ Alejandro Mirabal	(Archaeologist/ OPS Director/ Diver)
▮ Faure Cambiella	(OPS Manager/ Surveyor/ Diver)
▮ Alina Reyes	(Archaeological Registrar/ Administration)
▮ Sara Guerreiro	(AWW Representative / Administration)
▮ Manuel Navarro	(Dive Supervisor)
▮ Ramiro Pereira	(Diver)
▮ Yuri Romero	(Archaeologist / Diver)
▮ Danijar Morandin	(Diver)
▮ Boris Basnuevo	(Diver)
▮ Alessandro Lopez	(Archaeologist / Diver)
▮ Carlos Bosch	(Archaeological Registrar/ Diver)
▮ Alejandro Raul Mirabal	(Draftsman/ Diver)
▮ Jorge Ponce	(Senior conservator)
▮ Manuel Almeida	(Senior conservator)
▮ Grant Ruffel	(Skipper Zanj/ Diver)
▮ Gastón Bernal	(Engineer Zanj/ Diver)
▮ Otomane Valhale	(Boatman/ Diver)
▮ Salimo Djuma	(Conservation assistant)
▮ Wassia Sualehe	(Conservation assistant)
▮ Zuleida Russo	(Representative PI)
▮ Zinha Selemane	(Cook / housemaid)
▮ Carlitos Almeida	(Cook)
▮ Anifa Joao	(Cook)
▮ Mohanza Abdala	(Guard)
▮ Mustafa	(Guard)
▮ Machaka	(Guard)
▮ Amade Mustafa	(Supervisor from Marine Police)
▮ Mario Lima	(Supervisor from Marine Police)
▮ Maricano Denis	(Supervisor from Marine Police)
▮ Agostinho Assuate	(Supervisor from Ministry of Culture)
▮ Saide Gelane	(Supervisor from Ministry of Culture)